Who is Afraid of the Holy Ghost?

Religion in Contemporary Africa Series

The Religion in Contemporary Africa Series (RCAS) aims at publishing innovative research relevant to the diverse and changing religious scene in contemporary Africa. One of the principal objectives of the Series is to facilitate the dissemination of research by young African scholars. The Series includes books from a range of disciplines: the academic study of religions, anthropology, sociology and related disciplines in the human and social sciences.

Series editors are James L. Cox, Professor of Religious Studies in the University of Edinburgh, and Gerrie ter Haar, Professor of Religion and Development in the Institute of Social Studies, The Hague, Netherlands. They can be contacted at: <j.cox@ed.ac.uk> or <terhaar@iss.nl>.

Previous Publications in the Religion in Contemporary Africa Series

1. Abel Ugba. *Shades of Belonging: African Pentecostals in Twenty-first Century Ireland.*

2. James L. Cox and Gerrie ter Haar (eds.). *Uniquely African? African Christian Identity from Cultural and Historical Perspectives.*

3. Matthews A. Ojo. *The End-Time Army. Charismatic Movements in Modern Nigeria.*

4. Leslie S. Nthoi. *Contesting Sacred Space. A Pilgrimage Study of the Mwali Cult of Southern Africa.*

5. Gerrie ter Haar (ed.). *Imagining Evil. Witchcraft Beliefs and Accusations in Contemporary Africa.*

6. Asonzeh Ukah. *A New Paradigm of Pentecostal Power. A Study of the Redeemed Christian Church of God in Nigeria.*

7. Frieder Ludwig and J. Kwabena Asamoah-Gyadu (eds.). *African Christian Presence in the West: New Immigrant Congregations and Transnational Networks in North America and Europe.*

WHO·IS·AFRAID
of
THE·HOLY·GHOST?
PENTECOSTALISM AND GLOBALIZATION IN AFRICA AND BEYOND

Edited by

Afe Adogame

AFRICA WORLD PRESS
TRENTON | LONDON | CAPE TOWN | NAIROBI | ADDIS ABABA | ASMARA | IBADAN | NEW DELHI

AFRICA WORLD PRESS

541 West Ingham Avenue | Suite B
Trenton, New Jersey 08638

Copyright © 2011 Afe Adogame
First Printing 2011

Book and cover design: Saverance Publishing Services
Cover Photo (bottom) by Andrew Esiebo

Library of Congress Cataloging-in-Publication Data

Who is afraid of the Holy Ghost? : Pentecostalism and globalization in Africa and beyond / edited by Afe Adogame.
    p. cm.
Includes bibliographical references and index.
 ISBN 1-59221-803-2 (hard cover) -- ISBN 1-59221-804-0 (pbk.)
1. Pentecostals, Black. 2. Pentecostalism--Nigeria. 3. Pentecostalism--Africa, Sub-Saharan. I. Adogame, Afeosemime U. (Afeosemime Unuose), 1964-
 BR1644.3.W56 2011
 276.8'2--dc22
                                2011000404

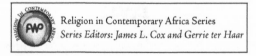

Religion in Contemporary Africa Series
Series Editors: James L. Cox and Gerrie ter Haar

DEDICATED POSTHUMOUSLY TO PROF. OGBU U. KALU
FOR MENTORING A LEGION OF YOUNG AFRICAN
SCHOLARS INTO GLOBAL ACADEMIC THEATERS!

TABLE OF CONTENTS

INTRODUCTION

Afe Adogame

The chapters that make up this book emanated from three scientific endeavors: two international, interdisciplinary workshops, Pentecostalism and Globalization (24-25 March 2001) and The Impact of New Communication Technologies on the Religions in West Africa (8 October 2001) organized by the Department for the Study of Religion under the auspices of the Sonderforschungsbereich / Kulturwissenschaftliches Forschungskolleg (SFB/FK 560) 'Local Action in Africa in the context of Global Influences' of the University of Bayreuth. Other contributions were drawn from papers presented within the Guest Lecture Series of the Department for the Study of Religion from 2000-2003. In spite of the wide scope covered by these very rich but diverse contributions, two issues that characterize their commonality center on the discourses of Pentecostalism and Globalization. The rhetorical subtitle 'Who is Afraid of the Holy Ghost?' was gleaned from one of the present contributions by Prof. Ogbu Kalu, a phrase that best encapsulates the overriding themes and debates in this book. It was appropriated as a suitable subtitle for the book with express permission and approval of the author. We owe immense debt and gratitude to him; and to him is this book dedicated posthumously.

The Pentecostal/charismatic movements represent some of the most popular, fastest growing religious movements within contemporary world Christianity. Pentecostals and charismatics have been estimated at over five hundred million adherents worldwide (Barrett & Johnson 2003: 24-25). Recent demographic statistics such as by the Pew Forum survey on Pentecostalism (2006), Philip Jenkin's *Next Christendom* (2002), and David Barrett's et. al *World Christian Encyclopaedia* (2001) are lucid indicators of the shifting contour of Christianity's center of gravity from the North to the South. It is estimated that two-thirds of Pentecostal and charismatic movement's 523 million adherents live outside the West in areas such as Africa, Latin America, Asia, and Oceania, as do most of the nine million who convert to it each year (Barrett & Johnson 2002: 284).

Pentecostal/charismatic Christianity has emerged as one of the most prevalent segments of world Christianity in ways that result in phrases such as 'Pentecostal power' (Pew Forum Survey 2006), to illustrate this trend and the dynamic nature of the phenomenon. As the survey indicates, "By all accounts, Pentecostalism and related charismatic movements represent one of the fastest-growing segments of global Christianity. At least a quarter of the world's 2 billion Christians are thought to be members of these lively, highly personal faiths, which emphasize such spiritually renewing 'gifts of the Holy Spirit' as speaking in tongues, divine healing and prophesying" (2006: 1). This survey which provides analysis of the religious demography of 10 countries including Nigeria, Kenya and South Africa demonstrates how Africa along with Asia and Latin America are assuming significant global players in the dramatization and appropriation of world Christianity.

Statistics on Pentecostal/charismatic movements, as with other religious movements in the world, are often fraught with controversy and imprecision. The projected demographic figures indicated in many existing works {can} be largely contested. So also is the criterion for categorizing these movements as Pentecostal or charismatic which, in itself, may be confusing as it varies from context to context. It actually depends on what definition of Pentecostalism and charismatic movements we adopt. Nevertheless, the value of any statistics is that it suggests that these movements have gradually carved out a niche for themselves within religious maps of the modern world, but also in terms of their demographic composition and geographical spread. It is even suggested that this brand of Christianity is now second in size to the Roman Catholic Church globally.

DEFINING PENTECOSTAL/ CHARISMATIC MOVEMENTS

Pentecostal/charismatic movements are indeed dynamic phenomena that have captured the scholarly attention of social scientists, historians of religion, theologians, policy makers, the media and other wide-ranging publics. What constitutes Pentecostal/ charismatic movements remain elusive just as explanations of their provenance are ever more contested in the face of newly emerging discourses and a revisiting of Pentecostal historiography. Their public visibility, mobility and social relevance in local-global contexts have attracted further interpretive and analytic approaches. There is a common tendency to talk about the globalization of Pentecostalism and charismatic Christianity or Global Christianity (van der Veer 1996, Dempster, Klaus, Petersen 1999, Coleman 2000, Jenkins 2002) and to give Pentecostalism the description 'a religion made to travel' (Dempster et. al 1999). These diverse academic scholarship, intellectual orientation and varied interpretations evident in a burgeoning literature have helped to reposition Pentecostal and charismatic movements from obscurity to center-stage of the global religious map. The various approaches to these religious movements are in themselves not mutually inclusive but have influenced and shaped each other in a dynamic way.

The emergence of modern Pentecostalism had earlier been located within religious events at the beginning of the 20th century. Two interrelated events, one in Topeka, Kansas on 1 January 1901 under Charles Parham, and the other, the Asuza Street revival in Los Angeles in April 1906 under a black Holiness preacher, William Seymour were traditionally recognized as the historical origins of these movements (Synan 2001; Burgess & Van der Maas 2002). However, recent scholarship has demonstrated that Pentecostal outbursts occurred in other parts of the world, notably in Africa, Europe, Asia and Latin America contemporaneously and to some extent even well before the 20th century. In global terms, Pentecostal origins are multifaceted, so are their opportunities, contexts and challenges. Thus, Pentecostalism as a global culture is to be understood in terms of parallel tracks and not simply as unilateral diffusion. Interpretations of Azusa Street as a birthplace of modern Pentecostalism have been relativized by growing awareness of other geographical foci. There are several developments independent of the Azusa Street narrative, although they may not have had the same resources and networks to globalize. Historically, the Azusa Street event was very significant in its capacity to launch into global networks, such as the pre-existing networks of immigrant and missionary networks. Thus, the human carriers of the Azusa street event were not only Americans, but immigrants from Europe, Latin America, Africa and Asia. From Los Angeles, news of the 'outpouring of the Holy Spirit' spread across the United States and around the world through social networks involving both word of mouth and printed literature (Burgess & Van der Maas 2002).

Pentecostal identity is obviously central to any definition of Pentecostalism and the description of its growth globally. Pentecostals and charismatic movements have been defined from a variety of sociological, historical, phenomenological, and theological perspectives. The collective identity of Pentecostals and charismatics also emerged from each group's self-identity. We can suggest that a common feature of these varied definitions is that they are not mutually exclusive. In the broadest sense, the term 'Pentecostalism' embraces what has been variously described as classical Pentecostals, neopentecostals, charismatics, neocharismatics, denominational Pentecostals (such as Charismatic Renewal groups), but also Christian and para-church organizations with Pentecostal-like experiences that have no specific traditional Pentecostal and charismatic denominational connections (see Burgess & Van der Maas 2002). In fact, the terms 'pentecostal' and 'charismatic' are often used loosely and interchangeably by churches in various contexts, thus complicating scientific attempts to achieve a precise definition. This complexity has therefore led some scholars to use both terms as a 'compound phrase' namely Pentecostal-charismatics or Charismatic-pentecostals. In fact, there is ample evidence of churches that describe themselves as both Pentecostal and charismatic in outlook, content and orientation. These varied definitions, meanings and contexts render a simple taxonomy of Pentecostal and charismatic movements almost impossible.

Nonetheless, Pentecostal/charismatic movements are identified by their central emphasis on spiritual rebirth (baptism of the
Holy Spirit) – evidenced by glossolalia, charismatic (spiritual) gifts,
healing, deliverance, prophecy, exuberant worship and a distinctive
language of experiential spirituality. In spite of these common features, they differ on the meaning, symbolism and level of emphasis
of each characteristic. Irrespective of differences in the composition
of these groups, their appeal and function are similar. In spite of
the extraordinary degree of affinity of liturgy, organization, ideology and ethic in various cultural contexts, Pentecostal/charismatic
churches should be viewed as diffuse global movements and not
as centralized, international organizations. One feature of Pentecostal movements is their relative religious autonomy permitting
them to develop independently within each local, cultural setting
as opposed to becoming a centralized bureaucratic organization.
The unprecedented growth of Pentecostal/charismatic movements
in their various forms also occasioned a remarkable growth of ritual
patterns, cultural attitudes, ecclesiastical structures, and complex
strategies of expansion.

The lack of definitional specificity and standardization in
such terms as Pentecostal and charismatic partly result from an
'elastic' and broad understanding of the phenomena. These terms
can become so general and broadly used as to be meaningless
(Corten & Marshall-Fratani 2001: 4; Droogers 2004: 46; Kamsteeg 1998: 10-11). Sociologists of religion can sometimes take for
granted the character of Pentecostalism without regard to its historical, phenomenological and theological dimensions. Sociological approaches to Pentecostalism investigate how Pentecostal and
charismatic movements respond to changes within a variety of local
and global contexts. The dynamics of religious change in different
cultural contexts enables a more exact insight into the nature and
impact of Pentecostal and charismatic movements. In short, this
terminological confusion among social scientists is partly a consequence of their lack of attention to the actual history of Pentecostal
and charismatic churches. As Joel Robbins argued, although a basic
historical framework cannot solve all definitional problems, it can
establish more adequate terminological parameters (2004: 119).
Social scientists who employ a variety of terms such as Protestantism, fundamentalism, evangelicalism, charismatic Christianity
and so forth, as analytic categories, sometimes mistakenly assume

that local meanings can be applied universally and will therefore be widely comprehended in different contexts. Such juxtaposition of terms in different contexts often obscures a clear definition of Pentecostalism.

FUNDAMENTALISM AND PENTECOSTAL/ CHARISMATIC MOVEMENTS

Since the 1970s the ascendancy to worldwide prominence of what was often described simply as 'religious fundamentalism' stimulated further sociological research into Pentecostal/charismatic movements. Debates about the rise of so-called fundamentalist religions in the United States and about new religions in a global perspective were significant in serving as the basis for reconfiguring our understanding of the significant place of religion in society. In a strict sense, fundamentalism refers to a specific development in the history of American Protestantism. Social scientists have been eager to learn who the religious fundamentalists are and what fundamentalism is. Why is resurgence taking place, and what are the distinctive characteristics, the global spread, and the possible connections to political violence? Exporting the American Gospel (Brouwer, Gifford & Rose 1996) demonstrates, though controversially, how new Christian fundamentalism has taken hold in many nations in Africa, Latin America, and Asia. This new kind of Christian fundamentalism – described as a transnational religious culture – was epitomized by 'a fresh hybrid of Pentecostal fervor, mainstream evangelicalism, and bible-believing millennialism distributed by modern means: innovative megachurches and parachurches, televangelism, and computerized churches' (Brouwer et al 1996). Unfortunately the interpretation of Pentecostalism and the charismatic movements has suffered from academic biases, because these religious movements do not measure up to secular scholars' notions about 'intellectual progress', 'progressive refinement', and religious ideas (Finke & Stark 1992: 4-5).

Although a survey of these and other related works over the past three decades reveals some progress in sociological research on such movements, there are evidently ongoing pitfalls in conceptualizing and understanding religious fundamentalism. Pentecostalism and fundamentalism may share certain affinities in that they both emerged in the early twentieth century and exhibit elements of the broader evangelical movement. The treatment of Pentecostalism as a branch of fundamentalism (Stoll 1990), its association with various brands of conservative Christianity (Woodberry & Smith 1998) and the assumption that they are the same can hardly suffice historically and analytically (Cox 1995, 1997; Martin 1990, 2002, Spittler 1994). In exploring global Christian fundamentalism, Brouwer, Gifford & Rose (1996) went too far in privileging a new and unique kind of American fundamentalism that is spreading across the globe. Such narratives of 'extraversion' and 'ecclesiastical externality' prevalent in earlier accounts on Protestantism in Latin America (Martin 1990) and of 'modern' or 'new' fundamentalist Christianity in Africa (Gifford 1998, 2004; van Dijk 2000), mask indigenous innovation and creativity. They also hide local experiences and expressions that shaped these contexts. More recent works are uncovering the local impulses and vitality of indigenous Pentecostal movements and how they are responding to rapid social change, modernity and globalization (Martin 2002; Kalu 2008).

THE GLOBALIZATION OF PENTECOSTALISM

Globalization as a concept and process has been employed by social scientists as an appropriate category for describing and interpreting the emergence of Pentecostalism as a cultural movement. In fact, Jenkins (2002: 7-8) defined it as 'perhaps the most successful social movement of the past century'. Religious traditions have the capacity for self-reflexive critical thinking about globalization (Beckford 2003: 105). The nascence and rapid expansion of the Pentecostal movement in the twentieth century lead to a recognition of Pentecostalism as an integral part of the globalization process but also as a product or consequence of it. The application of globalization to Pentecostalism therefore refers to its geographical expansion, demographic spread, and its cultural influence.

Robbins (2004) demonstrates how scholars 'use Pentecostals and charismatics to support theories that construe globalization as a process of Westernizing homogenization and those that understand it as a process of indigenizing differentiation'. Roland Robertson's (1992: 73) innovative concept of 'glocalization' is quite apt in exploring the interconnectedness between local and global contexts at the level of religious movements such as the Pentecostal and charismatic movements. Although the popular adage has been 'think globally, act locally', much of the thinking also takes place at the local level (Droogers 2001: 51). Thus, the globalization of Pentecostal/charismatic movements makes sense mainly in terms of its localization. As André Droogers aptly points out, 'this then is the somewhat gloomy globalizing world within which Pentecostal expansion occurs. In it, space and non-space intermingle, just as the global and the local – or even the fragmented...Religion is part of the globalizing forces, as well as of the local translations. It is part both of the global impact and the local reaction' (Droogers 2001: 51). In other words, the rich, local varieties, manifestations, expressions and experiences of Pentecostal and charismatic Christianity shed significant light on considering them as a global phenomenon or as a 'global culture' (Poewe 1994). Pentecostalism facilitates the translation from the global to the local and vice versa (Droogers 2001: 57).

It is within this context of globalization that questions about the 'why' and 'how' of Pentecostal expansion and success have become pressing and intriguing. To account for the success of Pentecostal/charismatic churches in terms of attracting converts in large numbers and of its phenomenal spread globally, sociological theories concentrate on the role of deprivation and anomie as causes of growth (d'Epinay 1969; Anderson 1979; Chesnut 1997; Corten 1999). Pentecostalism was largely described as the religion of the poor, the masses, the disinherited, and displaced persons. It was also categorized as an urban phenomenon. Such interpretations undercut and undervalue significant dimensions of Pentecostal/charismatic cultures. The narrow emphasis on the why of conversion undermines how Pentecostal/charismatic movements negotiate or transform the cultures into which they are introduced. Droogers aptly posits internal religious characteristics of Pentecostalism and their articulation within the external circumstances of globalization as causes of growth (2001: 41). He aptly remarks, 'In any case, now as before, whatever the theoretical framework, most attention is given to factors that are external to Pentecostalism itself. Only rarely are specific characteristics of Pentecostalism taken into account and a more idiosyncratic explanation sought...' (Droogers 2001:41). Thus, while not underestimating the influence of external conditions, Droogers underscores the fact that a far-reaching account of this expansion must necessarily commence from 'the particularities of a specific religion' and proceed from there to the impact of, and articulation with, external social processes, and not the other way round.

AFRICAN CHRISTIANITY AS A NEW
PENTECOSTAL/CHARISMATIC MOVEMENT

The most recent development within African Christianity is the emergence and proliferation of Pentecostal/charismatic churches, especially from the 1950s and 1960s onwards. There have been two waves of these Pentecostal/charismatic movements. On the one hand there are the indigenous Pentecostal groups such as the Redeemed Christian Church of God, the Deeper Life Bible Church, Zimbabwe Assemblies of God Africa, International Central Gospel Church, Church of Pentecost, Church of God Mission International, Winners Chapel, Rhema Bible Church, Mountain of Fire and Miracles Ministries, Latter Rain Assembly, and the Household of God Fellowship. On the other hand, there are those developments such as the Four Square Gospel Church, the Full Gospel Businessmen Fellowship International, Campus Crusade for Christ, Youth with a Mission, and Christ for all Nations, which exist as branches or missions of Pentecostal churches and organizations introduced from outside Africa. The former are largely independent and rely on hardly any external assistance, while some of the latter depend to a large extent on funds, literature, and sometimes personnel from their mission headquarters. The former have also embarked on transnational mission activities by planting branches in the United States, Canada, Europe, and other parts of the world.

The Pentecostal/charismatic churches have shaped African Christianity through their increasing involvement on the wider global stage. They have increasingly taken to proselytizing in North America and Europe, viewing the regions as 'new abodes' and promising 'mission fields' (Adogame, 2005: 504; 2007). There are also groups existing as branches of mother churches with headquarters in Africa; and others founded by African migrants in the diaspora. Examples include the Redeemed Christian Church of God, with headquarters in Nigeria and the Kingsway International Christian Center in East London. Both have a huge African membership with few non-Africans. The Embassy of the Blessed Kingdom of God for All Nations in Kiev in the Ukraine is a typical example of an African-led church with a majority non-African membership (Adogame 2008). Such African religious movements are significant within the framework of globalization, owing to the unique expression of African Christianity which they exhibit—a feature that could be described as their self-assertion and as the global preservation of their religious identity (Adogame 2003). They constitute international ministries that have implications on a global scale. As part of an increasing phenomenon of what they term 'mission reversed' or 'remissionization of Christianity to a secularized West', these African churches have systematically set out to evangelize the world. Notions of globalization and globality are appropriated as theological and ideological constructs, and thus feature prominently in their mission statements and strategies, as well as sermon rhetoric—although these notions are used and understood differently. It is common to find churches defining themselves as 'global churches' and their mission as 'global tasks'.

The literature on African Pentecostalism and charismatic movements has grown steadily in the past two decades. Until recently, research on the phenomenon in Africa has been dominated by social scientists from western countries. African scholars have now joined them to fill in this academic vacuum. Their varied methodologies and interpretations have opened up new vistas in research on the phenomena, but also contributed more broadly to knowledge of the field. Ogbu Kalu's recent book, African Pentecostalism (2008) remains the most comprehensive account of the role and social impact of African Pentecostal and charismatic Christianity, focusing on a broad range of issues such as identity, agency, gender and authority, media and popular culture, political discourses, and Pentecostal immigrant religiosity. Kalu critically engaged current scholarship, and was successful in balancing global processes with local identities. He combined the discourse on African Pentecostal and charismatic movements with a wide global, western historiography by revisiting the debate on genealogy, emerging themes, development and mobility of Pentecostalism.

THE CONTRIBUTIONS TO THIS VOLUME

Scholars' use, appropriation and application of the concepts 'pentecostalism', 'globalization' and 'fundamentalism' in this book were conceptually reflected upon in three opening contributions (Ulrich Berner, Afe Adogame and Asonzeh Ukah, Umar Danfulani). Some other papers tackled the vexed question of the provenance, historical development of Pentecostal/Charismatic churches (movements) in geo-ethnic contexts of Nigeria, South

Africa and the USA (Ogbu Kalu, Allan Anderson, Jacob Olupona). There was also a focus on thematic issues such as gospel music, new media – the Internet (Ezra Chitando, Afe Adogame), female religious leadership, deliverance and demonology, religious networking and revisiting the discourse of prosperity theology (Bolaji Bateye, Rosalind Hackett, Dapo Asaju, and Deji Ayegboyin) in African Pentecostalism. These varied perspectives demonstrate how brands of African Pentecostalism or Pentecostalism in Africa challenge, contest and negotiate modernity and globalization on the one hand, while they at the same time portray African pentecostalism or pentecostalism in Africa and beyond as a form of African modernity that is integrally engaged in the globalization process.

The contributors to this volume also have drawn attention to the spontaneous, multifaceted provenance and phenomenal expansion of Pentecostal and charismatic movements over the past 100 years, and they suggest that the movement will continue to reshape and reconfigure the global religious landscape of the twenty-first century and beyond (Barrett et. al. 2001). We can conclude that owing to the movement's mobility, public role and strategies of expansion, the pentecostalization and charismatization of world Christianity will be commonplace. This fluid, elastic nature of the phenomena, particularly its influence on mainline Christianity, will render a consideration of a distinctively Pentecostal identity more and more enigmatic. In fact, as new Pentecostal and charismatic movements continue to emerge, they will undergo, in the long run, institutionalization and bureaucratization processes likely to transform and change their nature, identity, texture, public (civic) role and modus operandi. Thus, the 'why' and 'how' of Pentecostal expansion and relative success globally will continue to pose critical issues relevant to sociologists and historians of religion as well as other social scientists, secular historians, theologians and policy makers in an era of increasing global insecurity and uncertainty. The movement's visibility, mobility and continued growth throws up future challenges to both Pentecostal/charismatic and non-pentecostals alike, to world Christianity and its interaction with other religions, and within the local and global public spheres. It is the intention of this book to shed important light on these dynamic movements, not just as they impact on Christianity in Africa, but on Christianity generally in its many global contexts.

References

Adogame, A.: 'Betwixt Identity and Security: African New Religious Movements and the Politics of Religious Networking in Europe'. In *Nova Religio: The Journal of Alternative and Emergent Religions* 7 (2) 2003: 24-41.

Adogame, A.: 'African Christian Communities in Diaspora'. In Ogbu U. Kalu (ed.) *African Christianity: An African Story*. (Pretoria: Department of Church History, University of Pretoria, 2005), 494-514.

Adogame, A.: 'Raising Champions, Taking Territories: African Churches and the Mapping of New Religious Landscapes in Diaspora'. In Trost, T.L., (ed.) *The African Diaspora and the Study of Religion* (New York: Palgrave Macmillan, 2007), 17-34.

Adogame, A.: 'Up, Up Jesus! Down, Down Satan! African Religiosity in the former Soviet Bloc – the Embassy of the Blessed Kingdom of God for All Nations'. In *Exchange: Journal of Missiological and Ecumenical Research*, 37, (3) 2008: 310-336.

Anderson, A.: *An Introduction to Pentecostalism. Global Charismatic Christianity* (Cambridge. Cambridge University Press, 2004).

Anderson, R.M.: *Vision of the Disinherited: The Making of American Pentecostalism* (Peabody, MA: Hendrickson, 1979).

Asamoah-Gyadu, J.K.: *African Charismatics. Current Developments within Independent Indigenous Pentecostalism in Ghana* (Leiden: Brill, 2005).

Barrett, D.B., George T.K. & Todd M.J., eds.: *World Christian Encyclopedia*. 2nd ed., 2 volumes (Oxford and New York: Oxford University Press, 2001).

Barrett, D.B., & Johnson, T.M.: 'Annual Statistical Table of Global Mission: 2003', in *International Bulletin of Missionary Research* 27 (1) 2003: 24-25.

Beckford, J.A.: *Social Theory and Religion* (Cambridge: Cambridge University Press, 2003).

Burgess, S.M., & Van der Maas, E.M., eds.: *The New International Dictionary of Pentecostal and Charismatic Movements* (Grand Rapids: Zondervan, 2002)

Brouwer, S, Gifford, P and Rose, S.D.: *Exporting the American Gospel: Global Christian Fundamentalism* (London: Routledge, 1996).

Bruce, S.: *Fundamentalism* (Cambridge: Polity Press, 2001).

Bruce, S.: *God is Dead: Secularization in the West* (Oxford: Blackwell, 2002).

Chesnut, A.: *Born Again in Brazil. The Pentecostal Boom and the Pathogens of Poverty* (New Brunswick, NJ: Rutgers University Press, 1997).

Coleman, S.: *The Globalization of Charismatic Christianity. Spreading the Gospel of Prosperity* (Cambridge: Cambridge University Press, 2000).

Corten, A.: *Pentecostalism in Brazil: Emotion of the Poor and Theological Romanticism* (New York: St. Martin's, 1999).

Corten, A. & Marshall-Fratani, R., eds.: *Between Babel and Pentecost: Transnational Pentecostalism in Africa and Latin America* (Bloomington: Indiana University Press, 2001).

Cox, H.: *Fire from Heaven: The Rise of Pentecostal Spirituality and the Reshaping of Religion in the Twenty-First Century* (Cambridge, MA: Da Capo Press, 1995).

Cox, H.: 'Into the Age of Miracles: Culture, religion and the Market Revolution', in *World Policy Journal*, 14 (1997): 87-95.

D'Epinay, C.L.: *Haven of the Masses: A Study of the Pentecostal Movement in Chile* (London: Lutterworth, 1969).

Dempster, M., Klaus, B. & Petersen, D., eds.: *The Globalization of Pentecostalism: A Religion Made to Travel* (Oxford and Irvine, CA: Regnum, 1999).

Droogers, A.: 'Globalization and Pentecostal Success', in Corten, A. & Marshall-Fratani, R., eds. *Between Babel and Pentecost: Transnational Pentecostalism in Africa and Latin America* (London: Hurst and Co., 2001), 41-61.

Finke, R. & Stark, R.: *The Churching of America: Winners and Losers in our Religious Economy* (New Brunswick, NJ: Rutgers University Press, 1992).

Gifford, P.: *African Christianity: Its Public Role* (London: Hurst and Co., 1998).

Gifford, P.: *Ghana's New Christianity: Pentecostalism in a Globalizing African Economy* (London: Hurst, 2004).

Hexham, I. & Poewe, K.: *New Religions as Global Cultures: Making the Human Sacred* (Boulder: Westview Press, 1997).

Hollenweger, W.: *The Pentecostals* (London: SCM, 1972; (reprint, Peabody Mass: Hendrickson, 1988).

Jenkins, P.: *The Next Christendom. The Coming of Global Christianity* (New York: Oxford University Press, 2002).

Kalu, O.U.: *African Pentecostalism. An Introduction* (Cambridge: Cambridge University Press, 2008).

Kamsteeg, F.H.: *Prophetic Pentecostalism in Chile: A Case Study on Religion and Development Policy* (Lanham: Scarecrow, 1998)

Martin, D.: *Tongues of Fire* (Oxford: Blackwell, 1990).

Martin, D.: *Pentecostalism: The World their Parish* (Oxford and Massachusetts: Blackwell Publishers, 2002).

'Pentecostal Power'. Pew Research Center Publications, October 5, 2006. Available at: http://pewresearch.org/pubs/254/pentecostal-power (accessed 13 July 2007).

Poewe, K., ed.: *Charismatic Christianity as a Global Culture* (Columbia, SC: University of South Carolina Press, 1994).

Robertson, R.: *Globalization, Social Theory and Global Culture* (London: Sage Publications, 1992).

Robbins, J.: 'The Globalization of Pentecostal and Charismatic Christianity', in *Annual Review of Anthropology* 33 (2004): 117-143.

'Spirit and Power' – Report of a 10-Country Survey of Pentecostals. The Pew Forum on Religion and Public Life, October 2006. Available at: http://pewforum.org/publications/surveys/pentecostals-06.pdf (accessed 13 July 2007).

Spittler, R.P.: 'Are Pentecostals and Charismatics Fundamentalists? A Review of American Uses of These Categories' in Poewe, K., ed.: *Charismatic Christianity as a Global Culture* (Columbia, SC: University of South Carolina Press, 1994), 103-116.

Stoll, D.: *Is Latin America Turning Protestant?* (Berkeley, CA: University of California Press, 1990)

Synan, V.: *Century of the Holy Spirit: 100 years of Pentecostal and Charismatic renewal* (Nashville, TN: Thomas Nelson, 2001).

Van der Veer, P., ed.: *Conversion to Modernities. The Globalization of Christianity* (New York & London: Routledge, 1996).

Van Dijk, R.: *Christian Fundamentalism in Sub-Saharan Africa: The Case of Pentecostalism*. Occasional Paper, (University of Copenhagen: Center of African Studies, 2000).

Woodberry, R.D., & Smith, C.S.: 'Fundamentalism et. al: conservative protestants in America', in *Annual Review of Sociology* 24 (1998): 25-56.

GLOBALIZATION AND RELIGION: SOME PRELIMINARY QUESTIONS

Ulrich Berner

INTRODUCTION

There has been much talk about globalization since the 1990s. Concepts such as 'global society', 'global village' and 'global culture' have become quite prominent in the social sciences. British sociologist Anthony Giddens, towards the end of a BBC lecture, said about globalization: 'It is the way we now live' (Giddens, 2000: 1). German sociologist Ulrich Beck in a similar way, stated: '*Globalität ist eine nicht hintergehbare Bedingung menschlichen Handelns am Ausgang dieses Jahrhunderts*' (Beck, 1997: 35). The reader of Beck's book has to wait for some time until the title question, 'What is globalization?' is answered. However, the reader will probably agree with Beck as far as the problem of definition is concerned:

> Globalisierung ist sicher das am meisten gebrauchte
> – mißbrauchte – und am seltensten definierte, wahrs-
> cheinlich mißverständlichste, nebulöseste und politisch
> wirkungsvollste (Schlag- und Streit-)Wort der letzten,
> aber auch der kommenden Jahre (Beck, 1997: 42)

This statement points among other things to the possibility of an ideological usage of the concept – an aspect that has been highlighted in a critical way by 'voices from the third world'. Kandiyur Pannikar has expressed the suspicion that the very concept of globalization is nothing else but a euphemism for domination (Pannikar, 1997: 49).

In any case, the talk about globalization has made its inroad into Religious Studies, giving rise to a number of new concepts, as, for instance, 'global religion' or 'global religious system'. These concepts seem to indicate that there are new religious phenomena arising in the context of globalizing processes. From the historian of religion's point of view, this talk of global religious phenomena is a challenge: the historian may ask himself whether there is really something new about the so called global religious phenomena. What is, for instance, the difference between a global religion and a world religion? (Berner, 2002). It can hardly be denied that Christianity, for instance, has always had a global aspiration.

Irving Hexham and Karla Poewe have rightly stated that Buddhism, Christianity, and Islam 'have always been global cultures'; they understand 'global culture' in this context as implying the ideal 'to spread a religious metaculture that was perfectly capable of remaining identifiable while being absorbed by local cultures' (Hexham and Poewe, 1997: 43). In order to distinguish the global culture of new religions from the global culture of old religions, they state that 'all new religions incorporate, often indiscriminately, insights from other cultures and traditions'. (Hexham and Poewe, 1997: 46). It might be asked, however, whether there were similar phenomena in the religious world of Late Antiquity. Apollonius of Tyana, for instance, according to the report by the pagan philosopher Philostratos, traveled the world as far as to India and Ethiopia in order to incorporate insights from other cultures and traditions into his Pythagorean system of religious philosophy (Berner, 1990).

In any case, identifying new global phenomena seems to be easy, as far as economics is concerned. According to Anthony Giddens, 'the current world economy has no parallels in earlier times'. He refers to the new global electronic economy: vast amounts of capital can be transferred 'from one side of the world to another at the click of a mouse', possibly destabilizing 'what might have seemed rock-solid economies' (Giddens, 2000: 2). British economist, Grahame Thompson has explained economic globalization in a most convincing way by distinguishing between a globalized world economy and an internationalized world economy. A globalized world economy, according to Thompson, is based on a new structure of disembedded economic relationships: 'The principle private actors here would be transnational corporations. These represent organizations that are disembodied from any national base' (Thompson, 1999: 140). Ulrich Beck has described the economic aspect of globalization in a similar way, referring to transnational corporations and to the breaking down of national boundaries, that is, the emergence of a new relationship between national unities and transnational agents (Beck, 1997: 28f).

Clear as it may be in the field of economics, the concept of globalization becomes vague when applied to culture in general. Beck tries to illustrate cultural globalization by giving the example of an Arabic chanson that is popular in France and Israel (Beck, 1997: 41f). Again, it may be asked, whether this is a new phenomenon at all. Perhaps there have always been transnational agents in the field of culture in general and in religion in particular. In any case, the question remains how to identify global religious phenomena as an equivalent of transnational corporations acting in a globalized world economy.

One could refer, perhaps, to the use of new media in religion, thus taking into account the technological globalization that is bound to globalization in economics (Hackett, 1998). The historian of religion, however, will have to ask whether the use of new media in religion is really an innovation or just acceleration? Does the electronic medium really shape the content of the religious message or only speed up its dissemination? The reflections on these questions, concerning globalization and religion, are subdivided into three sections: African new religious movements as local initiatives in a global context; religious pluralism as a global religious system; global problems and their impact on the religious traditions of the world.

AFRICAN NEW RELIGIOUS MOVEMENTS AS LOCAL INITIATIVES IN A GLOBAL CONTEXT

African Independent Churches, defined as 'Churches founded by Africans for Africans' (Turner, 1967; Ayegboyin and Ishola, 1997: 19), were quite a prominent subject of research, since the

1960s (Berner, 2000b: 267-269). Since the 1990s, researchers have embarked on a new field, focusing on the new wave of Pentecostalism that had reached the African continent (cf. Meyer, 2004: 447f.). Ruth Marshall begins her report on Nigerian Pentecostalism by stating correctly that all world religions are "transnational", Christianity in particular, having at its core an evangelical message which is to be spread to all peoples' (Marshall-Fratani, 2001: 80). The transnational character of contemporary Pentecostalism, however, according to Ruth Marshall, takes on a new significance in the context of globalization. She points to the use of the new media, and, most importantly, to the new attitude towards tradition – Pentecostals address the problem of evil forces, a problem that had been neglected in missionary Christianity (Marshall-Fratani, 2001: 91f, 99f.).

The last point already indicates that there may be some cultural continuity, despite the discontinuity brought about by the new processes of globalization. African church historian Ogbu Kalu has stressed this continuity, going back even to African traditional religion itself. He argues that modern Pentecostalism in Africa draws upon the traditional African worldview (Kalu, 2000: 103f.). Instead of summarizing Kalu's arguments, an historical example may be used as an illustration: the emergence and shaping of the Christ Apostolic Church in Nigeria.

After World War I, in the Anglican church of Ijebu-Ode, a prayer group emerged which might be regarded as the starting point of a movement that later grew into the Christ Apostolic Church. Apart from the local initiative – the local prayer group and the local prophet Babalola some time later – there was also a global connection from the very beginning of the movement: one member of the movement, Pastor D.O. Odubanjo, was corresponding with the Faith Tabernacle in the United States of America:

> From the very beginning of the historical development of CAC, he had played the role of the link-person between the church, at its various stages, and the western Pentecostal religious community (Omoyajowo, 1998: 211f.)

Seen against this background, taking into consideration the historical dimension, it is difficult to say what is radically new about Nigerian Pentecostalism in the 1990s, apart from the use of the electronic media (Cf. Hackett, 1998). This change of the media, however, could also be interpreted as an acceleration of communication rather than as an innovation, regarding the intercontinental correspondence that was functioning already in the 1920s.

RELIGIOUS PLURALISM AS A GLOBAL RELIGIOUS SYSTEM?

Since the 1970s there has been much talk about religious pluralism and interreligous dialogue. Christian theologians from different denominations, such as John Hick and Paul Knitter, have developed a pluralistic theology that would allow not only a friendly relationship towards other religions but also a mutual enrichment. John Hick has applied the formula 'Copernican Revolution' to this shift in the theological perspective of Christianity, and he has provided also the philosophical framework for such a pluralistic theology (See Hick, 1988: 120-132; Hick, 1980). It might be argued that the universal acceptance and institutionalization of such a pluralistic position can be interpreted as the emergence of a global religious system.

Looking for political efforts to institutionalize religious pluralism, one could think of the Pancasila system in Indonesia or, perhaps, also of the Ujamaa-system in Tanzania as it was put into practise by Nyerere in the 1960s (cf. Ludwig, 1999: 37f.). However, the question has to be asked again: Is religious pluralism, as an ideology and/or as an institution, really a new phenomenon in the religious history of humankind?

First of all, this recent development of pluralistic conceptions could be placed in a broader historical context, tracing it back at least to the World's Parliament of Religions that took place in 1893 at Chicago. Max Müller's appreciation of this event would be of special relevance here (Müller, 1993). A certain strand in Religious Studies itself might be regarded as a global religious system in this sense (Berner, 2002). Going back into the history of religions one may think of India and its great tradition of tolerance and pluralism. As early as the 3rd century B.C.E, Emperor Asoka established a peaceful relationship between all the religious groups and movements of his time. His system of religious policy was centered on the concept of dharma, an abstract concept that was intended to function as a universally acceptable basis (Berner, 2000a: 61f.).

Asoka has often been regarded as the first missionary of Buddhism which is misleading – what he tried to do might better be described as an effort to spread his pluralistic system globally.

Such an effort to establish religious pluralism could also be found in European history: Emperor Julian who is known as the Apostate from Christianity, might be regarded not only as an enemy of Christianity but could be described equally well as an adherent and defender of religious pluralism. In any case, a clearly pluralistic program was propagated by the pagan philosopher Themistios shortly after Julian's death, at that time however, such a program did not have a chance of being put into practise (*Themistios, oratio* 5. cf. Berner, 2002).

In view of these historical examples, it does not seem very reasonable to label the ideology of religious pluralism and its institutionalization as a 'global religious system', as a totally new phenomenon of the global age. However, it does seem reasonable to assume that the processes of globalization which are undeniably operating in the economic sphere have given or will give rise to new developments in religion as well. American sociologist of religion, James Spickard, has interpreted the Western human rights movement as a quasi-religious phenomenon that has come into existence in the context of globalization (Spickard, 1999). This movement, it seems, might be labeled as a global religious system, as a new phenomenon of the global age. However, there may also be some new phenomena that can be identified as religious in a narrower sense.

GLOBAL PROBLEMS AS A NEW CHALLENGE FOR THE RELIGIOUS TRADITIONS OF THE WORLD

A globalized world economy would not have been possible without new technologies – economic and technological globalization has been developing together. The computer and the World Wide Web have rightly been taken as symbols of the new global culture that has emerged in the Western world in the 20th century. Technological and economic developments in the 20th century, however, have created new problems that can reasonably be described as global problems.

One of these problems that became a much debated issue towards the end of the 20th century is environmental degradation. This is a global problem, indeed, since the warming of the atmosphere, for instance, is not limited to the countries that bear the responsibility for producing an increasing amount of CO_2. The growing awareness of such a global problem poses a challenge to the religions of the world. Canadian sociologist Peter Beyer has already drawn attention to this fact: since the 1960s and particularly since the 1980s, religious traditions and organizations, such as the World Council of Churches, have shown an environmental concern (Beyer, 1994: 209; cf. Robertson, 1994: 132). In addition to that, Beyer has also pointed to the fact that 'various portions of the secular environmental movement exhibit clear religious qualities' (Beyer, 1994: 212). Environmental movements, it seems, might also be designated global religious systems, as new phenomena of the global age.

However, this challenge caused by environmental problems may also lead to new religious phenomena in a narrow sense, as for instance, to new relationships between different religious traditions, clearly distinguishable from religious pluralism based on interreligious dialogue. A good example may be the activities of the Zimbabwean Institute of Religious Research and Ecological Conservation (ZIRRCON), initiated and documented by the missiologist Inus Daneel. The interesting point is that African Christians and African Traditionalists have been cooperating in their efforts of "Earth-keeping":

ZIRRCON's 'green army' consists of two sister organizations: AZTREC (Association of Zimbabwean traditional ecologists), the traditional wing, composed mainly of chiefs, spirit mediums, headmen, excombatants and tradition-oriented villagers; and the AAEC (Association of African Earthkeeping Churches), the Christian wing, comprising some 150 African Independent Churches, and led in the field by bishops, prophets, and women's associations of these geographically widespread movements (Daneel, 1998: 1).

There is a point for comparison: these joint ecological activities, based on different religious traditions, might be interpreted as the emergence of a trans-traditional religious system that is comparable to trans-national economic corporations acting in a globalized world economy. It should be noted that various religious traditions of the world have shown ecological concerns in the past.

Indira Gandhi, for instance, in an interview with Fritjof Capra, gave an example from ancient India, pointing to Emperor Asoka, some of whose edicts, in her view, 'foreshadow today's environmental concerns' (Capra, 1988: 315). The real danger of destroying nature and depriving humankind of its future, however, has become an issue often regarded as the age of globalization only towards the end of the 20ᵗʰ century.

Another new global problem that puts a challenge to all the religious traditions of the world is Gene-technology. Technological advance in this field of biology has created new ethical problems that call for solutions from the side of religion (see Schlieter; 2004 concerning Buddhism). This is a new problem which all religions, theistic religions in particular, have to respond to, since it challenges the hitherto predominant conceptions of human beings: the very identity of humankind would be altered, it seems, if human beings are going to take over the role of creator. Such a challenge may also lead to the emergence of new religious phenomena in the future.

These global problems, the danger of altering the identity and/ or destroying the existence of humankind, can be identified as side-effects of the process of globalization that may have a considerable impact on the development of religions. All religions have to respond to new type of problems that has been created by the economic and technological developments of the global age. This global situation may in the future give rise to new religious phenomena, as, for instance, trans-traditional religious systems. The decisive point would be the shift in the hierarchy of values, if in the long run global problems will gain priority over religious identities based on one particular tradition.

Bibliography

Ayegboyin, Deji and Ishola, Ademola, *African Indigenous Churches. An Historical Perspective*. Lagos: Greater Heights Publications, 1997.

Beck, Ulrich, *Was ist Globalisierung? Irrtümer des Globalismus. Antworten auf Globalisierung*. Frankfurt: Suhrkamp, 1997.

Berner, Ulrich, 'The Image of the Philosopher in Late Antiquity and in Early Christianity', in: Hans G. Kippenberg, Yme B. Kuiper and Andy F. Sanders (eds), *Concepts of Person in Religion and Thought*. Berlin and New York: Mouton de Gruyter 1990, pp. 125-136.

Berner, Ulrich, 'Kaiser Asoka – der "indische Konstantin". Wendezeiten im buddhistischen Denken', in: Peter Segl (ed.), *Zeitenwenden Wendezeiten. Von der Achsenzeit bis zum Fall der Mauer*. Dettelbach: Verlag J.H.Röll, 2000, pp. 51-70.

Berner, Ulrich, 'Reflections upon the Concept of New Religious Movement', *Method and Theory in the Study of Religion* 12, 2000, pp. 267-276.

Berner, Ulrich, Early Christianity as a Global Religion, in Armin Geertz, Margit Warburg (eds) *New Religions and Globalization: Empirical, Theoretical and Methodological Perspectives*. Renner Studies On New Religions Series. Aarhus: Aarhus University Press, 2008, pp. 145-161.

Beyer, Peter, *Religion and Globalization*. London, Thousand Oaks and New Delhi: Sage Publications, 1994.

Capra, Fritjof, *Uncommon Wisdom. Conversations with Remarkable People*. London, Melbourne, Auckland and Johannesburg: Rider, 1988.

Daneel, M L, *African Earthkeepers*. Vol.1 Interfaith Mission in Earth-care. Pretoria: Unisa Press, 1998.

Giddens, Anthony, 'Globalization', Available at: http://news.bbc.co.uk/hi/english/static/events/reith_99/week1/lecture.1.htm (03.07.2000).

Hackett, Rosalind, 'Charismatic/Pentecostal Appropriation of Media Technologies in Nigeria and Ghana', *Journal of Religion in Africa*, 28, 1998, pp. 258-277.

Hexham, Irving and Poewe, Carla, *New Religions as Global Cultures. Making the Human Sacred*. Boulder: Westview Press, 1997.

Hick, John, 'Towards a Philosophy of Religious Pluralism', *Neue Zeitschrift für Systematische Theologie und Religionsphilosophie* 22, 1980, pp. 131-149.

Hick, John, *God and the Universe of Faiths. Essays in the Philosophy of Religion*. Basingstoke and London: Macmillan Press, 1988.

Kalu, Ogbu U., *Power, Poverty and Prayer. The Challenges of Poverty and Pluralism in African Christianity, 1960-1996*. Frankfurt am Main: Peter Lang, 2000.

Ludwig, Frieder, *Church & State in Tanzania. Aspects of a Changing Relationship, 1961-1994*. Leiden, Boston and Köln: Brill, 1999.

Marshall-Fratani, Ruth, 'Mediating the Global and Local in Nigerian Pentecostalism', in: Andre Corten and Ruth Marshall-Fratani (eds), *Between Babel and Pentecost. Transnational Pentecostalism in Africa and Latin America*. Bloomington: Indiana University Press 2001, pp. 80-105.

Meyer, Birgit, 'Christianity in Africa: From African Independent to Pentecostal-Charismatic Churches', *Annual Review of Anthropology* 33, 2004, pp. 447-474.

Müller, Friedrich Max, 'The Real Significance of the Parliament of Religions', in: Eric J. Ziolkowski (ed.), *A Museum of Faiths. Histories and Legacies of the 1893 World's Parliament of Religions.* Atlanta: Scholars Press, 1993, pp. 149-162.

Omoyajowo, Justus Akinwale, *The Emergence and Shaping of an African Independent Church: Christ Apostolic Church, Nigeria.* Diss. phil., University of Bayreuth 1998.

Panikkar, Kandiyur N., 'Globalization and Culture', *Voices from the Third World* 20, 1997, pp. 49-58.

Robertson, Roland, 'Religion and the Global Field', *Social Compass* 41, 1994, pp. 121-135.

Schlieter, Jens, 'Die buddhistische Haltung zum Klonen des Menschen. Fragestellungen zwischen Religionswissenschaft und Bioethik', *Zeitschrift für Religionswissenschaft* 12, 2004, pp. 43-59.

Spickard, James V., 'Human Rights, Religious Conflict, and Globalization. Ultimate Values in a New World Order', *MOST Journal on Multicultural Societies* 1, 1999. Available at: http://www.unesco.org/most/vl1n1spi.htm (accessed on 24 September 2003).

Thompson, Grahame, 'Introduction: situating globalization', *International Social Science Journal* 51, 1999, pp. 139-152.

Turner, Harold, *African Independent Church, Vol. 1 – The Church of the Lord (Aladura); Vol. 2 – The Life and Faith of the Church of the Lord (Aladura),* Oxford: Clarendon Press, 1967.

Viewing a Masquerade from Different Spots? Conceptual Reflections on Globalization and Pentecostalism within Religious Studies

Afe Adogame & Asonzeh Ukah

Introduction

Our task in this chapter appears a simple one. We say so because we do not here intend to propound new theories or postulate new definitions of these two concepts, 'Globalization' and 'Pentecostalism', as there already abound a legion. Rather, what we have set out to do is an investigation of the scholarly discourses on the subject with a view to identifying and revealing varied strands and streams, which may in some way evince some complementarity of meaning and definitional affinity, but which may in more senses generate a whole gamut of academic confusion and scholarly agnosticism. In the context of our research located within the framework of 'globalization' and 'localization', a critical reflection on these discourses is therefore expedient with the end purpose of subjecting our data and findings to the 'acid test' of these conceptualizations.

Globalization is a term that has come from 'nowhere' to occupy almost 'everywhere' especially in the last decade. The term translates as *globalisierung* (Germany), *mondialisation* (France), *globalizacion* (Spain and Latin America). It has no doubt become a household name in both public and private domains. In a special investigative report, *The African Courier* (2000: 1) describes the 'Trafficking in African Women in Germany', a burgeoning international sex trade as 'the latest feature of globalization'. Women from poor parts of the world are imported for the sexual pleasures of men in rich countries. This shows the extent of usage of the term in both public and private discourses. It also shows that globalization is a dynamic process, still unfolding and revealing itself in many folds of social and private life. There can, therefore, be no final word on the epiphany of globalization. But what does this mean to us? Can this be understood in the same way as other usages and meanings of the term?

Anthony Giddens (2000) posits two completely opposite, extreme thought paradigms in debates about globalization, the one he calls 'the sceptics', and the other the 'radicals'. The former refer to scholars who raise eye brows about globalization in its entire ramifications. In their view, the import of globalization lies solely in and not beyond the talk about it. One of the major proponents of this 'sceptical approach' is perhaps Rodney Stark who discards outrightly the contemporary globalization debate with a wave of the hand as a 'bunch of intellectual nonsense'. Others in the category of 'globo-sceptics' include Paul Hirst and Graham Thompson (1996), and Immanuel Wallerstein (1999) who believe that globalization discourse is 'a gigantic misreading of current reality – a deception imposed upon us by powerful groups, and even worse one that we have imposed upon ourselves', a discourse that 'leads us to ignore the real issues before us, and to misunderstand the historical crisis within which we find ourselves'.

Giddens labels the other extreme position as 'radicals' because they tenaciously maintain that 'not only is globalization very real, but that its consequence can be felt everywhere'. In pitching his tent with the latter, he argues that 'globalization as we are experiencing it, is in many respects not only new, but revolutionary'. Collin Hay and Matthew Watson (1999) have chosen to introduce sceptical notes to a triumphalist model of the political economy of globalization discourse by insisting on a balanced perspective in the on-going debate. In order to provide a more complete picture on the phenomenon as highlighted by Giddens, it may not be out of place to add a third level in the debate. While globalization is perceived as a relatively recent phenomenon or that which is still in the process of emerging (Friedman, 2000), there are others who will view it as an age-long phenomenon, a feature which has always been identified with human history (Mazrui, 2000; Rudolph and Piscatori, 1997; Foreman-Peck, 1998).

Giddens rightly points out that it is a misnomer to narrow the phenomenon solely within the economic spectrum. Globalization must be situated in a broader frame within politics, technology, culture as well as in economics. According to him, 'It is wrong to think of globalization as just concerning the big systems, like the world financial order. Globalization isn't only about what is 'out there', remote and far away from the individual. It is an 'in here' phenomenon too, influencing intimate and personal aspects of our lives' (Giddens, 2000: 3). However, unlike Giddens' bipolar categorization of the discourse of globalization, Christopher Chase-Dunn (1999) has identified five different dimensions and meanings of globalization and their temporal characteristics. The types he gave are common ecological constraints, cultural globalization, globalization of communication, economic globalization and political globalization. To these, Keohane (2000) adds 'military globalization', meaning by this 'long distance networks of interdependence in which force and the threat or promise of force, are employed'. We dare to complicate this scenario by saying that there is a diversity of epiphanies within each sub-unit of globalization.

Although the focus on globalization is very diverse, what seems to run through this complexity is the view that 'the world is experienced as a single place, or even a non-place, an abstract sign space, or as subject to time-space compression' (Cf. Robertson, 1992; Augé, 1995). But this one world also has its shadow world. There is often talk of a tension between the universal and the particular, 'the clash of civilizations' (Huntington, 1996; 2000), the war of 'Jihad Vs McWorld' (Barber, 2000), the global and the local, the whole and the fragments, and this has led to terms such as 'glocalization' (Robertson, 1992: 73), 'globo-localism' (see Sklair, 1999: 150), 'fragmegration' (Rosenau, 1994). The fascination with globalization does not stem from the characteristics of the global, but from the attitude developed locally in order to survive in an era of globalization (Droogers, 1999: 11). Peter Kloos (1999) argues for a 'dialectics of globalization' as the context for reconciling the 'apparent contradictory processes'. For him, all globalizing neologisms suffer irredeemable explanatory inadequacy and should be replaced with the tested concept of 'transnational regimes' which captures the complexities of the present moment.

The stereotype is that the local disappears under the influence of Americanization, Cocacolaization, McDonaldization, Guinnessization, raggaefication and other common usages or what may be likened as synonyms. It is true that in a relative sense, one can find these commodities everywhere or that they are consumed by almost everyone and almost in every place. However, what needs to be borne in mind is the fact that the contents in real sense are not the same everywhere. The taste of coca-cola in Nigeria for instance is quite different from that in Germany just in the same way as the taste of Irish Guinness Stout is markedly different from Nigerian Guinness Stout. Furthermore, different cultural meanings are generated and attached to these items thus altering their primary symbolic signification. Why is this so even when they have the same brand names or appear to be from the same sources? What does this portend for our understanding and conceptualization of globalization? In a sense, what this may mean is that the quality, texture and structure of a particular phenomenon differ from one context to another (local) even though it is known, or it is familiar to people in all the different contexts (global). But in that case, can we talk of a 'global this and that'? What kind of meaning and understanding does this convey to us?

In our reflection and understanding of globalization in terms of space-time, global and local should be seen as the two faces of the same movement from one epoch. It is not static but dynamic, it is not unidirectional but multidirectional. A global space today can change to a local space and vice versa. Globalization, if it is to be of enduring analytical value, should transcend inferior/superiority boundaries. It is referring to influences at the level of elements and symbols, not entire structures but sub-structures. In this respect, globalization depends on where one is and what one is talking about. It is not only in terms of continents, countries or between the West and the rest of the world, or between the North and South. It could also be within a smaller entity/community/nation state. Thus, it can be seen at different levels. How can we under-stand the shopping for African football professionals by European clubs; or Swiss banks which serve as a haven for legitimate and illegitimate businessmen and thieves the world over (especially African despots, past and current mis-rulers and their collabora-tors within and without); artefacts or art works which were carted away, stolen or bought from Africa and are now lying in the world's famous museums and art exhibitions; music; 'multicultural' food choices and cuisines as seen in restaurants; and of course the growing dimension of ecumenical links and networks among old and new religious traditions? What about the worldwide shuffling of academics with their faculty culture?

RELIGION AND GLOBALIZATION

As Dawid Venter (1999) observes, 'the application of global-ization theories to religious movements is relatively undeveloped'. However, some notable attempts at linking or seeing the relation-ship between religion and globalization or globality are evident in the recent works of Roland Robertson (1985, 1987, 1992, 1994) and Peter Beyer (1994, 1998, 1999, 2001). Robertson is undoubt-edly the pioneer in this academic endeavor. Since the mid-1980s, he has written extensively on the theory and processes of globali-zation. He talks about 'the crystallization of the entire world as a single place', 'the emergence of the global-human condition', 'the consciousness of the globe as such'. On religion, Robertson based his analysis on how state-religion tensions across the globe arise from the politicization of religion, and the religionization of poli-tics, which result from the process of globalization.

Beyer (1994) attempted a theoretical and applied examina-tion of globalization and its application to religion by combining four world-system theorists to show globalization as resulting in a global economy (Wallerstein), a global culture (Robertson), a global society (Luhmann), and a global polity (Meyer). Beyer identifies Christian and Islamic fundamentalist forms as both flourishing in the new globalizing climate. The expansion of Christianity, prior to when the term 'globalization' gained wide currency, has always been viewed as a transnational phenomenon with globalizing tendencies.

The Roman Catholic Church for instance has been depicted as a religious multinational. It appears that most of the scholars who have attempted to see the link between religion and globalization have done that solely with references to the Christian and Islamic fundamentalist forms. This gives the impression that this is the only way we can see this connection. In our view, this is somewhat narrow and unrealistic. It is about time we started thinking about the slow but steady spread of African religions and other religious ideologies deriving from African indigenous spiritual ideologies as forms of 'globalization from below'.

Droogers (1999: 12) remarks that,

> the so-called "electronic" churches have fully embraced modern means of communication. For several decades already – and without using the word – Christian missiologists have been very aware of the "glocalization" concept, as in the case of local cultural translations of the universal message, stamped as "inculturation". In non-western contexts especially, Christian converts have shown how people can adopt a global view and at the same time remain faithful to their traditional identities.

Communication has become an integral issue on the question of globalization because it builds bridges between the universally human, the one global place, and local translations of the global (Axford, 1995: 28). The dramatic increase in the use of transport and communication facilities, suggests that we live in a global village in which each fellow-human being can be reached at short notice, if not instantly. World society is presented as a system of mutual dependency. People, nations, transnational corporations, and religions are all condemned to each other (Droogers, 1999: 11).

Globalization has stimulated post-modern interest in fragmentation, not so much in relation to the global, but much more in relation to the local translations of the global. Although the popular adagium has been: 'think globally, act locally', much of the thinking also takes place at the local level (Droogers, 1999: 12). Thus, we could add to the adagium by saying, 'think local, act global'. As Droogers rightly points out,

> this then is the somewhat gloomy globalizing world within which Pentecostal expansion occurs. In it, space and non-

> space intermingle, just as the global and the local – or even
> the fragmented…Religion is part of the globalizing forces,
> as well as of the local translations. It is part both of the
> global impact and the local reaction (Droogers, 1999: 13).

It is within this context of globalization that the talks about the 'why' and 'how' of Pentecostal expansion has become more and more intelligible and appreciated. Droogers thinks globalization is a ravishing illness that demands Pentecostalism as a cure. If globalization is a wind that breaks down cultural resistances, identities and wellbeing, Pentecostalism is a soothing balm that nurses and restores to good and full health. Are we not confronted by the same type of optimism, promises and dreams of modernization theories that left a great deal of emptiness in its wake? Is Pentecostalism not breaking homes and wrecking cultures in some places today? Is Pentecostalism, in some forms of its epiphany, not slowing and gradually transforming to a spiritual side of market capitalism? Can we not see the silhouette of the capitalist ethic and the spirit of Pentecostalism? In sum, it is not inappropriate to add that every medicine is a poison; it would depend on context and degree.

PENTECOSTALISM WITHIN THE AFRICAN CONTEXT

The origin, *raison d étre*, and explanations for the rapid proliferation and success of Pentecostalism has attracted varied interpretations depending largely on the academic persuasion and 'paradigmatic preference' of the author. Closely related to this is the fact that the nature, scope and what constitutes the basic and specific ingredients of Pentecostalism is rather complex, controversial, and somewhat confusingly aggregated. What is really understood as Pentecostalism? Is Pentecostalism synonymous with Charismatic Christianity or are they clearly different? Does Pentecostalism share some features with Charismatic Christianity, if so in what ways are these evident? What about Neo-Pentecostals? Where do we situate pentecostalist formations within the so-called mainline or mission Christianity? Where do we situate para-church formations which are waxing stronger and stronger in our contemporary religious landscape? Much more particular: Is African Pentecostalism indigenous or imported from elsewhere or a combination of both? To what extent have the various scholars taken sides on this? In what sense can we define Pentecostalism in Africa as 'African or Indigenous Pentecostalism'? Again, as research on Pentecostalism in Africa appears to be dominated by social scientists, what lessons or challenges does this pose to scholars (historians) of religion? How do their socio-scientific lenses portray and interpret their religious data? Do their methods becloud the realities of the data, alter the sense and meaning, or open new, enriching vistas in research on the phenomena?

Some scholars have made their take-off point from the theoretical premises of modernization and neo-Marxist perspectives in order to arrive at conclusions about the incipience and unprecedented expansion of the Pentecostal movement(s). The various explanations accounting for the genesis of this phenomenon may be subsumed under these somewhat loose categorizations. One dominant but very controversial argument is that which favours a process of unilateralism. Simply put, Pentecostalism is portrayed as born, packaged and transmitted or delivered from the West, particularly the USA (i.e. Azusa Street connections) to other parts of the world. This view asserts that these sporadic Pentecostal fires were planted in this way, 'flow' or 'spreads' irresistibly like 'wild fire' or 'hurricane' to the rest of the globe.

A second school of thought differs significantly from the earlier in that it emphasizes local, spontaneous and contemporaneous developments and manifestations of what could be identified as Pentecostalism. This view recognizes the Azusa street and other related events in the US as only one instance of the spiritual event that occurred spontaneously, contemporaneously and independently in different parts of the world. Such a view recognizes the occurrence of such similar local, indigenous, spiritual (Pentecostal) event but frowns at attempts at issuing a preponderance of one over the others, or the claim of one as a fore-runner and progenitor of other later developments or experiences. The third explanation, although somewhat related to the second, appears to occupy the middle position in that it places emphasis on what may be called a 'criss-cross development' of the phenomenon within and between cultural boundaries. This explanation does not necessarily posit the root of the spectacular spiritual event in Azusa but that several local, indigenous and spontaneous spiritual events have been transmitted to other contexts multi-directionally. Of course, it must be pointed out here that these categories are far from being exclusive. However, they are helpful in showing in a sketchy form the theoretical frameworks that are used in explaining this phenomenon.

The next pragmatic point to be made here is that the paradigmatic preferences of scholars have also influenced their analysis of these religious developments. It appears that this phenomenon has attracted the gaze of social scientists much more than historians of religion or scientists of religion. This is clearly evident from the volume of literature available on the subject. Apart from a few examples, most scholars seem to bury the religious factor or deny these movements their reality of the 'superhuman' in their attempt at explaining their *raison d étre*. André Droogers (1999), a cultural anthropologist of religion, took a cursory glance at the internal religious characteristics of Pentecostalism and their articulation within the external circumstances of globalization. He aptly remarks,

> In any case, now as before, whatever the theoretical framework, most attention is given to factors that are external to Pentecostalism itself. Only rarely are specific characteristics of Pentecostalism taken into account and a more idiosyncratic explanation sought...Since the supernatural is denied reality, the explanation is sought in the impact of non-religious factors – social, economic, or political – thus ignoring the role possibly played by the religious convictions of its believers...If the starting point is the prevailing external social processes, then we will never be able to do justice to the specifics of a particular religion such as Pentecostalism, because these social processes usually affect other religions as well, expanding or otherwise. The particularities of a specific religious situation are usually insufficiently explained in the light of these processes alone.

Thus, while not underestimating the influence of these external conditions, Droogers underscores the fact that, a far-reaching and wholistic account of the expansion must necessarily commence from 'the particularities of a specific religion' and proceed from there to the impact of, and articulation with, external social processes, and not the other way round.

Paul Gifford is one of the few scholars who had researched extensively on African Christianity, particularly on the phenomenon of Pentecostalism (Gifford, 1988, 1991, 1992, 1993, 1994, 1998). Maxwell's (2000) review article *In Defence of African Creativity* of one of Gifford's major works (Gifford, 1998) titled *African Christianity: Its Public Role* is indisputably apt here, in that it does not only reveal the skimpy and tenuous methodological framework Gifford uses but also hints at the lack of empathetic understanding, normativity and sweepy generalization inherent in such works.[1] In this (Gifford, 1998) and some of his earlier and latter works, he embraces the conspiracy theories which point to the role of the Central Intelligence Agency (CIA) in serving US capitalist expansion by the support given to North American missionary organizations (Droogers, 1999:10; see also Brouwer, Gifford and Rose, 1996). It may not be out of place to rehash here some of these remarks, but we should point out that this guilt must not be borne by Gifford alone. There are no doubt a handful of scholars who have adopted a similar theoretical approach to religion, thus giving a misrepresentation of their data and or falling into the 'academic trap of sociological reductionism'. Perhaps it is not out of place to ask to what degree the sources of research grants, publishers and editors as well as target intellectual/academic market influence the quality of research and the conclusions drawn from field data?

In examining contemporary developments in Africa Christianity *vis a vis* the 'public role', Gifford (1998) had sought to locate Africa's churches in their wider context employing socio-political concepts and tools in his data analysis. Using case studies of developments in Ghana, Uganda, Zambia and Cameroon, Gifford provides rich and vast material on the dramatization of Christianity on the African religious landscape, although he failed to realize the colossal diversity and complexity of African Christianity. This failure sometimes results in wide generalizations and insensitivity to the historico-cultural complexity of African religion. African Pentecostalism exhibits a baffling diversity that must be taken into account in any attempt at assessing the nature, practice, vitality and impact of Pentecostalism in Africa and beyond. In no mistaking terms, Gifford argues that scholars must 'attempt not just to describe current expressions of Christianity, but also to judge their adequacy' (p. 55). This was demonstrated in the same book where he provides an elaborate description of the growth of what he calls the 'born again movement', its public character, as well as an appraisal of its appeal. Here, he recognizes the popularity of the 'born-again theology', but concludes that this does not make sense in the way he would like. His appropriation and call for the imposition of value judgements raises very important and critical methodological problems for our discipline. One is tempted here to ask whether Gifford's work is shrouded in some kind of translucent theological agenda. Is it our task as scholars of religion to question the rightness and wrongness of our data if it does not tally with our sensibility, susceptibility and our 'hidden' academic agenda? What do we do when our data fail to meet the expectations of our sponsors?

Our second critical reaction to his work (see Maxwell, 2000: 469), lies in the preponderance of his argument on 'ecclesiastical externality'. He enthused that the American origins of the born-again upsurge, particularly its emphasis on the faith gospel or what has come to be known as 'gospel of prosperity'. He adds on the issue of externality that although the US evangelistic thrust (the agenda of the American New Religious Right) is undertaken on purely religious grounds (Gifford, 1998: 316), it is nevertheless part of a wider American cultural project. According to him,

> For all the talk within African church circles of localiza-
> tion, inculturation, Africanization, or indigenization,
> external links have become more important than ever.
> Through these links the churches have become a major, if
> not the greatest single, source of development assistance,
> money, employment and opportunity in Africa (Gifford,
> 1998: 308)

Gifford also glosses over indigenous religious creativity and innovation in his remarks that 'Creativity should not be so emphasized that it glosses over the West's cultural significance.'

Our reaction here is that the external factor (paradigm enforcing power of external agencies) should and must not be blown out of proportion in such a way that the local creativity as well as the independency of these movements is totally glossed over or undermined. In short, Gifford's analysis here is not bereft of exaggerations and analytical short-sightedness by taking some exceptions for the rule. The point being made here is that both internal and external factors are germane to the explanation of these developments, but our conclusions must emanate from the data and not as a consequence of any outstanding stereotypes. While not denying the fact that some 'born-again churches' rely or depend heavily, and some partially on external funding and resources and some Pente-costal elements (the influence of American Bible belt literature), examples abound of several Pentecostal movements in Africa, such as in Nigeria, which are self-financing and which demonstrate a high degree of indigenous religious vitality and innovation. Some of these movements are very conscious of external influences and its implications. Thus, Gifford's analysis and assertion are over-exaggerated on the one hand, and over-simplistic on the other. Also, the exaggeration of the influence of the Religious Right fails to square up with present realities both in the United States and in Africa (see Hick, 2000).

Rijk van Dijk has been conspicuously involved in the African Pentecostal discourse, with particular focus on Malawi, Ghana, and the Ghanaian diaspora in the Netherlands for a while (see Van Dijk, 1997, 1999, 2000, 2001a, 2001b). In one of his papers (Van Dijk, 2000), he attempts to make a definite departure from Gif-ford's agenda, (as evident from the special issue of ROAPE 1991) which was located within the political science study of African reli-gious movements to the growth of what it described as new sects of the religious right in Africa. As opposed to this 'new conservative, right wing forces' approach, Van Dijk places particular attention on the 'social meaning' of what he variously calls 'Christian funda-mentalism', 'charismatic Pentecostalism', or 'a religion of modernity' in sub-Saharan Africa. He examines the developmental history of charismatic Pentecostal churches as a fundamentalist turn in Africa Christianity, describes its basic ingredients and analyzes some of its 'essential ideological parameters', and shows how 'it draws its appeal from the ways in which it mediates, negotiates and mitigates modernity' (p. 2). Van Dijk concludes that,

> in essence, the articles that appeared in ROAPE proclaim-ing that the resurgence of Pentecostalism was inspired by right-wing, highly conservative, bourgeois ideals were wrong in their understanding of what this Pentecostalism, this form of Christian fundamentalism actually meant in a given African context (p. 24).

He adds that 'the public face of these new fundamentalist or Pen-tecostal movements should not deceive us as to their meaning and significance at a deeper level of social life in African societies' (p. 25). Although he talks about the initial development of the Pentecostal churches from black missionary efforts (and not white missionary), van Dijk argues that 'the Pentecostal churches and their many off-shoots and spin-offs certainly should be classified under the wider category of the African appropriation of Christianity' (p. 12). But what does 'African appropriation of Christianity' mean – African Pentecostalism or African Christianity?

In spite of the divergence in their views, Gifford and van Dijk seem to agree on one point, that is, their use and appropriation of 'Christian Fundamentalism' in reference to Pentecostalism and other 'new dimensions of African Christianity' (See Gifford, 1991, 1993; Van Dijk, 1993, 1995, 2000). Although, Van Dijk (2000: 5) attempts to make clear his use of the concept, his definition appears somewhat confusing, inappropriate and speculative. In what sense can we talk about Pentecostalism as a brand of fundamentalism or Christian Fundamentalism? Do the Pentecostals themselves refer to or identify themselves in these terms? When they do repudi-ate such categories, is it right for scholars to perpetually use them? How charged is the term especially considering its use for 'militant' Islam? What special meanings does its use for Christianity and Islam convey? Is fundamentalism a religious category or a social science construct? In our view, it is more of the latter than the former. Van Dijk also makes a somewhat rigid distinction between the worldview of the Pentecostal churches and the African Inde-pendent churches (AICs), thus rendering his argument loose and simplistic. For instance, Van Dijk (2000: 11) considers the essential difference between them that:

> the Pentecostals tend to take seriously the powers, spirits and occult forces that the missionary churches choose to ignore; on the other hand they have refused to follow a path of syncretism in which much of the traditional ritual and symbolic styles and repertoires would be adopted.

The apparent absence of ritual may only be a façade as Pentecostals are increasingly appropriating concrete ritual objects such as olive/anointing oil, prayer cloth or mantle, handkerchiefs, and holy water. We need to pay more attention to a more subtle use of or invention of ritual even within anti-ritual rhetorics.

Scholars should perhaps exercise some restraint on how and to what extent we push this 'making a complete break with the past' thesis (cf. Meyer, 1998), so as not to blur significantly the *weltaschauung* of these African religious initiatives. Van Dijk (2000: 14) further shares a similar view with Gifford and many other scholars (we shall discuss below) in his description of the 'charismatic Pentecostals' as 'primarily urban-based, with a focus on the influential middle classes of bourgeois, these churches are able to exert an unparalleled socio-political and moral influence on society'. As we shall highlight below, the first segment of this sentence is 'patronising' and 'selective' in a certain way, as it fails to capture the complex demographic structure and social composition of these movements. It shows more of a social construction of Pentecostalism than a reflection of the contemporary African religious landscape. It may not seem fair to judge Pentecostalism against the mission Churches who faced unique and unparalleled situations in introducing Christianity to 'unchristian' areas. It should be borne in mind that Pentecostalism is more a religion of 'reaffiliation' rather than of 'primary conversion' (see Stark & Bainbridge, 1996; Stark & Finke, 2000).

Other interesting treatments of African Pentecostalism are those of Ogbu Kalu (1998, 2000, 2002, 2003), Allan Anderson (1992, 1993, 1999, 2000a, 2000b, 2001), Karla Poewe (1994), Irving Hexham and Karla Poewe (1997); Ruth Marshall-Fratani (1998), Birgit Meyer (1998), David Maxwell (1998), Matthews Ojo (1988), Kingsley Larbi (2001), Cephas Omenyo (2002), and much more recently Kwabena Asamoah-Gyadu (2004). Kalu (1998: 3) calls this religious development, 'the third response', 'an implosion of the Spirit'. As he opines, 'we are witnessing the implosion of a third force, moved by the wind of the third Person of the Trinity in the triple task of re-evangelization, intensification and reconstruction of Christian experience in contemporary Africa'. Elsewhere, Kalu (2000) appraises the social face and force of African Christianity in the last three decades of the twentieth century. He argues vehemently for the uniqueness and peculiarity of African Pentecostalism and its unrelatedness to the Azusa street event and other external influences. In his view, 'as the third response by Africans to the Christian message, Pentecostalism actively reconstructs African spirituality according to Christian and biblical perspectives' (2000: 104). Kalu made very useful points in this book especially by locating the indigenous roots of African Pentecostalism. However, the contemporary Pentecostal terrain is so complex and diverse that some filets of external nexus within some strands of the classical and neo-Pentecostal movements cannot be easily explained off.

The gradual burgeoning of literature on Pentecostalism by African scholars has served to complement extant literature on the phenomenon, in a way that challenges the dominance of the field by largely European anthropologists. The works by Larbi (2001) and Omenyo (2002) is a remarkable instance of how Ghanaian scholars have contributed to a historical and contextual remapping of Ghanaian Pentecostalism. These works which largely echo Kalu (1998, 2000, 2002, 2003), place emphasis on the complex internal dynamics and indigenous creativities that characterize the contemporary forms and structure of the charismatic/Pentecostal phenomenon in the Ghanaian local context, a dimension largely undermined in several existing literature on the topic. From an insiders' perspective, Larbi (2001) dealt extensively on the origins, forms and development of Pentecostalism in Ghana, and explores the continuity and discontinuity between Ghanaian Pentecostalism and the indigenous religious imagination, as well as their peculiarities. Employing a theological perspective, he locates the movement's conception of salvation against the backdrop of Akan indigenous wordlview. Omenyo (2002) explores the Charismatic/Pentecostal phenomenon in Ghanaian mainline churches as one of the most challenging issues of Christianity in Ghana.

Anderson (2000b: 373) contends that 'the so-called 'prophet-healing' and 'Spirit' or 'Spiritual' African Instituted Churches (AICs), as well as other Pentecostal and Charismatic churches, both new and older varieties, are all different expressions of Pentecostalism in Africa'. Anderson (1999) adduces both internal and external roots in explaining the origin of African Pentecostalism. The external roots he explains also as 'predominantly African cultural features, evident in the leadership of William Seymour, whose spirituality lay in the past' (Anderson, 1999: 221). He remarks that 'one of the outstanding features of Pentecostals in the Third World (Africa) is their religious creativity and spontaneously indigenous character, a characteristic held as an ideal by Western missions for over a century'. In his earlier article on Pentecostal movements in Nigeria, Turner (1979) categorised the Aladura churches with the classical Pentecostals in describing the emergence of Pentecostalism in Nigeria. A point of convergence between Kalu, Turner and

Anderson lies in the tendency to lump all the so-called African Indigenous (Independent) Churches (AICs) under the Pentecostal umbrella. This wells up another typological enigma. While it may be possible, in some theological sense, to describe some indigenous Pentecostal churches as AICs, it may be confusing on a sociological level to aggregate all AICs as Pentecostals especially from the backdrop of the definitional ingredients that are provided.

Hexham and Poewe (1997) lash hard on Gifford and others who through arguments 'based on jumps of logic and the misuse of fragments of empirical evidence' engage in a superficial explanation of new religions (Pentecostal, charismatic Christianity). They attempted to highlight the intercultural dynamics involved in what they call the 'global culture'. Although, the extent to which they use a theological brush, imposing value judgments on their data remains controversial, yet they made a very useful point in saying that, 'in fact new religions (i.e. charismatic Christianity) are part of African life and must be interpreted as genuine expressions of African spirituality, not simply as a negative reaction to Europeans' (p. 53). Ostensibly in support of the multi-directional process of globalization, Hexham and Poewe aptly remark that 'Just as American religion is exported throughout the world, so large religious organizations abroad export their products to North America' (p. 45). Poewe's (1994) conceptualization of Pentecostalism as global religious culture is based on four main features: experiential, idealistic, biblical and oppositional. Although her methodological approach lacks merit in several respects, yet it may run the risk of delimiting the inherent dynamism of the phenomenon as well as the heterogeneity of the Pentecostal historiography.

Gunilla Oskarsson (1999) made an interesting summary of articles (by Rosalind Hackett, Ruth Marshall-Fratani, Birgit Meyer and David Maxwell) which were devoted to 'African Pentecostalism' in a special issue of the *Journal of Religion in Africa* (1998, vol. 28), and related these to relevant topics in the history of Pentecostalism in Burundi. In that volume, Hackett (1998) had her focus on religion and media, where she demonstrates how what she characterizes as Charismatic and Pentecostal movements in Ghana and Nigeria 'are increasingly favouring electronic media as suitable sites for transmission of their teachings and erecting of their empires'. She attributes the transformation of the religious landscape as a consequence of these developments. Hackett's recognition of the internal and external explanations for their growth is underscored with her assertion that majority of the charismatic movements are locally instituted, while some of their leaders were educated in the US and maintain some links and affiliations with leading American evangelists. She argues further that with extended viewing audiences and the enhancement of the electronic medium, evangelists with a powerful message and 'a good dose of charisma' can attract a much larger following, which might in part explain the development of 'mega-churches' in both Ghana and Nigeria in recent years (Oskarsson, 1999: 406). While Hackett concludes that 'the message and the media marry well for Africa's Charismatics and Pentecostals', Oskarsson (1999: 409) has shown that 'the media has obviously not been an important tool in the evangelization of the Pentecostal Church in Burundi'. A critical point in Hackett's paper is a terminological one. Although she tries to make a distinction between Charismatics and Pentecostals, she never provides a definition for the nomenclature 'Pentecostal'. Moreover, the characteristics she adduced for them make her comparison somewhat confusing. There is some muddling up of facts as far as the two contexts of focus (Ghana and Nigeria) are concerned. What she distinguishingly describes as charismatic in Ghana is more suitably understood as Pentecostal in Nigeria and vice versa. She prefers the use of 'charismatic' but, intermittently, both terms appear together, without any explanation why this is so (see Oskarsson, 1999: 414-415). The view that the focus of the Charismatics, 'the new type of religious collectivity' is 'healing, prosperity and experience' is in fact too narrow.

Ruth Marshall-Fratani (1998) locates Nigerian Pentecostalism within the purview of 'transnationalism', the nation-state and the media, and discusses the new situation in the world, created during the last decades. One of her main objectives was to show how and to what extent the current wave of Pentecostalism, in urban Nigeria, evinces an instance of the creation of subjects 'whose individual and collective identities seem to have been formed in terms of a new type of negotiation between local and global, one in which the media has a privileged role' (p. 281). Her second contention was with the relationship between Pentecostalism and the Nigerian nation-state. Marshall-Fratani concludes that even though Pentecostalism hardly faces the real issues behind the workings of power, it nevertheless entails a fairly bold attack on the Nigerian State. Interestingly, Oskarsson's (1999: 410) findings in Burundi reveal the exact opposite. Even in Nigeria, Pentecostalism is a diverse entity as to make unified 'bold attack on the Nigerian State'. If this was the state of affairs during the era of military dictatorship, can we still say the same thing today? Is there no difference between a critique of the socio-political culture of a society and an 'attack' on the state? There is need for caution, therefore, in the type of bold pictures we present about a still unfolding phenomenon. Marshall-Fratani (p. 280), just like Hackett, employs 'Pentecostalism' without a clear-cut definition or any suggestion on how to go about it. Without any explanation of the significance of the expression, she simply quotes van Dijk's use of 'the new charismatic type of Pentecostalism'. Another problem emanates from her sharp and narrow distinction on doctrine, between what she calls the 'older' churches and the 'new organizations'. She claims that the former lays emphasis on 'holiness and antimaterialism', and the latter 'place themselves firmly in the world'. One wonders how both can be located in the same group if they have such varied defining characteristics?

In her contribution to the African (Ghanaian) Pentecostal religiosity, Birgit Meyer (1998) discusses *inter alia* the connecting nexus between religion, memory and modernity in a globalizing world. She examines 'how Pentecostalism seeks to distinguish the present from the past, at the same time being engaged in a dialectics of remembering and forgetting, which has helped to construct the past'. Meyer was apt in her emphasis that 'the proponents of Pentecostalization regarded the local gods and spirits as authentic agents of Satan. They strove to exclude them, thereby placing themselves in a tradition of Africanization "from below"'. Meyer's distinction between Pentecostal and Charismatics also raises a typological problem. On the other hand, her reference to 'Pentecostal Churches' is 'not only to internationally spread Pentecostal Churches of American or European origin...but to all Churches in the Pentecostal spectrum, including the so-called Charismatic Churches'. As she points out, 'charismatic' stands for 'a newer type of Pentecostalism recently emerged, especially in urban areas' (p. 320). In spite of the doctrinal differences highlighted in her paper, she seems not to make any distinction between these newer ones and the old groups. It is again doubtful if the Pentecostals 'make a complete break with the past' and whether this is done in principle or in practice, and or in both.

David Maxwell (1998) had his attention on a particular version of the prosperity gospel as presented by the Zimbabwe Assemblies of God Africa (ZAOGA). He argues that the movement's leadership draws upon various American versions of the prosperity gospel to legitimize their excessive accumulation but its own dominant prosperity teachings have arisen from Southern African sources and are shaped by Zimbabwean concerns. In explaining the development of the prosperity gospel, Maxwell draws upon both external and internal roots with the latter playing a dominant role.

The concepts 'modernization' and 'urbanization' occupy special focus in the works of Gifford, Dijk, Hackett, Marshall-Fratani, Meyer and Maxwell. The modernization discourse is usually located within the context of the city, and urbanization is seen as an influential manifestation of the modernization process. There is always talk about personal uprooting and the loss of a social and cultural framework. The urban religions, including Pentecostalism, provide a new home and even a new family of 'brothers and sisters', albeit based on artificial kinship (Droogers, 1999: 9). As Droogers argues,

> Although it may be an important element in explaining Pentecostal expansion, this reasoning offers no help either in explaining its growth in rural areas, or its growth among long established and successful urbanities. It also does not answer the question of why some people choose one particular urban religion than another.

It is obviously problematic to generalize on the claim which explains away Pentecostalism simply as an urban religion. Most of the works we have treated here are guilty of this conclusion, an assertion that Oskarsson's findings prove to the contrary. In fact, Oskarsson concludes that,

> the Pentecostal Church in Burundi has always been, and to a greater part still is, a rural movement. It is only the two last decades that the congregations in Bujumbura and in Gitega have grown into what they are today. However, the biggest congregation is still to be found on the countryside, in the southern part, where in many villages the

Pentecostals constitute the majority of the population (Oskarsson, 1999: 414).

Research findings on large Pentecostal movements such as the RCCG, Deeper Life Bible Church, have shown that branches or parishes are concentrated in the rural areas as much as they are in the so-called urban centers. It must be recognised that there are even 'rural microcosms' within the 'urban macrocosms', especially in terms of the peri-urban and suburbs of the cities which now find themselves eclipsed in these urban enclosures. Researchers often concentrate on urban areas because that is where change is most dramatic and obvious. But rural environments have their own dynamism that yearns for attention as well.

WHICH WAY FORWARD?

We have asked more questions than providing answers. Our aim is that there is a need for a multi-disciplinary and multidimensional approach in the study of religion. No one approach says it all. And like the metaphor of a masquerade, no one view captures the total picture, the glamor, the splendor, the intricacies and nuances of a complex unfolding of religion and globalization. If theory is not helping us to properly understand a complex situation, we must not hold doggedly to it. These reflections call for more attention to the little items of our field work. It is data that helps to propound and expound theories and not the other way round. It is hoped that scholars would embark on empathetic understanding of whatever object they choose to study.

Bibliography

The African Courier, 10/11, October / November 2000, p.1.

Anderson, Allan, *Bazalwane: African Pentecostalism in South Africa.* Pretoria: University of South Africa, 1992.

Anderson, Allan & Samuel Otwang, *Tumelo: The Faith of African Pentecostals in South Africa.* Pretoria: University of South Africa Press, 1993.

Anderson, Allan, 'The Gospel and Culture in Pentecostal Mission in the Third World', *Missionalia,* 27/2, 1999, pp. 220-230.

Anderson, Allan, *Zion and Pentecost: The Spirituality and Experience of Pentecostal and Zionist/ Apostolic Churches in South Africa.* Pretoria: University of South Africa Press, 2000a.

Anderson, Allan, 'The Gospel and African Religion', *International Review of Mission*, LXXXIX/ 354, July, 2000b, pp. 373-383.

Anderson, Alan, *African Reformation: African Initiated Christianity in the Twentieth Century.* Trenton, NJ: Africa World Press, 2001.

Augé, Marc, *Non-Places: Introduction to an Anthropology of Supermodernity.* London, 1995.

Axford, Barrie, *The Global System: Economics, Politics and Culture.* New York: St. Martin's Press, 1995.

Barber, Benjamin, 'Jihad vs McWorld', in Patrick O'Meara et al (eds.), *Globalization and The Challenges of a New Century: A Reader*, Bloomington: Indiana University Press, 2000.

Beyer, Peter, *Religion and Globalization.* London: Sage Publications, 1994.

Beyer, Peter, 'Globalized Systems, Global Cultural Models, and Religion(s)', *International Sociology* 13, 1998, pp. 79-94.

Beyer, Peter, 'Secularization from the Perspective of Globalization: A Response to Dobbelaere', *Sociology of Religion*, 60, 3, 1999, pp. 289-301.

Beyer, Peter (ed.) *Religion im Prozeß der Globalisierung*, Würzburg: Erzon Verlag, 2001.

Brouwer, S, Gifford, P and Rose, S.D., *Exporting the American Gospel: Global Christian Fundamentalism.* London: Routledge, 1996.

Bruce, Steve, *Fundamentalism.* Cambridge: Polity Press, 2000.

Chase-Dunn, Christopher, 'Globalization: A World-System Perspective', *Journal of World-System Research*, 5, 2, 1999, pp. 165-185. <http://csf. colorado.edu/jwsr/archive/v...15_number2/htlm/chase-dunn/index. shtml>

Clark, Peter, 'Introduction', in Peter Clark (ed.), *New Trends and Developments in African Religions,* London: Greenwood Press, 1998.

Clark, Mary-Ann, 'Seven African Powers: Hybridity and Appropriation', <http://www.materialreligion.org/journal/candles.html>, 1999.

Droogers, Andre, 'Globalization and The Pentecostal Success', <http:// casnws.scw.vu.nl/publicaties/droogers-globpent.html>, 1999.

Foreman-Peck, James, *Historical Foundations of Globalization.* Chelten: Edward Elgar Publishing Ltd., 1998.

Friedman, Jonathan, 'Globalization, Class and culture in Global System', *Journal of World-Systems Research* 6, 3, Fall/Winter: 2000, pp. 636-656. <http://csf.colorado.edu/jwr>

Giddens, Anthony, *The Consequences of Modernity.* Stanford: Stanford University Press, 1990.

Giddens, Anthony, *Runaway World: How Globalization is Reshaping Our Lives*. New York: Routledge, 2000.

Gifford, Paul, *African Christianity. Its Public Role*. London: Hurts & Company, 1998.

Gifford, Paul (ed.) *The Christian Churches and the Democratisation of Africa*. Leiden: E.J. Brill, 1995.

Gifford, Paul, 'Ghana's Charismatic Churches', *Journal of Religion in Africa* 24, 1994, pp. 241-265.

Gifford, Paul, *Christianity and Politics in Doe's Liberia*. Cambridge: Cambridge University Press, 1993.

Gifford, Paul, (ed.) *New Dimensions in African Christianity*. Nairobi: All Africa Conference of Churches, 1992.

Gifford, Paul, 'Christian Fundamentalism and Development', *Review of African Political Economy* 52, 1991, pp. 9-20.

Gifford, Paul, *The New Crusaders. Christianity and the New Right in Southern Africa*. London: Pluto Press, 1988.

Hackett, Rosalind, 'Charismatic Pentecostal Appropriation of Media Technologies in Nigeria and Ghana', *Journal of Religion in Africa*, 28, 3, 1998, pp. 258-277.

Hay, Collin and Matthew, Watson, 'Globalization: "Sceptical" Notes on the 1999 Reith Lectures', *Political Quarterly*, 70, Oct.-Dec. 1999, <http://www2.vcsc.educgirs/publications/kiosk/articles9.html>

Hexham, Irving and Karla, Poewe, *New Religions as Global Cultures: Making the Human Sacred*. Boulder: Westview Press, 1997.

Hick, John, 'The Political Subsistence of the Religious Right: Why the Christian Right Survives and Does Not Thrive', 2000. <http://are.as.wvu.edu/jhicks.htm>

Hirst, Paul and Graham, Thompson, *Globalization in Question: The International Economy and the Possibilities of Governance*. Cambridge: Polity Press, 1996.

Huntington, Samuel P., *The Clash of Civilization and the Remaking of World Order*. New York: Simon and Schuster, 1996.

Huntington, Samuel P., 'The Clash of Civilizations?', in Patrick O'Meara, et al. (eds.), *Globalization and The Challenges of a New Century: A Reader*. Bloomington: Indiana University Press, 2000[1993].

Kalu, Ogbu U, 'The Third Response: Pentecostalism and the Reconstruction of Christian Experience in Africa, 1970-1995', *Journal of African Christian Thought*, 1, 2, 1998, pp. 3-16.

Kalu, Ogbu U., *Power, Poverty and Prayer: The Challenges of Poverty and Pluralism in African Christianity, 1960-1996.* Frankfurt am Main: Peter Lang, 2000.

Kalu, Ogbu U., 'Preserving a Worldview: Pentecostalism in the African Maps of the Universe', in *PNEUMA: The Journal of the Society for Pentecostal Studies,* 24, 2, Fall 2002, pp. 110-137.

Kalu, Ogbu U., 'Pentecostal and Charismatic Reshaping of the African Religious Landscape in the 1990s', in *Mission Studies,* 20, 2003, 1-39.

Keohane, Robert O, 'Globalization: What's New? What's Not? [And so What?]', *Foreign Policy,* Spring, 2000.

Kloos, Peter, 'The Dialectics of Globalization and Localization', 1999. <http://casnws.scw.vu.nl/publicaties/kloos-dialectics.html>

Larbi, Kingsley, *Pentecostalism. The Eddies of Ghanaian Christianity.* Accra: Center for Pentecostal and Charismatic Studies, 2001.

Marshall, Ruth, 'Power in the Name of Jesus', *Review of African Political Economy,* 52, 1991, pp. 21-37.

Marshall-Fratani, Ruth, 'Mediating the Global and the Local in Nigerian Pentecostalism', *Journal of Religion in Africa,* 28, 3, 1998, pp. 278-315.

Maxwell, David, "Delivered from the Spirit of Poverty?' Pentecostalism, Prosperity and Modernity in Zimbabwe', *Journal of Religion in Africa,* 28, 3, 1998, pp. 350-373.

Maxwell, David, 'Review Article: In Defence of African Creativity', *Journal of Religion in Africa,* 30, 4, 2000, pp. 468-481.

Mazrui, Ali, 'Pretender To Universalism: Western Culture in The Globalizing Age', Keynote address for the Royal Society of Art and the British Broadcasting Corporation, London, June 15, 2000. Text available at Columbia: University of South Carolina Press. <http://www.bbc.co.uk/worldservice/people/features/wor.../mazrui_lect.shtm>

Meyer, Birgit, *Translating the Devil. Religion and Modernity among the Ewe of Ghana.* Edinburgh: Edinburgh University Press, 1999.

Meyer, Birgit, 'Make a Complete Break with the Past: Memory and Post-Colonial Modernity in Ghanaian Pentecostal Discourse', *Journal of Religion in Africa,* 28, 3, 1998, pp. 316-349.

Ojo, Matthews, 'The Contextual Significance of the Charismatic Movements in Independent Nigeria', *Africa* 58, 2, 1988, pp. 175-192.

Ojo, Matthews, 'Deeper Christian Life Ministry: A Case Study of the Charismatic Movements in Independent Nigeria', *Journal of Religion in Africa* 18, 2, 1988, pp. 141-162.

Omenyo, Cephas, *Pentecost Outside Pentecostalism: A Study of the Development of Charismatic Renewal in the Mainline churches in Ghana.* Zoetermeer: Uitgeverig Boekencentrum, 2002.

Oskarsson, Gunilla Nyberg, 'African 'Pentecostalism', *Swedish Missiological Themes,* 87, 3, 1999, pp. 405-418.

Poewe, Karla (ed.), *Charismatic Christianity as a Global Culture,* 1994.

Review of African Political Economy, Special Issue, 52, 1991.

Robertson, Roland, 'The Sacred and the World System', in Philip E. Hammond (ed.), *The Sacred in a Secular Age: Toward Revision in the Scientific Study of Religion,* Berkeley: University of California Press, 1985.

Robertson, Roland, 'Church-State Relations and the World-System', in Robertson, R. and Robbins, T. eds., *Church-State Relations: Tensions and Transitions.* New Brunswick: Transaction Books, 1987.

Robertson, Roland, *Globalization, Social Theory and Global Culture.* London: Sage Publications, 1992.

Robertson, Roland, 'Religion and the Global Field', *Social Compass,* 41, 1, 1994, pp. 121-135.

Rosenau, James N., 'New Dimensions of Security: The Interaction of Globalizing and Localizing Dynamics', *Security Dialogue* 25, 3, 1994, pp. 255-281.

Rudolph, S.H. and J. Piscatori (eds.), *Transnational Religion and Fading States.* Boulder: Westview Press, 1997.

Rudolph, Susanne Hoeber, 'Introduction: Religion, State, and Transnational Civil Society', in S.H. Rudolph & J. Piscatori (eds.), *Transnational Religion and Fading States.* Boulder: Westview Press, 1997.

Sklair, Leslie, 'Competing Conceptions of Globalization', *Journal of World-System Research,* 5, 2, 1999, pp. 143-162. <http://csf.colorado.edu/jwsr/archive/vol5/vol5_number2/html/sklair/index.html>

Stark, Rodney and Roger Finke, *Acts of Faith: Explaining the Human Side of Religion.* Berkeley: University of California Press, 2000.

Stark, Rodney, and William S. Bainbridge, *The Future of Religion: Secularization, Revival, and Cult Formation.* Berkeley: University of California Press, 1985.

Stark, Rodney, William B. Bainbridge, *A Theory of Religion.* New York, 1996.

Turner, Harold, *Religious Innovation in Africa: Collected Essays on New Religious Movement.* Boston: G.K Hall and Co., 1979.

Van Dijk, Rijk, 'Contesting Silence: The Ban on Drumming and the Musical Politics of Pentecostalism in Ghana', *Ghana Studies* 4, 2001a, pp. 31-64.

Van Dijk, Rijk, 'Time and Transcultural Technologies of the Self in the Ghanaian Pentecostal Diaspora', in A. Corten and R. Marshall-Fratani (eds.), *Between Babel and Pentecost. Transnational Pentecostalism in Africa and Latin America*. London and Bloomington, IN: Hurst Publishers and Indiana University Press, 2001b, pp. 216-234.

Van Dijk, Rijk, *Christian Fundamentalism in Sub-Saharan Africa: The Case of Pentecostalism*. Occasional Paper, University of Copenhagen: Center of African Studies, 2000.

Van Dijk, Rijk, 'The Pentecostal Gift: Ghanaian Charismatic Churches and the Moral Innocence of the Global Economy', in R. Fardon, W. van Binsbergen and R. van Dijk (eds.) *Modernity on a Shoestring*. London, SOAS and Leiden ASC: Anthony Rowe, 1999.

Van Dijk, Rijk, 'From Camp to Encompassment: Discourses of Transsubjectivity in the Ghanaian Pentecostal Diaspora', *Journal of Religion in Africa*, 27, 2, 1997, pp. 135-159.

Venter, Dawid, 'Globalization and the Cultural Effects of the World-Economy in a Semiperiphery: The Emergence of African Indigenous Churches in South Africa', *Journal of World-Systems Research*, [http://csf.colorado.edu/wsystems/jwsr.html], 5, 1999, pp. 105-126.

Wallerstein, Immanuel, 'Globalization or Age of Transition? A Long-Term View of the Trajectory of the World-System', Fernand Braudel Center, 1999. <http://fbc.binghmton.edu/iwatrajws.htm>

Note

1. See Maxwell (2000) for an exhaustive critique of Gifford. See also criticisms of Gifford in Hexham (1997: 42-43).

Globalization, Fundamentalism and the Pentecostal/Charismatic Movement in Nigeria

Umar Habila Dadem Danfulani

Is Charismatic Pentecostalism Global and/or Fundamentalist?

The term 'Pentecostal' derives from the 'Day of Pentecost' experience of the second chapter of Acts (Anderson, 2001: 18; cf. 1992: 2-6, Cox, 1995: 3). The Pentecostal movement emerged and spread rapidly with a popular appeal to virtually five continents of the world within the first decade of, and continued throughout the 20th century, constituting a challenge to the historic certainty of traditional Protestant and Catholic churches (cf. Cesar, 2000: 5; Lehmann, 1996: 122). The astonishing rise of Pentecostalism and its associated penumbra of Charismatic Christianity represent the largest global shift in the religious market place over the last forty years (Martin, 2002a: xvii). It boasts of a quarter of a billion people globally, being the most widespread form of non-Roman Catholic Christianity, claiming one out of every eight persons from the Christian constituency of nearly two billion, and one in twenty-five of global population (Martin, 2001: 1).

In Africa, the new independent Pentecostal/Charismatic churches and 'ministries' have a more recent historical origin, emerging from the evangelical-Charismatic renewal of the 1960s and 70s. They are regarded as 'Pentecostal' movements because they too, as the African Initiated Churches (AICs) emphasize the power and the gifts of the Holy Spirit, though they do not always refer to themselves as Pentecostals, in some cases preferring the terms 'Charismatic' and/or 'evangelical' (Anderson, 2001: 19). Despite their recent origins, however, some of these churches are already among the largest and most influential denominations in their respective countries, especially in West Africa, with some becoming huge churches in less than a decade after their emergence (Larbi, 2001: 295). Concerning this mesmerizing development, Gifford observed that they are found in every major city in Africa (Gifford, 1994: 513-533). The growth of the Pentecostal/Charismatic churches over more than two decades has seen the momentous attraction of even founders and membership from old evangelical (mainline) fellowships, African Zionist-Ethiopian types and prophet healing churches. They are not united in their beliefs, practices, and identity; but each congregation is independent of the other with no central authority, with only the Pentecostal Fellowship of Nigeria (PFN) a loose umbrella body uniting them.

Some scholars have described the Pentecostal/Charismatic phenomenon in terms of religious fundamentalism (Van Dijk, 2000; Brouwer et al, 1996), while others see them either as agents of globalization or as institutions that are already globalized, thus referring to the process of 'the globalization of Pentecostalism' (Droogers, 2001: 41-61; Van Dijk, 2001: 216-234). The questions we raise in this chapter refer to the characteristics of religious fundamentalism in general and the extent to which we may describe Nigerian Pentecostal Charismatic groups as fundamentalist. This approach fits into the current globalization-localization debate, as we examine the global characteristics of Pentecostal Charismatic churches vis-à-vis the local or traditional tendencies some of them tend to exhibit even in this 21st century.

Furthermore, Pentecostal/Charismatics in Nigeria react to the challenge of globalization in various ways. Some Pentecostal-Charismatic movements in Nigeria, such as the Synagogue Church of All Nations of T.B. Joshua and the Deeper Life Bible Church of

Pastor William F. Kumuyi have remained conservative, non-innovative and anti-modernist (Gaiya, 2002: 1) in direct contradiction to the assertion by Van Dijk that charismatic Pentecostalism can in a very real sense be considered a religion of modernity itself' (van Dijk, 2000: 2). This chapter examines the extent to which we may refer to Pentecostal/Charismatic movements in Nigeria as globalized and/or local. The chapter proceeds by examining the term globalization, followed by an analysis of the term fundamentalism and the characteristics it exhibits in most religions. The nature of charismatic Pentecostalism in Nigeria is examined, together with a description of its characteristics. It concludes by analyzing the questions concerning the nature of globalization and fundamentalism to the innovative localization process going on in Pentecostal-Charismatic churches in Nigeria today.

Globalization and Transnationalism

Globalizing structures are interacting with individuals, households and communities and are delivering modernity to some, but not all peoples formerly far removed from meaningful participation in cross-border flows of capital, knowledge, information, and consumer goods. A massive transformation is thus being compressed in a short time, a few years rather than many generations and often despite officially managed processes (Mittelman, 1996: 1). In Nigeria, the older African ways of communication are giving way to faster satellite-compliant gadgets such as computers, cell phones, fax machines, internet and other cyber spaces, television facilities such as DSTV, CNN, M-net and MTV. For Robert Cox, these forces turn globalization into an inevitable ideology, 'presented as a finality, as the logical and inevitable culmination of the powerful tendencies of the market', and where 'the dominance of economic forces was regarded as both necessary and beneficial' (Cox, 1996: 23). To grasp the nature of change that has taken/is still taking place will demand phenomenological description, a severely empirical register of what is happening to the frames of meaning in people's lives as globality, globalism and globalization take hold. This means finding ways of registering the way the experiences of people under globalized conditions operate through recognizable social forms and relate to cultural ideas. The trans-historical relations and relevance and cross-cultural potential is significant as the New Age tries to make sense of new experiences and link individual fate with historical experience (Albrow, 1996: 73-77).

Albrow employs the term 'globality' to refer to the total set of inscriptions of or references to the global. He differentiates between 'modern' and 'global'. He describes 'modern' as a time reference that highlights innovation and obsolescence, with its production and consumption of time being its space of reference. While the global is a space reference and the product of the location of the earth in space; it is a material celebration of the natural environment on which human beings depend, the evocation of the concrete wholeness or completeness of existence, embracing humanity rather than dividing it. Thus the term global now carries connotations of the commercialization of humanity (Albrow, p. 82ff.). Globalism brings to the forefront of attention the 'idea of the forces', which are important in market ideologies and in all thought where human projects are subject to pressures and constraints, which are unavoidable and only partially controllable. Forces may arise in the natural environment, in the human organism (such as cancer, HIV/ AIDs, SARS) or as undirected outcomes of collective action or of aggregated individual acts that do not respect human boundaries, whether territorial, moral or aesthetic. Boundary, however, is one of the main ways in which human beings seek to control forces (p. 84). However, because forces by nature breach human boundaries, the quest for their limit encompasses the globe as a whole.

This is where globalization has significantly and effectively altered the framework of human action. It has done this by bringing about a global interconnectedness of human relations, thus bringing awareness of the globe in its train and makes it possible to conceptualize global risks. Globality becomes an ever present aspect of human calculations once the limits of action are the globe itself. The globe as the 'risk society' in the words of Ulrich Beck seeks to reflect the significance of risk, not merely as a local individual matter but as a global concern of profound importance (Beck, 1992). A tremendous transformation has taken place and the word which is perfectly descriptive of that is globalization. It conveys a change of a profound social and cultural transition from one state to another. The term has become a point of focus of concern for diverse groups, among them politicians, historians, geographers,

business persons, management consultants, economist.
critics, publishers and the media (Beck, p. 85).

In relation to religion, Lehmann, however rejects 'a n.
globalization as the inexorable spread of a homogenous, ra
ized, standardized "modern culture"' as a model generated when the
spread of global capitalism is taken to be the model for all globalization. This he says has given birth to two interconnected views
of religious globalization, namely, the spread of standard, homog-
enized forms of religion across the globe and the assertion of local
religious identities in reaction to such globalization (Lehmann,
2002: 299-315). For Lehmann, religion is 'the original globalizer'
and it does this on two levels. First, is the level of 'cosmopolitan
globalization' that is characterized by erudite and institutionalized
forms of religion, and which involves attempts to introduce into
the clash of religious systems a historical contextualized theory of
other cultures. This according to him predates modernity, though
it is still active in the modern world (Lehmann, p. 299). In this
case religion serves as a natural accompaniment of conquest and
colonization. Religion thus legitimates the power of the conquer-
ing people over their new subjects and serves as a resource in the
imposition of power. On the other hand, the transmission of religion is dependent on the will to appropriate and even domesticate
the powers and virtues of the conquered or invading 'Other'. A con-
quering people are made aware that those with whom they enter
into alliance or confrontation have a place in history and location
in space; they are made aware of this in relation to themselves as
well. In a nutshell, some theory of history is required and a concept
of history, of origins and of social causation is, of course, a feature
of modernity. The generation of such a theory about the position
of dominant power in relation to the 'Other' is a defining feature of
the cosmopolitan variety of religious globalization (Lehmann, p.
302f.). The best example of this is cited in Catholicism.

Second, is the much more disorganized form of globalization,
which is characteristic of the contemporary forms of religion that
was labelled 'fundamentalist' or 'Charismatic'. Such religion is driven
not by elites but by a mass of independent actors, who pick and
choose elements from different cultures (modern and pre-modern)
without regard to the constraints of regulating of official religious
hierarchy (Lehmann, p. 299, 305f.).[2]

DEFINING RELIGIOUS FUNDAMENTALISM

According to Lehmann,

> The term fundamentalism carries a wide range of meanings, some of them pejorative. Here it is used to refer to what the French call 'integrism', meaning a religious code which encompasses and governs with its prescriptions the entire private and public life of individuals and the collectivity. The prime examples in the contemporary world are Muslim renewal; the innumerable Evangelical and Charismatic churches, sects and tendencies descended from the Protestant tradition... (p. 305)

Martin rejects the use of the term to represent the huge shifts such as observed among Christians in the Pentecostal revolution and elsewhere in Islam as a 'catch-all category, quite apart from its journalistic misuse and its pejorative overtone' (Martin, 2002a: 1). First, while Pentecostalism is attached to Christian 'fundamentals' and to a conservative understanding of Scripture, the heart of its distinctive appeal lies in empowerment through spiritual gifts offered to all. Second, whereas Islamic revivalism pursues an organic relation between law, society, and faith, Pentecostalism represents a fissiparous and peaceable extension of voluntarism and competitive pluralism. The third relates to understandings that view 'fundamentalisms' as reactions against modernization, whereas, in most parts of the world where Pentecostalism is most expansive, notably Latin America and Africa, any extension of pluralistic voluntarism is arguably a manifestation of modernity. In fact Pentecostalism manifests and advances modernity in many other ways, than pluralistic voluntarism, having historical links with the US, and representing a variant of the North American model of the separation between state and church, territory and local community, exhibiting a partnership between voluntary denominations (including revivalist movements) and modernity (Martin, pp. 1-2). Such a unity and cooperation between church and state is never fathomed by Islamic fundamentalisms.

Religious fundamentalism has a rather short history, initially stemming from Christianity, when early in the twentieth century a group of orthodox Protestants in the United States published a series of pamphlets under the title *The Fundamentals: A Testimony* to the *Truth* between 1910 and 1912, in response to a number of social ills of the time. They freely referred to themselves as *fundamentalists* (Ter Haar, 2003: 2; An-Na'im, 2003: 28). The term is applied today to Christians who strongly and emphatically propagate a return to the fundamentals of life as experienced and practiced by early Christians and expressing a firm and total belief in Christ, not only as Son of God but as God incarnate in Himself. Such strong Christian fundamentalisms are expressed by Howard A. Kelly and the 1878 Niagara Creed (Marsden, 1988: 123-126; Sandeen, 1970: 273-277). The term, however, came to the fore front of world wide Islamic resurgence, when the fantasies of militant or political Islam came into reality in the 1979 Iranian Islamic revolution. The history of this shift in perception, according to Ter Haar dates back to the Iranian revolution under Ayatollah Khomeini in 1979, when the term *fundamentalism* was applied by journalists to describe the nature of the revolution process in Iran (Ter Haar, 2003: 1). Soon after, it was used to denote other religious groups with certain political interests, particularly those who use religion as a legitimate basis for seizing or holding on to power.

Contemporary use of the term almost always coincides with a type of belief associated with or possessed by 'Others', different from the belief possessed by 'Us'. This marks a point of departure, which has created a shift from the original Protestant usage of the term for ('our') self-definition, identity and legitimization to outside imposition on ('them') others. This shift portends grave implications for the relationships and interaction between adherents of different faith communities or people living in religiously and culturally pluralistic and diversified societies. This is particularly the relationship between Christian and Muslim in Nigeria (Ter Haar, p. 2). The original American Protestant fundamentalists chose their description, but the shift observable in the recent application of the fundamentalist label is imposed by outsiders, notably those journalists and academics who adopted it for Islam wholesale in uncritical fashion. Thus the term is used nowadays as a general term for a whole range of rather diverse phenomena (p. 3). Its present usage has been quite negative, irresponsible, unacceptable by 'the Other' and anti-sociable in nature.

CHARACTERISTICS OF RELIGIOUS FUNDAMENTALISM

Though the use of the term 'fundamentalism' may be problematic, Ter Haar stressed that there seem to be enough common features amongst these types of religion to justify its usage. Particularly significant is the reality that all these fundamental bodies can be grouped together as the prime instances of a second main type of modern religious globalization. Homogeneity (sameness) is a much more striking feature of fundamentalist globalization than heterogeneity (variety). Homogeneity is achieved by reliance on common authoritative texts rather than on traditions or institutions. Yet despite its universalizing tendencies, fundamentalist form of globalization is also characterized by a remarkable ability to adopt and adapt to local customs, and established local forms of identity (Lehmann, 2002: 305-306; Ter Haar, 2003; An-Naim, 2003). Considering different levels, these will include ideological or theological, social and cultural characteristics. Ideologically, the focus is on the past, socially it is on alternative structures, and culturally, it is on *asabiyya* identity. Fundamentalist forms of globalization possess an extraordinary ability to 'plug in' to local cultural practices and to incorporate them into their ritual and symbolic procedures, but without 'theorizing' them (in the manner of the cosmopolitan forms of globalization) and to provide a frame work for coping with serious social ills among or impoverished populations, again in a wide variety of cultural contexts. They have the ability to jump over existing political, linguistic and ethnic frontiers and to create transcultural communities of individuals without regard to these prior attachments. They also possess an obsessive attention to the control of sexually, especially female sexuality, a belief in the literal ('inerrant') truth of every word in the holy text and place emphasis on conversion as a crisis and rupture in the life of individuals. Some fundamentalist groups centrally focus attention on the inerrant word-for-word truth of the sacred text, while others focus on 'gifts of the Holy Spirit' such as healing, speaking in tongues and inspired oratory (Lehmann, p. 306).

Social change, particularly modernization, urbanization, technological innovation, other agents of globalization and localization, ethnic and religious pluralism and the creation of the nation state have brought about radical structural changes that imply a disruption of traditional society world wide. These have effected changes in myth and cosmology (worldview), cultural matrix and ritual leading to erosion of identities and stimulating a return to or re-enactment of a 'pristine', 'golden' or 'utopian' past to find solutions for current problems (Ter Haar, 2003: 5). Such reconstructive attempts by champions of re-enactment of pristine and utopian moments are often times undermined by those members who usually resort to violence to achieve desired objectives, thus contributing to the notoriety of religious fundamentalists. This becomes heightened and urgent when it is regarded as a divine directive to a holy people running out of time (p. 5). Religious fundamentalism, generally speaking refers to 'an identifiable pattern of religious militancy in which self-styled true believers attempt to arrest the erosion of religious identity by outsiders, fortify the borders of the religious community, and create viable alternatives to secular structures and processes' (p. 5). Ter Haar discerns a display of three patterns: first, a return to traditional values (viewed as golden, pristine) and an accompanying sense of restoration, stimulating and contributing to the building of alternative structures. Second, the search for new identity, *asabiyya* often at the expense of minority groups or outsiders; third, a preoccupation with moral (sometimes legal) concerns that tend to have adverse effect on women (human rights violations, revival of absurd anti-women and dehumanizing policies). Fourth, a spirit of militancy with which these objectives are pursued provides religious legitimacy for them, which may include the use of physical violence (p. 6).

In the process of evaluating the (golden pristine) past, a sense of yearning for restoration, which involves a careful sieving and selective process (from written or oral sacred history), whereby only those (divine) elements are retained, which are considered helpful in furthering the specific agenda of religious fundamentalists is pursued (p. 7). In all cases of religious fundamentalism, sacred (divine) history is contrasted with worldly history, in terms suggestive of a moral-ethical opposition between virtuous (positive) 'tradition' and devilish (negative) 'modernity'. Tradition divinely symbolized all that is virtuous, moral, utopian and hence identified as the source of all good in human history, while modernity epitomizes all of society's ills, identified with all evil, Satan, the immoral and chaotic; a deviation from original tradition, thus causing moral decay in society. Morality is at the center of the agenda of fundamentalists, thus their preoccupation with purity and separation into own monolithic societies becoming visible in the role given to women and the treatment meted to those considered outsiders (p. 7).

Religious fundamentalism aims at empowerment (acquisition of power, *charismata*) based on memories of a golden glorious past, whether historically accurate or mythical, projected into the future and believed to be within reach through transformative action. A return to this alternative society is possible either for the leader or for all members in this present time (p. 8). This ultimately leads to the establishment of a holy congregation or community (*umma*), in solidarity, unity, identity and communion *asabiyya* with God and with one another. Furthermore, economic and political goals are pursued in the establishment of independent constructive and developmental pursuits such as the establishment of practical life provisions such as social, educational, health, economic-trading networks and religious renewal leading to the establishment of some aspects of civil society (p. 9). Since fundamentalisms emerge as gradual historical processual developments over time, it implies that they possess histories that can be reconstructed. Sometimes such histories may emerge in layers, while on the other hand, they may historically develop along narrower paths, leading to schismatic/splinter churches (p. 10).

BRIEF HISTORY OF PENTECOSTALISM/ CHARISMATISM IN NIGERIA

The literature on the impact of globalization on Pentecostal/ Charismatic churches in Africa is enormous, with significant contributions from Paul Gifford and Ruth Marshall on its influence on socio-economic development of Africa (Gifford, 1998; Marshall, 1983), Ruth Marshall-Fratani and Rosalind Hackett focussing on innovation and creativity; particularly the use of media (Marshall-Fratani, 1998: 278-315; Hackett, 1998: 258-277), while Afe Adogame (1998a, 1998b 2000a, 2000b, 2002a, 2002b, 2002c), Gerrie ter Haar (1998a, 1998b), Clifford Hill (1971), Roy Kerridge (1995), Jack Thompson (1995), Roswith Gerloff (1992, 1999) and Rijk van Dijk (1997, 1999, 2001, 2002) study the impact of non-Western Pentecostalism and AICs in the Western world among many other works on African immigrant religions in diaspora.

46

Olupona aptly stated that the international status of Pentecostal/Charismatic movement in Nigeria is not in doubt. For some it is a part of their self image as they very often add such terms as 'global', 'international' and 'continental' to their titles (Olupona, 2002: 309, 15; cf. Peil and Opoku, 1994: 21). Secondly, the Pentecostal/Charismatic movements of Nigeria are engaged in a reverse mission to Europe, the US and other parts of the world, thus proving that the African church, which was the target of Western Christian missionary enterprise over a century ago have come of age, exporting 'authentic' and urgently needed Christian spirituality back to a morally eroded Western world today. These international branches abroad channel huge resources back home to their headquarters in Nigeria (Olupona, p. 15). The *World Christian Encyclopedia* estimates that there are 83 million 'Independents' and 126 million Pentecostals-Charismatics in Africa in 2000, representing about 20% of all Christians (Barrett, Kurian and Johnson, 2001: 1-13; Barrett and Padwick, 1989: 9). The Pentecostal/Charismatic group is the fastest-growing movement in West Africa, at least from the numbers of buildings and the large number of people attending Pentecostal assemblies. The Pentecostal/Charismatic movement in Nigeria has indeed had a phenomenal rise in membership, being reckoned by the *New International Dictionary of Pentecostalism and Charismatic Movements* to have a population of approximately 3.03 million, that is, 8% (Pentecostals), 9.79 million, that is, 27% (Charismatics) and 23.06 million, that is, 64% (Neocharismatics), giving a total of 35.885 million as members of renewal movement (Burgess, 2002: 192).

Charismatic Churches are evangelical churches founded by African leaders who have adopted a radical spiritual conversion, 'the born again' syndrome, through baptism of the Holy Spirit, re-enacting the Day of Pentecost of speaking in tongues, divine healing and miracles. They also profess that material success and prosperity of members are signs of divine grace and benevolence. The leadership of Pentecostal/Charismatic in Nigeria is entirely of a local autonomous nature. Most founders, though older now, are still in charge of affairs and can be termed younger than founders of AICs. They are mostly elitist, relatively educated, ranging from college graduates to university professors and professionals such as chemists, engineers, physicists and mathematicians, but very seldom in theology or religion. This marks a shift from founders of prophetic African churches who are in general semi-illiterates.

The Charismatic movement originated in Nigeria in the 1970s, with the first being those that started as college and university student ministries out of the Student Christian Movement (SCM), Scripture Union (SU), and Campus Christian Fellowship (CCF). Many of these students had become Pentecostals before coming to college/university. As university students, many read literature on charismatics from Europe and the US, among them are the works of Kenneth Hagin, Oral Roberts, Robert Tilton, and Kenneth Copeland. The Universities of Ibadan and Ife became hotbeds of Pentecostalism. This later shifted to house prayer cells, ministering to youths and others as some of the leaders graduated from college. Then some of the house churches expanded into full-fledged ministries in urban centers; the most successful being the Deeper Life ministry of William F. Kumuyi and Redeemed Church of God of Pastor E.A. Adeboye (Olupona, 2002: 15; Ojo, 1988a, 1988b, 1988c: 26; Gaiya 2002: 4). These youths traveled all over the country and some of them soon establish contacts abroad. Their enthusiasm, zeal and aggressive evangelism tremendously aided the growth of Christianity in Nigeria (Ojo, 1988c: 28). They soon attracted young English-speaking Christian civil servants and business persons to their fold. For instance, most members of the Christian Worker's Association (CWA) who met regularly at the Jos Township School (Nigeria) for Wednesday mid-week prayers and Bible studies became the first members of the Redeemed Christian Church of God in the late 70s.

The second level involves those that originated from overseas, especially the US. The Charismatic movement began within the mainline churches in America, within the Protestant Church of Rev Dennis J. Bennet, an Anglican minister of St. Mark's Episcopal Church in Van Nuys, California in 1960. It became known within the Roman Catholic Church in 1966 when some faculty members of Dusquesne University in Pittsburg sought the experience of speaking in tongues. This led not only to the emergence of the Catholic Charismatic Renewal movement, but to the holding of annual meetings from 1967 that grew in numbers year after (Larbi, 2001: 80-81; Connelly, 1977; Hollenweger, 1972; Quebedeux, 1983). These were established initially as national branches of international religious groups, for example The Full Gospel Business Men's Fellowship International typifies success stories of movements belonging to this platitude.

The third level constitutes those that originated from Nigeria, but quickly spread to other countries of West Africa. The Church of God Mission International of the late Archbishop Benson Idahosa (1938-98), who trained at Christ for the Nations Institute in the US where he received a great deal of funds, and The Living Faith (a.k.a) Winners' Chapel of Pastor David Oyedepo belong to this category. He trained and ordained some disciples who founded other charismatic churches. Nicholas Duncan Williams of the Christian Action Faith Ministry International, and Charles Ayim Asare of the World Miracle Bible Church in Tamale, Ghana are Idahosa' protégés and successful charismatic leaders (Olupona, 2002: 15-16; Gifford, 1994).

Pentecostal/Charismatic are essentially 'a liberation movement through which the Holy Spirit sets free many people held in bondage by Satan'. The healing, exorcism and deliverance from sin which adorn the Gospels and Acts are re-enacted in modern Ghana. According to Larbi, 'I have myself witnessed blind, deaf, and paralytics healed and the dying resuscitated'. The movement derives its power and success from Christian spirituality, the exercise of the gifts of the Holy Spirit, and from the development of indigenous Church life-style using local language, music, liturgy, symbols and personnel. It emphasizes laity leadership in worship as well as mass evangelism, periodical congregational revival meetings, women's participation in the ministry, pastoral care, and solidarity with the poor. Although its teachings and preachings demonstrate concern with political matters, it believes more in secret intercessory prayer than matters political (Larbi, 2001: 97).

GLOBALIZED CHURCHES?

There is a Western, especially North American Pentecostal influence in these churches both in liturgy and leadership patterns and the North American 'prosperity preachers' are not only often times promoted, but even invited, which sets Charismatic Pentecostalism against the spirit of fundamentalism, which is essentially anti-modern and anti-West (Anderson, 1987: 72-83; Larbi, 2001: 295; Dovlo, 1992: 60). Participating in church services produces evidence for an identity of success and provides a social space for performing positive social status. Charismatic churches appear cosmopolitan since English is the main language of communication and a globalized middle-class dress code prevails, implying that even the dress code is globalized. Pastor, elders, deacons dress in suits and ties, while deaconesses and ladies dress in suits, skirts, caps or hats, everybody is dressed up. Many pastors appear on stage more like pop stars (not that of the humble servant of God), an American style of religious service, 'modern' and 'entertaining'. This attraction of the Americanized style of service is alluringly modern, and it fits better with modern life. This 'modernism' that is closely connected to material success and its attendant symbols, is a part of the image presented of the Pentecostal/Charismatic churches.

However, most Pentecostal/Charismatic churches that want to attract a certain class of persons reject a 'backward' or merely simple type of dressing as a Christianity lacking in faith and class. To attract the correct class of people (the middle-English speaking income earners or their children), God must be presented as 'a blessing God, a promoting God and a prospering God' who is prepared to elevate those who serve him faithfully from a lower level (with regards to status, wealth, promotion in the work place, excelling in school work, business and other areas materially) to a higher level. The church must, therefore, appear 'attractive' or 'modern' to the believers because an attractive, modern appearance represents the power of God internalized within, together with its potential capability in transforming the life of the individual for the better. A Pastor asserts, 'In my church, I want to be surrounded by successful people'. This message works in two directions, first it works as a promise, becoming a part of the church is a means of becoming successful and second, being a member of the church is a claim or guarantee (by faith) to be successful already (Nieswand, 2005).

The preaching emphasizes an empowering moral code and tends to be sharply opposed to traditional practices, prohibiting tobacco, alcohol, use of symbolic healing objects (some use holy/anointing oil, sanctified handkerchiefs), any form of ancestor veneration, title taking (outside the church), polygyny and the wearing of uniforms. They are thus often regarded by the older AICs as mounting a sustained attack on traditional African values (Anderson, 2001: 19). The membership is not from the very poor in society (cf. Corten, 1999: 63), but tends to consist of younger less economically deprived middle class and more formally educated as in the West and globally (Martin, 2002a: 1). One no doubt recognizes the boost of these churches as a part of the failure of the state in Nigeria, with unstable economies, creating an economic crunch and political instability that gave way to ethnic conflicts and the emergence of ethnic militias for years (Gifford, 1998; Marshall, 1993: 213-246). A confused state created by long military (mis) rule, birthing extremely difficult conditions for human existence in a contingent world made more difficult by the scourge of HIV/AIDs, the worst kind of STIs/STDs, massive unemployment and high inflation rates among other factors. Many become so desperate that they seek for solace in churches that can show tender loving care and the Pentecostal/Charismatic churches do take care of their Christian *umma*, through creating conducive environment for *asabiyya* group solidarity and identity.

GLOBAL/FUNDAMENTALIST

Pentecostal/Charismatics in Nigeria assert identity and solidarity since members have experienced a renewed and shared life in Christ and have been born again. They exhibit exclusivist tendencies, regarding members of other churches as nominal Christians, spiritually dead or lukewarm, for whom genuine Christian living is far from being a way of life. For this reason, Olupona referred to them elsewhere as the Christian *umma*, community (Olupona, 1997), while in asserting their self-identity and solidarity with each other, they have developed a unique Christian *assabiyya*, solidarity, unity and platform for identity. By living a life of holiness, they see themselves as a separate *umma*, community linked by holiness, 'twice born' or 'second birth' identity *assabiyya*, different from non-charismatics.

There is a preoccupation with reading, seeking for and displaying identity symbols/relics of church life, which we have called Christian *assabiyya*. This emphasis on reading is displayed in the purchase and reading of books, tracts, Bible Commentaries, magazines, and newsletters, written and published by the founder. They purchase and listen to recorded messages, drama and songs on cassette, video, CD and DVD, all sold in the church bookshop or shopping center. Signs bearing the identity of members (*assabiyya*, solidarity) are exhibited in the form of car stickers, T-shirts, with inscriptions such as 'Jesus Is Lord', 'Are you Saved?', 'The Blood of Jesus', 'I Am A Winner', etc. are conspicuously displayed in homes, on TV, door posts, walls, refrigerators, cars and in work places. The production and sale of these items has become a very lucrative business indeed. The use of e-mail, web sites and other internet facilities demonstrates that they put technology to rigorous use. Pentecostalism also takes the media seriously. Televangelism is carried out on TV with the groups buying air time to showcase their programs for the viewing public. For instance, the late Archbishop Benson Idahosa was inspired by the likes of Jim Bakker, Freda Lindsay, Oral Roberts, and T.L. Osborn, leading him to begin 'Redemption Hour' as the first TV evangelist in Nigeria. His All Nations For Christ Bible School, fashioned after Christ For The Nation Institute, is the most successful school established by any Pentecostal group in Nigeria and is christened 'Father of Prosperity Gospel' in Nigeria (Gaiya, 2002: 9).

Pentecostal/Charismatics publish a great deal in newsletters, magazines, and the print media. Church members distribute tracts on buses, along the street, and through house to house evangelism where they are also seen to be actively engaged in public preaching. Many revival meetings are announced on bill boards, TV advertisements, hand bills, posters, decorated on large pieces of cloth pasted at gates and walls of college and university campuses announcing special crusades, healing and miracle sessions, revival meetings, night vigils, or their weekly activities. Such events are usually attended by thousands of peoples traveling from far and near (Olupona, 2002: 14-15).

There is emphasis on prophecy, dreams, visions, prayer healing and the possession of the Holy Spirit play central role in their theology and worship. This is the crux of Pentecostal/Charismatic Christian *umma*. Glossolalia is the most visible sign of divine, Holy Spirit possession, prophetic utterances, signs of divine revelation, and a divine gift from God in Pentecostal/Charismatic Churches. Acts 2 is used as a defence for this practice (Olupona, pp. 16-17). Pentecostalism in the early church exhibited being filled by the Holy Spirit and pure living through three stages. First is a testimony of the acceptance of Christ, second is water baptism by total immersion and third is 'baptism in/by fire', the eruption of glossolalia. This 'twice born' *erlebnis* is the initiation into spiritual militancy, leading to revelation in dreams, visions, prophecy, healing and speaking in new tongues. It is the most unique form of religious *charismata* found among Christian Pentecostals the world over (Holm, 1991: 135-151). The baptism of Pentecostal/Charismatics is not primarily sacramental; but an emotional baptism in the Holy Spirit; an intense, mystical feeling of contact with God. This feeling is expressed through 'speaking in tongues', which the church witnesses. For Pentecostals, this emotional experience (*Erlebnis*) is an element of the religious – the *homo religiosus*. Pentecostalism is a *sui generic* phenomenon resulting from trans-nationalization (Corten, 1999: 25-26, 37ff., cf. Kelsey, 1981; Burgess and McGee, 1988: 334-441). Speaking in new tongues is a gift from God, a language of the Holy Spirit in communication between the homo-religiosus and God (cf. Brandt-Bessire, 1986: 174). It is a divine language, when displayed it exhibits an exclusive relationship between God and the believer. It is open and available to everyone who desires to have it. It is a sign of Christian *communitas* as much as a breaking point with the outside world. It is thus viewed by outsiders as 'anti-social', 'anti-clerical' and 'the anti-establishment of Protestantism'.

Corten refers to this as 'ritual fundamentalism' that ensures cohesion (communitas, *assabiyya*, solidarity) amongst the believers. A stress is placed on Matt. 3.11 '...He will baptize you with the Holy Spirit and with fire'. Acts 1.8 'But you shall receive power when the Holy Spirit has come upon you; and you shall be witnesses to me...' centrally characterizes Pentecostalism (Corten, 1999: 38f.). It is a fundamentalism seeking perfection. Perfection is sought in withdrawal from the world to the life of an ascetic renouncer (in the form of a yogi, sanyasin or *sadhu*) in Hinduism and within the confines of monastic – convent life in Catholicism and Buddhism. The pursuit of holiness in the holiness movement is an immediate consciousness of salvation, 'the Holy Spirit actualizing the image of God in each person', a pursuit carried out both individually and collectively in camp meetings where emotions are released. This first level leads to repentance from sin during the conversion experience, and in turn gives birth to the second level of experience of crisis, the fruit of a total personal experience of the 'Charismatic emotion' and in the 'experience of plenitude' it brings. In Pentecostalism a third stage appears (Hollenweger, 1988: 25), 'speaking in tongues' (Corten, 1999: 39). Men and women from the lower classes experience 'speaking in tongues' as well as others from higher social classes. Surveys of Burgess and McGee show that up to a fifth of Pentecostal/Charismatic members received this gift (Burgess and McGee, 1988: 144).

Liturgical practice and worship mode is another aspect of the *assabiyya* identity and solidarity. Worship is not as quiet as the old established evangelical or orthodox churches, but is characterized by 'raising a loud shout unto God in worship'. They use rather heavy musical instruments, shouting, aggressive and high pitched tone. Songs sang are mainly pop gospel songs, from the US. People clap and dance in their conspicuously dressed-up form, with a whole band, singers and background choir performance, like a party or concert attendance, everyone is dancing. Songs and speeches (prayers, lamentations, preaching, blessings, collections, information, healing) come out of sophisticated instruments, a complete band – guitar, a drum set, the mandolin, synthesizer, praise worship – spiritual songs, jazz, rock, disco, romantic style, baroque music (Cox, 1993: 181-187). According to David Martin, 'Born-again Christianity [in West Africa] opens on to the modern world, equipped with synthesizers and contemporary music, screens and videos, radio and television ministers, open-air preachments and large scale rallies. It wears suits and ties...' (Martin, 2002b: 11). The singing when prolonged produces a rise in the emotional climate, a heightened climate that is likely to produce harmony.

FUNDAMENTALISM

Pentecostal/Charismatic movements in Nigeria place emphasis on a return to Bible-based faith in Christ, a re-enactment of the days of Christ on earth thus directly challenging members to meet Him face to face. God, Jesus and the Holy Spirit solved or will solve all human problems. All sicknesses will be cured, food will arrive, money will be multiplied, and children will be born to the barren women. In the words of Waldo Cesar, converts to Pentecostal churches can cope with the daily contingencies in life because they have experienced a great deal of extraordinary, cathartic transformation of life. This catharsis is so powerful that it leads them to a radiant acceptance of the providential salvation of God through Christ. It enables them to build up a new self-esteem of a vibrant hope that transfigures situations normally associated with frustration and despair into victory – call it alienation, fanaticism, naivete or fundamentalism (Cesar, 2000: 33). Moreover, there is usually a strong urge to re-enact the Pentecostal church life of the golden pristine era when Christ was on earth and during the life time of the early disciples and apostles.

There is also a strong eschatological teaching about the nearness of the end of the times, and Jesus Christ can give meaning to life in this age that is too close to the Armageddon, the time of the tribulation and the End of Age. There is the firm belief that in these 'end-time' days, those who place their belief in Christ 'find relief on every side'. Thus one of the informants of Cesar could confess with a radiant confident face:

> After I entered Universal everything changed. Even with my very rigid boss it was also possible to change. I used to work very depressed and then I started to take everything in a natural way. I went on to have Jesus alive as I do, so why worry about it. If the boss only knew the God I know today, he wouldn't be like he is... And also the doctor said that I would never be a mother. So I took part in a prayer chain at the church and by the seventh session I got pregnant.

There is a preoccupation with the other transcendental world, heaven as a reality now and simultaneously as a reality that will soon be consummated with the eminent second coming of Christ to the earth, thus relating Pentecostal/Charismatics with deviant behavior. The fundamentalist and militant protest here, should however, be understood as a spiritual not physical warfare, though described in vivid battle caricatures (Cesar, 2000: 33-34).

The rise of Islamic fundamentalism and militancy in the form of search for self assertion and identity has brought Nigerian Muslims, particularly those in the far north and the Middle-Belt, into violent confrontation with Christians since the 1980s. This has made Christianity in the area to become more and more intolerant towards Islam, a trend becoming more characteristic of northern Nigerian Christian life. The recent Shari'a crises that started from 1999 gave sharp impetus to the rise of this intolerant type of Christian fundamentalism, birthing the doctrine of the 'third slap' or 'tired cheek', which urges Christians to be ready to bear arms according to the principle of self-defence. This has

given birth to a general growing militancy amongst the youth of the
Evangelical and Catholic churches, and in some cases, even those of
Pentecostal/Charismatics throughout northern Nigeria. However,
this development is not so much as a direct result of the teaching of
the church leaders as it is a reaction to what is happening in society,
that is, the provocative Shari'a campaigns, lectures and utterances
of Muslims and the direct and other subtle ways in which Shari'a
Muslim law is affecting Christians in northern Nigeria generally.
Credit is given to leaders of Pentecostal/Charismatics in controlling their massive youth population through an emphasis on
'spiritual' rather than 'physical' warfare, or else the situation would
have gone out of hand. This was greatly aided by the dependence
on oral theology, sayings, deeds, and instructions of their founders, who exert great influence on members. For example, members
of The Living Faith may not travel or embark on a project if they
are not specifically instructed by the Pastor, whom they refer to as
Papa (Father) to do so. Members of most Pentecostal/Charismatic
groups are taught to be obedient to church and political authority,
and while the Papa is preaching, shouts of 'Yes Sir' could be heard
from the membership throughout the sermon.

The Pentecostal/Charismatics operating in northern Nigeria
are of course opposed to the spread of Islam in the area as their
other Christian counterparts. They however believe that aggressive
preaching of the Gospel of Christ, unceasing prayer, with fasting
should be pursued towards checkmating the 'spirit of Islam' and
Islamic fundamentalism. They often pray for the government and
the political elite, irrespective of whether they are Christians or not.
They are thus not keen on fighting a physical battle in Nigeria to
acquire physical space, but prefer to control the situation on their
knees in prayer. They consider 'the Spirit of Islam' as a part of the
demonic world that must be conquered. It is a spiritual battle; and
not a physical warfare that is fought with guns, machetes, axes,
clubs, grenades, vigilante groups, ethnic youths and/or mercenar-
ies. The members are thus urged to:

> Finally, build up your strength in union with the Lord and
> by means of his mighty power. Put on all the armour that
> God gives you, so that you will be able to stand up against
> the devil's tricks. For we are not fighting against human
> beings but against the wicked spiritual forces in the heav-

enly world, the rulers, authorities, and cosmic powers of this Dark Age. So put on God's armour now! Then when the evil day comes, you will be able to resist the enemy's attacks; and after fighting to the end you will still hold your ground (Ephesians, 6:10-14).

The whole of life is a spiritual warfare and the believer must be filled by the Holy Spirit and lead a life of pure living in order to face the enemy, Satan, his demons and human disciples successfully in battle. A non-member listening to them may mistakenly think that they are planning a physical battle against the Muslim *umma*, or even other Christians.

AGAINST GLOBALIZATION/LOCALIZATION?

However, not all Pentecostal/Charismatic churches in Nigeria allow a great deal of Western influences to penetrate them. The Deeper Life Church of William F. Kumuyi and the Synagogue Church of all Nations of Prophet Temitope Balogun Joshua, the Sabbatharians, classical Pentecostals and the AICs are not totally flexible to the 'wind' of globalization. The Deeper Life Church even prescribes a 'holy' life style for its members. Members are taught not to 'dress up', or 'over-dress', but to appear simply neat and modest. Women do not wear facial make-up, jewellery such as necklaces, bangles, rings on the fingers and the ears, not to speak of nose and eyebrows. Members are discouraged from watching TV at home, and like some Sabbatharian movements, church music is bereaved of the heavy rhythm usually present in other Pentecostal churches, with emphasis on the use of the organ and accappella (cf. Ojo, 1988).

The theology of Pentecostal/Charismatics take over several aspects of the African worldview since their cosmology are filled by *ogbanje/abiku* (born-to-die) children, mammy water spirits, witches, sorcerers, spirit mediums and possession, divination, secret society, ancestor veneration, traditional healing methods and their apparatus, occultism and the force of evil is vividly present and considered real. The Trunk Room Ministry of Rev. Kure of Kafanchan, Southern part of Kaduna State, Nigeria, have been engaged in spiritual cleansing of lands and communities believed to have been polluted and cursed by the evil spirits. Demons are perceived as the causes of lack of success and prosperity, misfortune such as barrenness and childlessness, bad harvest, STIs/STDs particularly HIV/AIDS and political oppression. The pervasive presence of demons in the Pentecostal/Charismatic movements is described in this way, 'the devil's presence is doctrinal, practical and ritual' (Olupona, 2002: 17; Lehmann, 1996: 139). Doctrinally, according to Olupona, it is an unwritten article of faith, 'to proclaim the power of Jesus, to liberate individuals from the power of the devil and from possession by the devil', since a belief that the devil and his demonic spirits are ever present and are considered a concrete truth and constitute a threat in the lives of members and the Christian *umma* and its *assabiyya*, solidarity and identity (cf. Ojo, 1988). Thus members must be, individually and collectively, regularly on guard. This could be achieved only through rituals of fasting and prayer of deliverance (elsewhere regarded as exorcism, casting out of demons), prayer of prevention, prayer for strength, etc (Olupona, p. 17; cf. Lehmann, p. 139). Gifford remarks that Nigerians' accounts of demonic powers are exaggerated, 'frightening', bizarre, and possibly untrue compared to those of Ghanaians (Gifford, 1994: 255). Peil and Opoku (1994) support this view when they assert that witchcraft and other forms of mystical principles and powers are not commonly emphasized in sermons.

Thus, emphasis on Satanic origin of sin and all evil, appealing as an anti-dote to every ill in a society that believes in witchcraft, Satanic or occultic wealth, demon belief – *ogbanje/abiku* spirit, mammy water, demon or spirit possession, a cosmology in keeping with traditional beliefs, has not merely survived to contemporary times, but is currently gaining a renewal, spread and acceptance throughout Nigeria. Such a cosmology is quite frightening and can create low self-esteem and what Meyer calls a sense of 'false consciousness' (Meyer, 1995: 237). These evil forces are discussed and regarded as concrete and real in the lives of many (Olupona, 2002: 15). Church attendance implies 'importing' a specific mode of self representation. Thus, the essential embodied experience of Charismatic religious practice is empowerment, towards overcoming the obstacles hindering achievement and self-realization.

Healing is a holistic attitude, involving spiritual, physical and emotional or psychological aspects of well being. In principle, it is a gift of the Holy Spirit, to every born-again Christian. In practice, it is the prerogative of the founder – part of his/her charisma. Church members/elders with the gift of 'anointing' lay hands on the sick after they have received their healing. Healing is not individualistic and secretly performed, but rather publicly and corporately. This is a positive element in Charismatic movements' approach to healing, as it serves in strengthening the spirit of Christian *assabiyya* (solidarity, identity, a sense of belonging and victory) within the Christian *umma*. As opposed to the individualistic approach of Western bio-medicine, the charismatic method is closer to the African holistic method of corporate, group and community approach to healing and rehabilitation. Healing and exorcism draws throngs of people to Charismatic assemblies because people expect to receive healing, see miracles (the lame walk, the blind see, the barren received assurance of fertility, the demon-possessed delivered, etc). People with various life problems, infirmities and disabilities patronize healing arenas such as 'Miracle Night Crusade', 'Power Night Crusade' – miracle and or/healing centers (Olupona, 2002: 17).

Pentecostal Charismatism has the ability to respond to the existential and pragmatic problems, including domestic and economic, faced by modern, urban congregation. They aspire towards healing both 'the soul and the body' – prison, hospital ministries, counseling for women, welfare programs, child ministry, nursery and secondary schools, in Nigeria the Covenant University owned by Living Faith Church, Benson Idahosa University at Okada (Olupona, p. 18; cf. Gifford, 1994: 243). The emergence of Ghanaian charismatic churches in response to economic crises, as exemplified by MacLean, is also applicable to the Nigerian situation, where there is a rather heavy emphasis on 'prosperity' and 'material success' (MacLean, 1997). The charismatic churches target educated, English-speaking new urban dwellers, lower and upper middle income earners, and successful business persons. Their emphasis on individual progress and high achievement in life, individual success and prosperity has a great appeal for this bracket of urban dwellers. This appeal has propeled them into other regions of Africa, Europe and the US (Olupona, p. 18-19).

There has been a return to the rendition of African 'ethnic' songs, and the provocative almost 'erotic' Yoruba, Makossa and Congo dance steps, highlife, traditional songs in local Nigerian languages in Pentecostal/Charismatic songs. Such dance steps and the use of instruments makes it impossible to say that they have been completely globalized. In another vein, the activities of some so-called Pentecostal/Charismatic movements have generated much public criticism and skepticism. The Overcomers' Christian Mission of Owerri founded and led by Rev. Alexander Ezeugo Ekwuba was allegedly involved in ritual murders. Riots broke out in the city of Owerri in September 1996, when some rich persons who worshiped in this church were allegedly accused of the crime. It did not help matters when rampaging youths found two human skulls within the church premises (Gaiya, 2003: 21). Such scenarios do not actually signal a break with traditionalism. This also shows that some members may consider Christianity alone as incapable of combating all existential problems in human life. This mere fact that these problems are still combated through extra-traditional methods shows that local strains are still very much present. Tension generated by political and issues of a controversial nature are sometimes visible within the Pentecostal fold. For instance, the refusal to register Prophet T.B. Joshua, founder of the Synagogue Church of All Nations into the Pentecostal Fellowship of Nigeria, the umbrella body of Pentecostal/Charismatic churches in Nigeria. This is in spite of its popularity, attracting thousands of people including traditional rulers, top politicians and foreigners such as Frederick Chiluba, Zambia's former President. The church has attracted the highest numbers of visitors seeking healing from Europe and the US. At one time, it boasted of 400 foreigners from ten different countries (Gaiya, p. 23).

CONCLUSION

Gifford uses the terms 'Charismatic/Pentecostals', 'evangelicals' and 'fundamentalists' interchangeably in Africa (Brouwer, et. al, 1996: 155). In any case, none of the Nigerian churches, including Pentecostal/Charismatics would accept being described as fundamentalists. Furthermore, as we have seen, not every aspect of Nigerian Pentecostal Charismatism was imported from abroad (Europe and the US). It appears that Pentecostal/Charismatics are globalized, if by this we mean the balancing of the interplay between the global/local elements towards producing a transglobal picture. The emphasis on faith teaching, miracle-healing, speaking in tongues, the notion of being born again and the dress code strongly keep them on the global scene. However, this is not a sort of religious imperialism that has wiped out all local influences as the belief in demons, witchcraft and notion of the devil is still prevalent. Some characteristics of fundamentalism are strongly present in the sense of going back to pristine times, biblical traditions and being filled with the Holy Spirit. The concept of militancy is spiritual, but physical militancy in the sense of Christians fighting back, regarded against the back drop of the doctrine of the 'third slap' and 'tired cheeks' continue to keep fundamentalism of the violent type amongst Christian youths in northern Nigeria, notwithstanding the teachings of church leaders against it. Pentecostal/Charismatics in Nigeria are therefore far from being homogenous, some are conservative, others are innovative, some tend towards traditional religious practices, thus becoming syncretic in the process.

Bibliography

Adogame, Afe, 'A Home away from Home: The proliferation of Celestial Church of Christ in Diaspora-Europe', in *Exchange – Journal of Missiological and Ecumenical Research*, 27, 2, 1998a, pp. 141-160.

Adogame, Afe, 'Building Bridges and Barricades', *Marburg Journal of Religion*, 3, 1, 1998b, pp. 1-13.

Adogame, Afe, 'Missions from Africa: The Case of the Celestial Church of Christ in Europe', in *Zeitschrift für Missionswissenschaft und Religionswissenschaft*, 84, 1, 2000a, pp 29-44.

Adogame, Afe, 'The Quest for Space in the Global Religious Marketplace: African Religions in Europe, in *International Review of Mission* 89, 354, 2000b, pp. 400-409.

Adogame, Afe. 'African Initiated Churches (AICs) in Dispora-Europe', in Stanley M. Burgess (ed.), *The New International Dictionary of Pentecostal and Charismatic Movements* (revised and expanded edition). Grand Rapids, Michigan: Zondervan, 2002a, 309.

Adogame, Afe, 'Pentecostalism in Germany', in Stanley M. Burgess (ed), *The New International Dictionary of Pentecostal and Charismatic Movements*, 2002b, pp. 109-111.

Adogame, Afe, 'Traversing Local-Global Religious Terrain: African New Religious Movements in Europe', *Zeitschrift für Religionswissenschaft*, 10, 2002c, pp. 33-49.

Adogame, Afe, 'Engaged in the task of 'Cleansing' the World: Aladura Churches in 20th century Europe', in Klaus Koschorke (ed.), *Transkontinentale Beziehungen in der Lateinamerika des Außereurpäischen Christentmus* (Asien, Afrika, Lateinamerika)/*Transcontinental Links in the*

History of Non-Western Christianity, vol. 6, Wiesbaden: Harrassowitz, 2002, pp. 73-86.

Albrow, Martin, *The Global Age: State and Society Beyond Modernity*, Cambridge and Oxford, UK: Polity Press, 1996.

Anderson, Allan, *African Reformation: African Initiated Christianity in the 20th Century*. Trenton, New York and Asmara, Eritrea: Africa World Press, Inc., 2001

Anderson, Allan, *Bazalwane: African Pentecostals in South Africa*. Pretoria: University of South Africa Press, 1992.

Anderson, Allan, 'The Prosperity Message in the Eschatology of some new Charismatic Churches', in *Missionalia* 15, 2, 1987, pp. 72-83.

An-Na'im, Abdullahi Ahmed, 'Islamic Fundamentalism and Social Change: Neither the "End of History" nor a "Clash of Civilisations"', in Gerrie ter Haar and James J. Busuttil (eds.), *The Freedom to do God's Will*, London and New York: Routledge, Taylor and Francis Group, 2003, pp. 25-48.

Barrett, David B., George T. Kurian and Todd M. Johnson (eds.), *World Christian Encyclopedia*, 2nd ed., 2 volumes, Oxford and New York: Oxford University Press, 2001.

Barrett, David B. and T. John Padwick, *Rise Up and Walk! Conciliarism and the African Indigenous Churches, 1815-1987*. Nairobi, Kenya: Oxford University Press, 1989.

Beck, Ulrich, *Risk Society: Towards a New Modernity*. London: Sage, (1986) 1992.

Berger, Peter (ed), *The Desecularization of the World*, Grand Rapids, MI: Eerdmans, 1999.

Beyer, Peter, *Religion and Globalization*, London: Sage, 1994.

Burgess, S.M., and McGee, G.B. (eds.), *Dictionary of Pentecostal and Charismatic Movements*, Grand Rapids, Michigan: Regency Reference Library, 1988, pp. 334-441.

Brandt-Bessire, Daniel, Aux sources de la spiritualite pentecotiste, Geneva: Labor et Fides, 1986).

Brouwer, Steve, et. al, *Exporting the American Gospel: Global Christian Fundamentalism*, New York: Routledge, 1996.

Bruce, Steve, *Fundamentalism*, Cambridge: Polity Press, 2001.

Cox, Harvey, *Fire from Heaven: The Rise of Pentecostal Spirituality and the Reshaping of Religion in the Twenty-First Century*. Cambridge, MA: Da Capo Press, 1995.

Cox, Harvey, 'Jazz and Pentecostalism', *Archives de sciences sociales des religions*, 84, October/December, 1993, pp. 181-187.

Cox, Robert W., 'A Perspective on Globalization', in James H. Mittelman (ed.), *Globalization: Critical Reflections. International Political Economy Year Book*, volume 9. Boulder and London: Lynne Rienner Publishers, 1996, pp. 21-30.

Cesar, Waldo, 'Part 1: Daily Life and Transcendence in Pentecostalism', in Richard Shaull and Waldo Cesar, *Pentecostalism and the Future of the Christian Churches: Promises, Limitations and Challenges*, Grand Rapids, Michigan and Cambridge, UK: William B. Eerdmans, 2000.

Connelly, James C., *Neo-Pentecostalism: The Charismatic Renewal in the mainline Protestant and Roman Catholic Churches of the United States, 1960-1971*, PhD Diss., University of Chicago, 1977.

Corten, André, *Pentecostalism in Brazil: Emotion of the Poor and Theological Romanticism*. (trans. by Arianne Dorval) Houndmills, Basingstoke, Hampshire and London: Macmillan and New York: St. Martin's Press Inc., 1999.

Dovlo, Elom, 'Comparative Overview of Independent Churches and Charismatic Ministries in Ghana', *Trinity Journal of Church and Theology*, 2, 2, December 1992, pp. 55-73.

Droogers, André, 'Globalization and Pentecostal Success', in André Corten and Ruth Marshall-Fratani, *Between Babel and Pentecost: Transnational Pentecostalism in Africa and Latin America*. London: Hurst and Co., 2001, pp. 41-61.

Gaiya, Musa, *The Pentecostal Revolution in Nigeria*, Occasional Paper, Center for African Studies, University of Copenhagen, 2002, p. 1.

Gerloff, Roswith, 'Pentecostals in the African Diaspora', in Allan Anderson and Walter Hollenweger (eds.), *Pentecostals After a Century: Global Perspectives on a Movement in Transition*, Sheffield, England: Sheffield Academic Press, 1999, pp. 67-86.

Gerloff, Roswith, *A Plea for British Black Theologies: The Black Church Movement in Britain in its Trasatlantic Cultural and Theological Interaction* (2 vols.), Frankfurt a.M: Peter Lang, 1992.

Gifford, Paul, 'Some Recent Developments in African Christianity', *African Affairs*, 93, 373, 1994, pp. 513-533.

Gifford, Paul, 'Ghana's Charismatic Churches', *Journal of Religion in Africa*, 24, 3, 1994, pp. 241-265.

Gifford, Paul, *African Christianity: Its Public Role*. London: Hurst and Co., 1998.

Hackett, Rosalind I.J., 'Charismatic/Pentecostal Appropiation of Media Technologies in Nigeria and Ghana', *Journal of Religion in Africa*, 28, 1998, pp. 258-277.

Hill, Clifford, *Black Churches: West Indian and African Sects in Britain*, London: Community and Race Relations Unit of the British Council of Churches, 1971.

Hollenweger, Walter, *The Pentecostals*, London: SCM, 1972 (reprint, Peabody Mass: Hendrickson, 1988).

Holm, Nils G., 'Invited Essay-Pentecostalism: Conversion and Charisma', in *The International Journal for the Psychology of Religion*, 1, 3, 1991, pp. 135-151.

Kelsey, M., *Tongue Speaking: The History and Meaning of Charismatic Experience*, New York: Crossroad, 1981.

Kerridge, Roy, *The Storm is Passing Over: A Look at Black Churches in Britain*, London: Thames and Hudson, 1995.

Larbi, E. Kingsley, *Pentecostalism: The Eddies of Ghanaian Christianity*, Accra: Center for Pentecostal and Charismatic Studies, SAPC Series 1, 2001.

Lehmann, David, *Struggle for the Spirit: Religious Transformation and Popular Culture in Brazil and Latin America*, 1996.

Lehmann, David, 'Religion and Globalization', in Linda Woodhead, Paul Fletcher, Hiroko Kawanami and David Smith (ed.), *Religions in the Modern World*, London and New York: Routledge, 2002, pp. 299-315.

MacLean, L.M., 'The Moral Economy of the Urban Middle Class: The Rise of Charismatic Churches in Ghana since the 1980s', *African Traditional Religion*, Seminar Paper, University of California, Davis, 1997.

Marsden, George M. (ed.), *The Fundamentals: A Testimony to Truth*, Vol. 1, New York and London: Garland Publishing Inc, 1988, pp. 123-126.

Marshall, Ruth, '"Power in the name of Jesus': Social Transformation and Pentecostalism in Western Nigeria Revisited', in Terence Ranger and Olufemi Vaughan (eds.), *Legitimacy and the State in Twentieth-century Africa: Essays in Honour of A.H.M. Kirk-Greene*, London: Macmillan, 1983, pp. 213-246.

Marshall-Fratani, Ruth, 'Mediating the Global and Local in Nigeria Pentecostalism', *Journal of Religion in Africa*, 28, 1998, pp. 278-315.

Martin, David, *Pentecostalism: The World their Parish*, Oxford and Massachusetts: Blackwell Publishers, 2002a.

Martin, David, 'Africa: A Mission Accomplished?', *Christianity Today*, November/ December 2002b.

Meyer, Birgit, 'Delivered from the Power of Darkness: Confessions of Satanic Riches in Christian Ghana', *Africa*, 65, 2, 1995, pp. 237.

Mittelman, James H., 'The Dynamics of Globalization', in J. H. Mittelman (ed.), *Globalization: Critical Reflections. International Political Economy*

Year Book, volume 9. Boulder and London: Lynne Rienner Publishers, 1996, pp. 1-19.

Nieswand, Boris, 'Charismatic Christianity in the Context of Migration: Social Status, the experience of Migration and the construction of selves among Ghanaian Migrants in Berlin', in Afe Adogame and Cordula Weißköppel (eds.), *Religion in the Context of African Migration*, Bayreuth: Bayreuth African Studies Series, 2005, pp. 243-265.

Ojo, Matthews A., 'The Contextual Significance of the Charismatic Movements in Independent Nigeria', *Africa* 58, 2, 1988a, pp. 175-192.

Ojo, Matthews A., 'Deeper Christian Life Ministry: A Case Study of the Charismatic Movements in Western Nigeria', *Journal of Religion in Africa*, 18, 2, 1988b, 141-162.

Ojo, Matthews A., 'The Church in the African State: The Charismatic/Pentecostal Experience in Nigeria', *Journal of African Thought*, 1, 2, December, 1988c.

Olupona Jacob K, 'West Africa', in Stanley M. Burgess (ed.), *The New International Dictionary of Pentecostal and Charismatic Movements* (revised and expanded edition). Grand Rapids, Michigan: Zondervan, 2002, pp. 309, 15.

Olupona, Jacob K. 'Prophetic Movements: Western Africa', in John Middleton (ed.), *The Encyclopedia of Africa South of the Sahara*, 1997.

Peil, M. and K. Asare Opoku, 'The Development and Practice of Religion in an Accra Suburb', *Journal of Religion in Africa*, 24, 3, 1994, pp. 201.

Poewe, Karla (ed.), *Charismatic Christianity as a Global Culture*, Columbia, SC: University of South Carolina Press, 1994.

Quebedeux, Richard A., *The New Charismatics II.* San Francisco: Harper and Row, 1983.

Robertson, Roland, *Globalization: Social Theory and Global Culture*, London: Sage, 1992.

Sandeen, Ernest R., *The Roots of Fundamentalism: British and American Millenarianism, 1800-1930*, Chicago and London: The University of Chicago Press, 1970.

Ter Haar, Gerrie, 'Religious Fundamentalism and Social Change: A Comparative Inquiry', in Gerrie ter Haar and James J. Busuttil (eds.), *The Freedom to Do God's Will*, London and New York: Routledge, Taylor and Francis Group, 2003, pp. 1-24.

Ter Haar, Gerrie, *Halfway to Paradise: African Christians in Europe*, Cardiff: Cardiff Academic Press, 1998a.

Ter Haar, Gerrie (ed.) *Strangers and Sojourners: Religious Communities in the Diaspora*. Leuven: Peeters, 1998b.

Thompson, Jack, 'African Independent Churches in Britain: An Introductory Survey', in R. Towler (ed.), *New Religions and the New Europe*, Aarhus: Aarhus University Press, 1995, pp. 224-31.

Van Dijk, Rijk, 'From Camp to encompassment: Discourses of Transsubjectivity in the Ghanaian Pentecostal Diaspora', *Journal of Religion in Africa*, 27, 2, 1997, pp. 135-139.

Van Dijk, Rijk, 'Christian Fundamentalism in Sub-Saharan Africa: The Case of Pentecostalism', Occasional Paper, Center of African Studies, University of Copenhagen, 2000.

Van Dijk, Rijk, 'Time and Transcultural Technologies of the Self in the Ghanaian Pentecostal Diaspora', in André Corten and Ruth Marshall-Fratani, *Between Babel and Pentecost, Transnational Pentecostalism in Africa and Latin America*. London: Hurst and Co., 2001, pp. 216-234.

Van Dijk, Rijk, 'The Soul is the Stranger: Ghanaian Pentecostalism and the Diasporic Contestation of "Flow" and "Individuality"', *Culture and Religion* 3, 1, 2002, pp. 49-65.

Zaleha, Sharifah, 'Strategies for Public Participation: Women and Islamic Fundamentalism in Malaysia', in Gerrie ter Haar and James J. Busuttil (eds.), *The Freedom to do God's Will*, London and New York: Routledge, Taylor and Francis Group, 2003, pp. 49-74.

Notes

1. For more information on religion and globalization, see Robertson (1992), Poewe (1994), Beyer (1994) and Berger (1999).

2. For more discussion on 'Religious Fundamentalism', see An-Na'im (2003: 25-48), Zaleha (2003: 49-74), and Bruce (2001).

3. See Psalm 95.

4. See Matthew, 24-25.

5. Quoted in Cesar (2000: 33).

GLOBALIZATION AND AFRICAN IMMIGRANT CHURCHES IN AMERICA

Jacob Olupona

OVERVIEW

African immigrant churches in America play a unique role concerning the question to what extent globalization is a preeminently secularizing phenomenon. In this chapter, I wish to refer to my present research on African immigrant communities to refine and in many respects counter the assumption that globalization is an inevitable and unstoppable force towards standardizing values of work, cultural identity, class strata, voluntary associations, family and religion.[1] I wish, in other words, to perform a kind of exorcism that will cast out the notion that the world is becoming one place with its diversity of identities and socio-cultural legacies on an eventual decline (Robertson and Garret, 1991: ix). I proclaim that in the case of America's African immigrant churches, globalization has been as much a force for the promotion and expansion of religion than it has been a force for its secularization. We can see living examples of these counter cyclical tendencies within the local/global dynamics of America's African immigrant churches as conduits of what is increasingly being referred to as transglobalism within the African Diaspora. By transglobalism, I refer here to a new conceptual framework that rejects the former paradigms of assimilation and 'cultural imperialism' (Wilson and Dissanayake, 1996). In essence, this new way of looking at globalization recognizes that religious traditions and faiths are remarkably adaptive and resilient (Rapport and Dawson, 1998: 42-33). In the case of the African Diaspora, the very technologies of modernity itself are serving to maintain strong cultural linkages between African communities within the United States, Europe, and Africa itself. In this context, it is the connection between America and Africa that is of the greatest interest in conceptualizing the relationship between religion and globalization.[2]

In utilizing a transglobal framework to examining the special relationship between African immigrant communities and globalization, this chapter will be divided into two parts. The first part will address the broad themes of globalization, African identity, gender and changing roles of African Christianity and American civil society within the African Diaspora. This background addresses only some of the major issues of African Immigrant churches but will enable us to better conceptualize their unique dynamics. For the second part of this discussion, I will develop a brief taxonomy that characterizes these churches and I will explore each type in the context of the theoretical issues previously identified. These African churches are divided in three broad categories I will call African independent, African Pentecostal or charismatic churches and ethnic and national congregations allocated to mainline churches.

PART ONE

Globalization

The concept of globalization is often confused with a simplifying assumption of modernity. In many cases both are one and the same but in some cases they are quite distinct. This confusion between globalization as a unifying and simplifying force of world capitalism and globalization as a force for transglobalism reflects a fundamental misunderstanding that there is not just one modernity but there are in actuality multiple modernities. To understand the dominant view of globalization as modernity, we can look towards Anthony Giddens' work, *The Consequences of Modernity* (Giddens, . 1990: 1). Giddens defines modernity as the trend of modes of social life or organization which emerged in Europe from the 17th century onwards and which subsequently became more or less worldwide in their influence. Modernity is associated with the secularization of Protestant Christianity, humanism, and the prominence of scientific thought in Western culture. This notion of modernity challenges tradition and faith as rival sources of truth and authority within society. American television for example, has led us to the belief that what is ancient, indigenous and non-Western is superstitious, unchanging and even childlike (McPhail, 1987).

In rising in opposition to this view, scholars such as Robin Horton have challenged the notion that there is a fundamental difference between modernity and indigenous belief (Horton, 1993). He maintains that there is a basic continuity of structure and intentions between traditional religions and modern scientific thought. In essence, the solution of the traditionalists to the challenge of modernity has not been a complete rejection of scientific humanism. Rather, Horton argues the 'traditionalists' have demonstrated their own cognitive efficiency through the creation of adaptive mechanisms and institutions. Because these adapted or 'hybrid' mechanisms and institutions serve communal needs and functions, Horton questions whether they can be deemed inferior to scientific theorizing. Flexibility, awareness, and coexistence of alternatives are part of the African response to modern Western materialism. They are values that constitute the African mind, body and spirit as expressed through the African church. This process of globalization is not a limiting but in fact it is an expanding influence that utilizes technologies, resources and networks of communication to reinforce, adapt and re-energize indigenous traditions and values. This is nowhere more prominent in the formulation of distinct African identities.

Identity

Faced with the secularizing trends of modernity and Americanization, African immigrants are maintaining their cultural identities through communal links with African Americans, religion and the development of new institutions and support structures. Being an American does not entail the abandonment of indigenous identity. As stipulated by Dr. Sulayman Nyang, the image has changed from the 'Great American Melting Pot' to the Salad Bowl. This new paradigm of recognizing the role of diversity and culture helps to provide us a better understanding of the Diasporic communities that are developing pluralistic linkages. However, the development of new communal links through the vehicle of the African immigrant church does not mean that there are no changing roles. Traditions are maintained but they are also adapted to reflect the practical concerns of the new environment. For example, globalization has fundamentally altered the traditional roles of women as well as has encouraged the nature of the church to change from a source of spiritual worship to a source of civil and secular support. Traditions do not disappear, but the relations and the balance between them shifts in the context of globalization. I believe this to be an important part when examining the socio-cultural issues behind the African immigrant church. We should not assume that globalization like Marxism is an inevitable force that will one day replace all traditional values within the world with one common consumerist mass culture. Instead I maintain that globalization does incur a significant impact upon African traditions and cultural values but traditionalism at the same time retains aspects of resiliency and adaptability that enables them to maintain cohesion in non-Western environments.

Traditions are adaptable. Often they provide the frameworks for how we view and process information. Once a new piece of information is provided that does not exist within an existing framework, that information can be used to modify but not significantly alter the existing framework. For example, a form of taboo can be put in place to process the new challenge until the old existing framework can adapt.[3] What is of interest to note in the case of African immigrant communities is not so much what traditions have been abandoned as the question of how traditions have adapted.

Women

One of the most prominent of these adapting traditions is the question of how the global/local dynamic will affect the role of women within the immigrant church. This question is especially important among women in immigrant communities since they commonly 'are expected to preserve culture and traditions, immigrant mothers are expected to be the carriers of culture for their children in the new country' (Espin, 1999: 149). Frequently these traditional roles call upon women to be supportive helpmates, enabling their children and their husbands to function in accordance to prescribed traditions (Warner and Wittner, 1998:172-173). As a consequence of these paradigms we see that a significant proportion of Africans who are involved in African immigrant churches are women. Depending upon the composition of the church in question, these largely female congregations demonstrate a wide variance in their participation from very limited and traditional roles to leadership roles within the church itself. In part, this dichotomy can be attributed to the nature of the African Diaspora itself as American society has come to challenge the traditional roles of women within African immigrant communities. As stated by Filomina Steady in her article, 'Women of Africa and the African Diaspora: Linkages and Influences',

> In some ways the development of African feminism has been aided by a number of factors. One of these is the tendency for African societies and societies in the African Diaspora to develop "limited" rather than "absolute" patriarchal traditions. In doing so, external political and economic factors have been important to some extent. Among these factors are the limited participation of black men in the public sphere of authority and political power in multiracial societies; high unemployment among black men; the prevalence of female-headed households, and the generally subordinate position of black men and women in the racist world economic system (Harris, 1993: 183).

Although we can surmise that the general tendency is for women to maintain strong traditional roles within immigrant communities within the United States, economic, political and societal factors can challenge these roles within Western societies. James Clifford in his work, *Routes: Travel and Translation in the Late Twentieth Century*, also addresses this issue by asking,

Do diaspora experiences reinforce or loosen gender subordination? On the one hand, maintaining connections with homelands, with kinship networks, and with religious and cultural traditions may renew patriarchal structures. On the other, new roles and demands, new political spaces, are opened by diaspora interactions. Increasingly, for example, women migrate north from Mexico and from parts of the Caribbean, independently or quasi-independently of men. While they often do so in desperation, under strong economic or social compulsion, they may find their new diaspora predicaments leading to renegotiated gender relations. With men cut off from traditional roles and supports, with women earning an independent, if often exploitative, income, new areas of relative independence and control can emerge. Life for women in diaspora situations can be doubly painful – struggling with the material and spiritual insecurities of exile, with the demands of family and work, and with the claims of old and new patriarchies. But despite these hardships, they may refuse the option of return when it presents itself, especially when the terms are dictated by men (Clifford, 1997: 259).

In my own research, I have seen these trends played out a number of times. For example, in examining the roles of women among some of the Christian African churches in seven major US cities, we saw a significantly disproportionate amount of participation among women members as opposed to men. In many cases, women within these churches have come to assume leadership roles as a result in part of American influences.[4]

Civil Society

Finally, we must examine how globalization is affecting the nature of the African church and civil society itself.[5] The African church as a source of identity and continuity may soon become better associated as a source of secular aid and support with the imposition of President George W. Bush's 'Faith Based Clearing House.' The promise of direct state support for the secular activities of religious institutions may fundamentally change the boundaries between the state and the civil society. This has substantial implications for both African immigrant and African communities since the continual expansion of America's African immigrant churches into providing services serves not only to strengthen the stature of these institutions within the United States, but has also began to develop a trend towards immigrant churches providing services for congregations within Africa itself.[6]

PART TWO

From this brief sketch of some of the themes of globalization, African identity, gender, civil society and changing roles, I would like to address the specifics of emerging African immigrant communities and their corresponding African immigrant churches within the U.S. In understanding the relationship between religion and globalization, I believe there are three key reasons why contemporary African immigrant communities are of special interest. Firstly, in terms of a local/global dynamics, African American communities in the US retain a strong desire to retain distinct African identities, religions and traditional values after their immigration to the United States. Secondly, since the passage of the Hart Act in 1965, more Africans have migrated to the United States than during the entire period of American slavery. Lastly, recent African immigrants have become significantly wealthy in American society. As a result of retaining greater resources of wealth, expertise and skills, African immigrant churches are increasingly developing ties between Africa and the United States. This has addressed a new factor to the perception of blacks in America.

The resiliency to retain African identities, the increasing numbers of African immigrants who arrive in the US each year as well as the significant degree of resources within the American society have all led to a strong propensity to preserve, maintain and even enhance a distinct African identity within American society. Globalization in this context does not refer to the destruction of African tradition and values. It instead applies to an increasing global connection of travel, communication, and an awareness of Africa. African Americans for example, who had become forcefully separated from their African origins, are beginning to utilize the conduit of the African immigrant religious churches and traditional religious centers as a means of re-establishing and re-orienting themselves. We can see these trends occurring by examining the Christian tradition of the new African religious institutions as evolving from one of three traditions that I refer to as the African independent churches, African Pentecostal or Charismatic churches and accommodating mainstream American churches.

African Independent Churches

African independent churches such as the Celestial Church of Christ, Christ Apostolic Church and Cherubim and Seraphim are unique in that they reflect the nexus between African indigenous beliefs and Christianity. In order to understand this tradition, we must recognize that conversion to Christianity in Africa, like in Latin America, is an evolving process that retains significant aspects of indigenous faith and cultural practices. Many of the first mission converts were social outcasts who later became the new local elites with the rise of colonialism. As a reaction to the continued dominance of the mission churches by African Christian elites, African spiritual leaders emerged who claimed they have been called by God to begin authentic African churches. As a result of this reversal of status, these African leaders were composed of both those who relied upon Christian and indigenous traditions as the source of truth and authority. It is not surprising, therefore that as indigenous Christianity evolved in Africa, the African independent church would retain aspects of indigenous tradition and belief. Images of Jesus as a leader, the Holy Spirit and the idea of faith healing for example, allowed many Africans to integrate aspects of their own spirituality into the new faith. African ideas of community, ancestor veneration and revelation continue to persist in the independent church traditions.

Traditionally oriented African churches provide linkages to African identities. We often see individuals engaging in a form of religious pluralism by participating in more than one tradition and one institution at the same time or combining aspects of multiple traditions. These efforts constitute an attempt towards accepting aspects of American and African traditions by adapting them both part and parcel. A naming ceremony for example, can be utilized to incorporate significant aspects of indigenous and traditional beliefs within the framework of an American church. Hymns spoken in African languages can be selected to incorporate indigenous sayings or values. Finally, special or secondary services can be created to supplement or modify existing English sermons.

These crossovers of tradition are not limited to Africans abandoning their indigenous beliefs and traditions in exchange for an African American identity. In other words, the adoption of belief, rituals and practices can go 'both ways' in the sense that not only are African immigrants becoming 'Americanized' but African-Americans are at the same time becoming Africanized. At the Ghanaian Presbyterian-Reformed Church of Brooklyn for example, Ghanaians are moving away from translated hymns created by German missionaries to ones with African Christian compositions and biblical renditions of praise in the context of more contemporary music and cultural expressions of identity. The inclusion of African immigrants and their demands into existing structures of American churches may be creating tensions, especially within African American communities, in that these new members seek to redirect existing institutions to adopt a more pluralistic outlook and thus incorporate African immigrant values.

The African church and its emphasis on African tradition and culture offer a means to redefine identities. It is an opportunity to learn to sing the African Christian derived songs in America. In the Aladura Celestial Church of Christ in Miami, I counted a number of African American couples wearing the white flowing garments of the church. A number of women were also spouses of Nigerian members. Likewise, in examining African churches in Los Angeles, I saw many of the same flavors of African tradition such as the usage of the Shebshba dance among member of LA's Ethiopian Christian Fellowship.

With the current influx of African immigrants, we are beginning to see another peak emerging to develop African identities among African immigrants. These immigrants who predominantly reside in the urban areas of America's largest cities are becoming integrated in schools, businesses and are becoming a growing presence within African-American communities. As more African Americans are becoming exposed to African immigrants, this influence is responsible for a resurgence of interest in Africa. The African independent church with its strong focus on African culture and traditional practices is especially attractive to large numbers of African Americans to participate in African immigrant churches. Though more African Americans are devotees of Orisa, Yoruba indigenous religions than Aladura Christianity, this movement is part of a general trend of African Americans to rediscover their own identities.

The process however is not a coordinated one as one of the dilemmas of African independent churches is that their uniqueness has also left these churches divided within African Diasporic communities. The individuality of these churches has helped to fine tune aspects of specific African cultures and traditions but has also served to some extent to keep these churches separated from other African churches. As a result, we see that they must overcome the challenge of logistical and coordination difficulties to expand their efforts beyond the initial congregation. These efforts to promote African traditions and values are occasionally plagued with many of the same ethnic and political divisions that have separated Africa itself within the current African crisis.

African Pentecostal or Charismatic Churches

We should acknowledge that African Pentecostal or Charismatic churches are a growing and fundamentally important trend among the African immigrant communities. Unlike the previous discussion of African independent churches as the nexus between African tradition and Christianity within the African diaspora, the Charismatic church is reflective of the trend towards modernity within Christianity. Modernity as a product of western culture emphasizes a sense of western rationalism and scientific/logical reasoning. In the case of these churches, aspects of African spirituality such as divination, witchcraft and polytheistic beliefs are strongly discouraged and are even portrayed as a product of the devil's influence. However, within these same churches, we see that in many instances views of spirit possession are officially tolerated and promoted in the tradition of 'speaking in tongues'. This leads me to an interesting observation. Scholars of African charismatic movements are very quick at declaring that the new Pentecostal charismatic churches represent a radical departure from the independent African churches precisely because of their radical departure form African indigenous religious worldview.

The truth is that there is no rapture with African religious worldview. Rather, what exists is a pre-packaging of the old structure in a new modern structure. Scholars should be more concerned with what the African Pentecostal churches practice than what they claim they are doing. Pentecostal or 'born again' styles of worship are prominent in African immigrant communities in that it is perceived to allow better incorporation of African beliefs such as spirit possession, fervent prayer, pragmatism and proximate salvation. For example, in an Los Angeles interview with pastor Joseph Dosumu of The Gospel Faith Mission International Church, the pastor indicated that he had converted from serving as an Anglican priest in Nigeria to a Pentecostal pastor in the US since Pentecostalism for him was closest to the indigenous systems of worshipping while evoking the spirits of the Most High'. At Chicago's African United Methodist Church (AUMC), I saw that as the church body slowly grew, those who came in while the church is clapping, dancing, and testifying would naturally follow the flow or rhythm of the activity. Some women would dance out of their church pews by rejoicing and clapping their hands higher in the air to evoke the Holy One, while other members would kneel down by their seats and praise God, and still others would stay in their seats jumping and calling out God's name. These situations are not what one would find in 'higher Anglicanism'.

However, we must be careful to qualify these assertions by 'born again' adherents with an understanding that they may in fact place little actual emphasis on the values of African indigenous traditions. Often these same 'advocates' of spirituality can at the same time be the greatest critiques of traditional African beliefs as evil, superstitious and contrary to the teachings of Christianity. To some extent, the claim that 'born again' styles of worship are closer to African styles is an attempt to pull African immigrants away from their indigenous beliefs towards beliefs in conjunction with the values of modernity.

Ethnic and National Congregations allocated to Mainline Churches

In recognition of the new demographic trends of African migration, many mainstream American churches such as the Episcopal, Baptist or Catholic churches are beginning to offer services that better reflect the interests and concerns of these immigrant communities. These churches in the US have been steadily developing their 'Ethnic Ministries', ethnically and nationally specific ministries (for example, Irish, Polish, Vietnamese, Haitian, etc.) that minister for a wide range of immigrant communities. The most prominent example of these accommodations focuses on the use of African or indigenous language services. These services can take on various forms from the use of indigenous language hymns to services conducted entirely in non-English languages. Often these services are Saturday or Sunday evening services conducted after English services.

A typical example of this trend is reflected in the efforts of Igbo Father Charles Onubogu, for example, who heads the Igbo Catholic

Foundation at San Francisco's Sacred Heart parish. While Father Charles is responsible for leading mass at the Mission Dolores in San Francisco, working with a white and Latino congregation, he also works with the Igbo Catholic Foundation, an Ethnic Ministry that aims to:

> reconnect Igbo immigrants in the US to their Igbo culture in Nigeria. By teaching the language and other cultural practices (like dances, music, etc.), the foundation aims to instill in its participants the positive aspects of Igbo and Nigerian life. Celebrating the Igbo language is a great entry into developing an understanding and appreciation for the culture (Onubogu 7/28/00).

The San Francisco Bay Area Igbo community thus comes together during the last Sunday of every month for mass and community support. A member of the congregation, quite impressed with Father Charles' sermon remarked, 'When we attended the Igbo mass, Father Charles and his associate led the entire mass in Igbo, including songs, except for the sermon'. Unfortunately, the coordination of these services is difficult in that unlike Latin American services where the whole immigrant congregation speaks Spanish, African immigrant communities are substantially divided along linguistic, cultural and at times political lines. Only in cases where there are significant concentrations of African languages such as Igbo, Yoruba or certain Ghanaian and Ethiopian communities are there sufficient concentrations of Africans to merit special language services.

Beyond the creation of ethnic and natural congregations is another significant trend in African immigrant religion. This is the increasing number of African priests ministering to American congregations. While this is strongest among the Catholic churches, there are evidences of African priests in Episcopal, Baptist and Methodist mainstream churches. I was particularly struck by an Igbo Reverend Father in Miami who ministers to a Catholic Spanish church just a stone throw from where I lived in the South during my field research. Several of the African ministers in all these three types of African churches analyzed above present the notion of a reverse mission to America as a way of justifying their call to minister to American congregations. They argue, Africa has become one of the centers of Christianity and is ripe enough to send missionaries abroad. These African ministers hope that these religious communities will discover their transnational identity in the complex relationships between communities within metropolitan centers, local communities and the global environment.

CONCLUSION

The presence of vibrant African immigrant communities within the United States is serving as a new conduit for transglobal linkages of African Diaspora culture, expression and identity. The causal arrow of this influence is not unidirectional. Just as African Americans are rediscovering their African traditions in the United States, Africa itself is becoming better acquainted with its lost communities in America. Within my research I have seen a number of examples where both international and African churches have branched out to communities in the United States as well as the reverse. We are beginning to see a number of African American churches establishing themselves in Africa itself. The result of the process is a reawakening of culture, communication, travel and expertise that rejects the notion of assimilation in favor of transglobality and diversity within America's changing and dynamic Christian communities.

Bibliography

Abdul-Raheem, T. (ed), *Pan Africanism: Politics, Economy and Social Change in the Twenty-first Century.* London: Pluto, 1996.

Cesaire, Aime, *Return to my Native Land. Presence Africaine.* Paris, 1971.

Clifford, James, *Routes: Travel and Translation in the Late Twentieth Century.* Cambridge, Mass: Harvard University Press, 1997.

Espin, Oliva, *Women Crossing Boundaries: A Psychology of Immigration and Transformations of Sexuality.* New York: Routledge, 1999.

Giddens, Anthony, *The Consequences of Modernity.* Stanford: Stanford University Press, 1990.

Gilroy, Paul, *Small Acts: Thoughts on the Politics of Black Cultures.* London: Serpents Tail, 1993.

Harris, Joseph, *Global Dimensions of the African Diaspora.* (2nd ed.) Washington: Howard University Press, 1993.

Horton, Robin, *Patterns of Thought in Africa and the West: Essays on Magic, Religion and Science.* Cambridge: Cambridge University Press, 1993.

Keane, John (ed.), *Civil Society and the State*. London: Verso, 1988.

McPhail, Thomas, *Electronic Colonialism*. London: Sage Publications, 1987.

Olupona, Jacob K., 'African Immigrant Religious Communities: Identity Formulation in America's Pluralistic Society'. Ford Foundation Report (forthcoming).

Rapport, Nigel and Dawson, Andrew (ed.), *Migrants of Identity: Perceptions of 'Home' in a World of Movement*. Oxford: Berg Publishers, 1998.

Redkey, E.S., *Black Exodus: Black Nationalism and Back to Africa Movements*. New Haven: Yale University, 1969.

Robertson, Roland and William, Garret (eds.), *Religion and Global Order*. New York: Paragon House Publishers, 1991.

Segal, R., *The Black Diaspora*. London: Faber and Faber, 1995.

Warner, Stephen and Judith, Wittner (eds.), *Gathering in Diaspora: Religious Communities and the New Immigration*. Philadelphia: Temple University Press, 1998.

Wilson, Rob and Wimal, Dissanayake (eds.), *Global/Local: Cultural Production and the Transnational Imagery*. London: Duke University Press, 1996.

Notes

*   I acknowledge with thanks the Ford Foundation Grants that have enabled me to collect the data for this paper. The assistance of my research assistant Mark Davis is also gratefully acknowledged.

1.   I refer here to a Ford Foundation Project I completed some years ago, entitled African Immigrant Religious Communities: Identity Formulation in America's Pluralistic Society. Within this project I examined how African immigrant and African religious institutions are developing networks of mutual assistance and support within America's second wave of mass migration.

2.   By African-American connection I refer both to the presence of African-American churches that have evolved from a four hundred year tradition among America's first wave of African slave immigrants and to African immigrant churches that evolved during the past 15 years as part of Africa's second mass migration to the US.

3.   These notions of the malleability and adaptability of tradition can be found throughout the works of Robin Horton.

4.   An interesting consequence of the study of gender relations in African Immigrant communities is the light these results may throw on race relations in America. A number of African men who were breadwinners at home suddenly found themselves in America unemployed while

their wives have assumed the role of breadwinners. The situation has partly led to a higher divorce rate in the USA than in Africa.

5. By civil society I refer to the organized and collective efforts within the state that are not directly associated with state power.

6. See Ford Foundation Report, African Immigrant Religious Communities: Identity Formulation in America's Pluralistic Society (forthcoming).

WHO IS AFRAID OF THE HOLY GHOST? PRESBYTERIANS AND EARLY CHARISMATIC MOVEMENT IN NIGERIA, 1966-1975

Ogbu U. Kalu

INTRODUCTION: THE SCREAM IN THE NIGHT

A new trend in African Christianity occurred in the early 1970s. In one country after another, young puritan preachers appeared in urban contexts all over the continent, as if they were maggots from the woodworks, preaching fire and brimstone sermons. They were members of mainline churches. Soon, some of the charismatic groups consolidated into Pentecostal churches. The implosion of the Pentecostal and the Charismatic movements has caused much stir among mainline churches in Africa. Quite often, ministerial retreats devote attention to the matter, either to map counter-insurgence or to formulate policy on damage control measures. The Presbyterian Church in Nigeria witnessed such a challenge following a spiritual revival that had started during the Civil War, 1966-1970 (Burgess, 2004; see Kalu, 2003: chapter 11). The title of this reflection is taken from a scream that broke through the protracted debate in a holy conclave of clergymen who met to discuss the state of the church amidst the outbreak of this phenomenon. The year was 1966. The holy conclave had lasted into the night. Passionate speeches flowed about the potential threat constituted by young men and women who spoke in tongues, rolled on the ground allegedly slain by the spirit, and challenged the rule of the elders. Suddenly, a pastor jumped to his feet, sought the permission of the Moderator and queried his compeers: 'Who is afraid of the Holy Ghost?' He wondered why they should continue to bury their heads in the sand when the gusty wind of God was blowing away the sand and many congregations were losing members to the Pentecostal movement and many more congregations battled with charismatic young people seeking an enlarged space, challenging the polity, testing liturgical boundaries, and critiquing the ethical behavior of churchly people. He vigorously urged his colleagues to accept the new context for being a church and the intensified competition in the religious market, and accept the reality of the charismatic/Pentecostal reshaping of the religious landscape.

The candid admission was stunning because the church had struggled to hold her grounds since 1970 and, now it appeared that the rampart was shaken, deserving a scholarly inquiry. A summary of the profile of The Presbyterian Church in Nigeria provides a background for appreciating the enormity of the awkward challenge (Kalu, 1996). It came to Nigeria in 1846 when the Jamaican branch of this Scottish church was so moved by Fowell Buxton's book, *African Slave Trade and Its Remedy* (1841) that they sought to contribute to the redemption of the motherland through missionary enterprise. In a century and a half of arduous witness, the church has left indelible and noble marks in education and medical work but her witness concentrated in the southeastern zone around the Cross-River basin. After political independence in the 1960s this church dared to open satellite branches in other regions of the country. The slow pace could be explained by a combination of cautious missionary policy and a delimitation agreement between Methodist, Anglicans and Qua Iboe Mission that divided the eastern Nigerian theater into mission zones and quarantined the Presbyterians in a certain zone of the country. It was hoped that the constituent churches would unite in a single mega church to eschew the scandal of church disunity and competition. The cultural nationalism that followed political independence fuelled the project. It crashed in 1965 and the failure of the church union movement between these churches re-opened the rivalry of yester-years (Kalu, 1978). The religious field was suffused with competition between Protestants, Roman Catholics and the African Independent Churches before the Pentecostal/Charismatic dimension became crucial. Presbyterian numerical strength in 1996 was about a quarter million.

When the Pentecostal wind was gathering, from 1970, soon after the Civil War, the Presbyterians and Anglicans appeared to support it while the hostility of The Roman Catholics under the leadership of Archbishop Francis Arinze was loud and clear. He was already countering the growth of the Aladura that became alarming during the disruptive civil war period. Arinze had commissioned Father Ikeobi to start a prayer and healing service on Tuesdays in Onitsha to encapsulate the distressed urban dwellers who needed charismatic support in the effort to cope with the aftermath of a traumatic civil war. The Protestant churches had a history in the pre-war years for supporting evangelical fellowships such as the Scripture Union, which functioned in secondary schools, Boys' Scouts in primary schools, and Students' Christian Movement that flourished in both Secondary Schools and Universities. After the war, the Scripture Union regrouped and attracted large numbers of young people. Soon it became obvious that the Scripture Union, like the proverbial hen that grew teeth in the night, had become charismatic during the trauma and spiritual revival that sprouted during the Civil War period, 1967-70. At St. Andrew's Presbyterian Church, Enugu, the elders nipped the rebellion in the bud by driving away the fellowship from the church compound. All pleadings to the contrary, the elders–in–session stood firmly on the decision that the Scripture Union should no longer use the church facilities for their meeting on Sunday afternoons. In the heartland of Presbyterian presence, matters got out of hand. For instance, in Ohafia Presbytery, located in Cross River or eastern Igboland, a conflict forced the elders to physically barricade the church building against the truculent young charismatics. This compelled the young people to establish their own church, The Church of the Evangel. This body of energetic evangelical youth grew faster than the Presbyterian Church in an area that they had monopolized since 1910. Since these heady events, the battle for orthodoxy had taken many turns before the stunning and disruptive scream in the night.

STUDYING THE CHARISMATIC CHALLENGE

Two facts make this reflection important: the 'Wind of God' has continued to blow with increasing force all over the continent of Africa and has catalyzed the charismatization of the mainline churches. The first problem is an adequate methodology for understanding what happened and how the opposition collapsed. The nature of the problem is important because the counter response of the Presbyterians remained ambiguous and inconclusive precisely because the challenge arose from the interior of the faith claim. It was built on what the church had been teaching through the years. The charismatic movement that gave rise to Pentecostalism was rooted in the affirmations of the Reformed tradition and its emphasis on reliance on the Bible only (*sola scriptura*). It was like a replay of the old dispute between Luther and the Muntzerites or left-wing of the Reformation saga. The new Christianity could be profiled as the third dimension of African response to the gospel, a 'setting to work' of missionary message, and a reconstruction of Christian experience in Africa (Marshall-Fratani, 1991: 21-37). Unlike the pneumatic challenge of the Aladura movement or African Indigenous Churches that absorbed much from the indigenous religious tradition, this was a pneumatic challenge emerging from within the teachings of the mainline churches and propagated by the products of their schools and churches. For, indeed, Pentecostalism in contemporary Nigeria started as charismatic movements, with membership drawn from within various churches, as young people sought to create a new religious space for themselves. Despite all control mechanisms, it held the cutting edge of contemporary African church history. The phenomenon did not only challenge the Presbyterian Church in Nigeria, it affected all mainline churches. In the early 1970s, the Baptist Church set up a committee to examine the phenomenon. In the preamble, the report observed that:

> The reason why the executive committee embarked on this exercise is due to various occasional allegations and accusations by some Baptist youths and adults that worship services in Baptist Churches are very lukewarm. They have alleged that our prayer is weak and not "hot enough", that we do not heal the sick nor raise the dead. They have also alleged that in the Baptist Churches miracles are not

happening and people are not baptized by the Holy Spirit neither are they able to speak in tongues. They have also accused the elders of hypocrisy. For above reasons some people have left for churches that practice and encourage such things which they think we have neglected. But surprisingly enough of these people still stay in the Baptist Churches and insist on forcing those Pentecostal beliefs on members (cited in Olorunfemi, 2004: 21).

It should be clear that charismatic movements operate within the churches while Pentecostals refer to the institutions that consolidated as the charisma was routinized outside the mainline churches. One method could study the various clashes that have occurred in the churches between 1966-1975, and through the analysis of the theological and personality clashes paint a canvass of the impact of the Wind. But a conflict theory analysis suggests that church conflicts tend to operate on three layers: at the surface level is what happened or the immediate cause; underneath this is what is going on or the remote causes that may have sedimented below the surface. These tend to rise to the manifest level sooner than later; at all times these influence the responses of individuals to a particular issue. Often, there is a third layer beneath; that is the ideological core of the conflict. It may not be easily articulated because it is buried in the psyches of the combatants.

Phillip Turner has argued that traditionalism serves such an ideological function as people who imbibed the traditions fostered by the early missionaries essay to culture, nurture and sustain these against the battering rams of change. Tradition begins to determine what people expect from the worshipping communities. All Christian forms are basically cultural and missionaries installed a certain identifiable tradition that they maintained through a tight control over the affairs of the church during a century. Each mission sought to transplant its identity crafted in the foreign metropoles. Such efforts spawned rivalry that suffused the missionary scene and bred denominationalism as each group sought to install its version of the gospel as the standard revised version (Turner, 1971: 45-68; Kendall, 1978). Felix K. Ekechi, therefore, argued that rivalry in the missionary enterprise explains the patterns of vertical growth and the investment in charitable institutions (Ekechi, 1971). Rivalry encrusted an institutional perception of the church that detracted from concern for people. It bred disunity. The Kenyan novelist, Ngugi wa Thiongo, paints an image of Christianity that became a 'River Between'; instead of serving as the water of life, it became a force that balkanized and divided communities. For the most part, ecumenism was more mouthed than practiced among missionaries. As the proverb says, when adult rats steal, little rats watch and imitate; so rivalry became worse among their protégés. Traditionalism, the sustenance of the heritage from the missionary ancestors, encrusted patriarchy, and compelled the church elders to treat the youth as rebellious upstarts instead of listening to them. The elders expelled the youth from the churches in one place after another. This exposed the fundamentally patriarchal ethos of African churches because the bulk of the charismatic demography consisted of young people and women. It also created a dilemma because the strategy could not continue for long. The hemorrhage forced policy to gyrate because of the need to encapsulate or protect the exodus of youth and women.

At decolonization, rivalry assumed a different face. The new problem was how to retain influence in the post-Independent political space especially as missions were forced to indigenize their manpower. A more disturbing scenario was the attack by nationalists which posture missions as pathfinders to imperialists and collaborators to the crimes committed against Africans. The albatross of sub-serving foreign interests, of being vestiges of neo-colonialism, hung over the spires. In response, missions encouraged their lay people to get involved in nationalist politics and to use their influence to promote the cause of denominations. As Elochukwu Amucheazi has shown, the churches became political pressure groups; educational and charitable institutions, and pulpits were pressed into the service of mobilizing votaries into the political machinery as new political parties fought for dominance in those heady days (Amucheazi, 1986). This particular version of encapsulation strategy has led to the laicization of power in the churches. In later years, it would be enhanced by the creation of knighthood orders that served as a reward agency of social control as well as a mobilization strategy. Social control theory suggests that this strategy enhances the status of those who have 'stakes in conformity' and in preserving inherited institutions through a social network of the elite bonded with a religious cord, and oiled with a sense of heavenly mission. To such people, charismatism appeared as deviance. Among other unpleasant habits, charismatism forces attention to spirituality and away from institution maintenance. This attack on inherited vision naturally offended.

Moreover, as children of their times, missionaries transplanted traditions woven around the intellectual and cultural milieux of the metropoles and which included the Enlightenment worldview and a certain jaundiced perception of the religion and culture of the indigenous communities. The gospel-culture interface became a contested space right from the inception of the missionary encounter with African communities. Missionaries tended to institutionalize, build structures and create a certain moral economy that absorbed enormous resources to maintain. Their cultural baggage often conflicted with their spiritual vision. The task became a struggle to balance vision, civilization project and adequate response to the personhood of the host communities. This, it will be argued, informed the muted doctrine of the Holy Spirit in the missionary arsenal. Weaving culture, gospel and the role of the Third Person of the Trinity constituted a key aspect of the ideological core of the Presbyterian/Pentecostal conflict. From this core, other cleavages and conflicts would emerge over aspects of doctrine, challenges to liturgy, polity and ethics. Such conflicts are often strengthened by patterns of ministerial formation, generational gap and sometimes by misrepresentation. The focus on the third layer in conflicts does not neglect the imperatives of the religious landscape and the socio-political and economic backdrops of the conflict. Periodization is, therefore, important as the contours of the conflict changed through time. From this perspective, an adequate method should examine the third layer of the conflict, where the bone touches the marrow. It is the challenge to doctrine, liturgy, polity and ethics of the mission churches that exacerbated the conflict. The executive committee of the Nigerian Baptist Convention catalogued it accurately.

Cephas Omenyo has recently validated this approach in his work, *Pentecost Outside Pentecostalism*, that examined the charismatisation of the mainline churches in Ghana (Omenyo, 2002). Cephas Omenyo who teaches in the Department for the Study of Religion at the University of Ghana, Legon, has written on Pentecostalism in Ghana through the years with much insight.[1] His elegant title captures the emergent dimension in African Christianity as the old battles between traditionalized mainline churches and youthful charismatic movements begin to ebb. He demonstrates how the mainline churches chose the better part of valor to join the youth. Nowadays, he argues, the liturgical environments in Pentecostal and mainline churches look alike: songs, dance, hot sermons, night vigils, fasting and tithing. The key question is whether the enlargement of space to both young people and charismatic spirituality is an encapsulating strategy or a measure of the rapid religious changes occurring in the continent. The ramparts may have collapsed around liturgy and ethics as Omenyo shows, but in many West African mainline churches, the battle to protect polity and doctrines continues. In the rainy season of 2004, the Clerk of the General Assembly of the Presbyterian Church in Nigeria toured the presbyteries to remind them that many of the charismatic practices offend the Reformed Tradition.

Omenyo's method is to start with the socio-political and religious setting. This indicates that the attraction to charismatism and changes in the religious sphere are both embedded in the indigenous worldview and arose in response to the new socio-economic realities characterized by unemployment and political crises that are side effects of the consolidation of democratic processes. He historicizes the presence of the eight missionary groups, namely, Roman Catholic, Moravian United Brethren, Netherlands Reformed Mission, Anglican, Basel Mission, Wesleyan Methodism, Bremen Mission and Presbyterians. Each sought to replicate the structures, doctrines and character of the home bases. Thus, the emergent charismatic forces would contest these traditions that may have been little affected by liberal changes in Europe. The conservatism of African mainline churches has become proverbial. But Omenyo shows that revival movements invaded the religious landscape early in the 20th century, the same time frame as in Nigeria, planting the seeds of modern Pentecostal and charismatic movements. Interestingly, he profiles the global charismatic renewal before tracing the indigenous wave in Ghana. This may leave the wrong impression that the indigenous ones owed their origins from Europe. Some did; others did not. It is crucial to privilege this aspect of African religious initiative because the literature is stuck in the debate within North American historiography whether Pentecostalism has a black or white origin. However, Omenyo uses a typology to show that Pentecostalism is a movement with different shades; that there is a distinction between charismatics and Pentecostals.

Omenyo provides in-depth analyses of the charismatic movements in the various mainline churches: Roman Catholic, Anglican, Presbyterian, Methodist, the conflict-ridden Evangelical Presbyterian and Baptist. Initially, these bastions fought valiantly to contain, control and channel the charismatic waves. He attempts a comparative analysis that uses polity and spirituality as the controlling indices to show the flow of charismatisation. For instance, the spirituality and non-connexional or autonomous polity of the Baptists explain the ease of the spread. For each context, he examines the capacity for networking among different branches of a movement, leadership, ethos and challenges to inherited polity and doctrines. The degree of the enlargement of space to charismatism may vary due to its acceptance as Biblical, appropriate to the missional goals of the denominations and in helping stem 'the drift of its members to Pentecostal churches'. It became clear that analysis that focuses on the first and second levels might miss the core of the matter, namely what happens at the third layer. He found that some churches deployed charismatic movement and liturgical renewal as a model of local assertion or agency, and as a cultural signifier indicating maturity and independence from foreign control.

He, therefore, delved into analysis of the spirituality, doctrine, ecclesiology and practices of the charismatic movements: praying (especially aloud), fasting, frequency and style of each of these, holiness ethics and such-like. Three points are emphasized here: by privileging prayer, the charismatic movements created a decline of the African Indigenous Churches that are called Aladura (meaning, the Prayer People) in Nigeria. Second, these youthful movements have woven an identifiable spiritual culture; therefore, they are not an extension of the American electronic church. Rather, they are re-negotiating inherited traditions. Third, what is their specific spirituality? As Omenyo observes, the movement critiques the mainline churches and 'emphasizes and exhibits aspects of general Christian religious experiences and expressions, which can be used as bases to distinguish charismatic specificities within the respective churches'. His focus is narrowly on the youth but in fact they need the support of pastors. Often, the clerical cadre is widely split over the support for the movement. Hilary Achunike's study of Catholic renewal movement analyzes a crucial dimension by examining the debate in the publications by pastors (Achunike, 2001). The capacity of ministers to adjust to the new trend depends on age, training and location in the hierarchy. Younger pastors tend to favour the movement except the ambitious, sycophant ones who want to please the leaders.

All the chickens come to roost when he examined the origins and sources of the groups, the level, rationale for formal recognition, the danger of schism, and the significance and prospects of charismatisation of the churches. All the churches constituted committees to study the problem at various points in time. The evangelical programs won the respect of some committees because they tackled the problem of decline and catalyzed growth. Other committees acknowledged the need for self-criticism and the Biblical bases of the youthful challenges. Omenyo needed to show the extent to which the charismatic movements actually changed the growth pattern of any denomination. For instance, the Ghana Evangelism Committee issued an update of its nation-wide survey of Christian forms in 1993. It showed that the Roman Catholics declined by 2% between 1987-1993, Methodists grew by 2%, Evangelical Presbyterians declined by 14%, Presbyterians grew by 17% and Pentecostals grew by 99% while the African Indigenous Churches declined by 20.8%. What has been the effect of the enlarged space for charismatic movements that occurred in the 1990's on this trend? This dimension could not be attempted for Nigeria because the data do not exist. Finally, Omenyo shows that the young people were motivated by both Aladura spirituality and the ministry of Pentecostals but the greatest source of inspiration came from evangelical traditions within the mainline churches such as the New Life program that spread in the late 1950's and early 1960's. Thus, he confirms the comparison with Nigeria that contemporary charismatic movements may be the old evangelicalism writ large.

ANATOMY OF A CONFLICT IN THE PRESBYTERIAN CHURCH, NIGERIA

Quite often, sociologists tend to diminish the force of doctrine in both conversion to Christianity and conflicts within churches. It is assumed that interpersonal relationships and social networks explain the route to conversion to new religious movements; that beyond deprivation theory, instrumentalist explanations still wield much force. For instance, conversion has been explained as the indigenous African's quest for education, status, wealth, and modernity. Rodney Stark's *The Rise of Christianity* advocates a market economy discourse as converts exercise free choice from a variety of religious products packaged to attract. The conflicts could, therefore, be explained by competition in supply and demand, or other non-doctrinal factors (Stark, 1997). But, as Omenyo demonstrated, while instrumentalist background factors are certainly very important, the heartbeat of the conflict was the negotiation over doctrines and polities of the particular denomination. For instance, in the cases of the Evangelical Church of West Africa (formerly Sudan Interior Mission) and the Nigerian Baptists, the doctrine was firmly cessationist, that refers to the denial that the charismata listed in 1Corinthians 12 and 14, Romans 12, and Ephesians 4 still operate within the contemporary household of faith. These churches, like many evangelicals, argued that the charismata have ceased to function; that they served the survival of the church at a certain point in time or dispensation. The Presbyterian Church in Nigeria was built on the rock of Reformed Tradition, a heritage that had preached cessationism.

The key issue in the conflict is what the Reformed Tradition said about the role of the Holy Spirit and the manifestation of the charismata, the graces or power gifts. The founding father, Luther posed the question as the relationship between the Word and Spirit. Escaping from the anvil of 'traditions' that was the bastion of Roman Catholic ideology, Luther raised the Word as the canon, the boundary of acceptability, the litmus test on the validity of spiritual manifestation. On this touchstone, he could desert the Muntzerites and the Peasant Rebellion in 1525 by denying the Scriptural basis for their egalitarianism, appeal to the Spirit and emphasis on experience. His response was not merely based on how far one should obey secular authorities or the use of violence in Christian matters. He addressed these vexed issues but saw some real dangers: the left wing of the Reformation had, like Tertullian and the Montanists in an earlier period of church history, given the role of the Holy Spirit and the charismata much greater latitude. The question would be the degree to which a church could give primacy to the *experience* of the Holy Spirit and the *practice* of the gifts. The social implication, argued Luther, would cause disorder and endanger the new reformation program that he pioneered. He needed to protect the Godly cause from political interference. Of course, he could not hedge it enough from the instrumentalist concern of the German princes who used him as a fodder in their rivalry with the Emperor.

Luther was also concerned with control and the egalitarianism of 'Herr Omnes'. Authority was an essential ingredient in both church and state; he asserted the supremacy of the Word as the vehicle through which the Spirit operated. Those drunk in the Spirit threatened order. It may well be argued that Luther was driven more by strategy rather than doctrinal concerns. He himself gave a high prominence to the Holy Spirit in spiritual life such as prayer and fasting. Ironically, the Roman Catholics used the same anvils of tradition, order and control to clobber the rhema given through Luther for edifying the body of Christ, for opening a new vista in God's relationship to man, and for exposing the corruption within the institution. Even Catholic historians admit that a reformation was needed, was already in progress, and, therefore, Luther did not need to act as a boar in the vineyard. The Council of Trent proceeded to impose control. Latin Christianity not only banished the manifestation of the charismata but in 1000 AD drew up the *Rituale Romanorum*, a ritual for exorcism that branded such manifestation as demonic. Eastern Christianity continued to practice its manifestation especially in the monasteries.

A similar trend appears in Calvin, who claimed to have enjoyed an identical experience as Paul in the 'third heaven'. But Calvin was concerned about abuse to the point of relegating the charismata to the Apostolic Age. He agreed that speaking in tongues facilitated the preaching of the word in an earlier period. It had ceased. This ambivalent posture contrasted sharply with the democratic principles as priesthood of all believers and parity of all ministers. It must have surprised listeners who held to the belief in further reformation in a church open to the principle of 'semper reformanda'. Here again, concerns for control and order countered creativity. Luther and Calvin followed Augustine in arguing that the spiritual gifts were given for certain dispensation and had ceased as the church institutionalized. This institution was now the vehicle of grace. From this, the Roman Catholics could affirm that *extra ecclesiam nulla salus est* (there is no salvation outside the church).

At the turn of the century, Karl Barth encrusted the theological tradition that has guided Reformed theology until the recent challenge. At the root of this was not just the enlightenment world

view which restricted the mode of knowing and posed a dialectics between revelation and experience, but the political challenge
posed by the rise of National Socialism in Europe. Constraints of
space would not permit a comment on this dialectic; suffice it to
say that theory of knowledge has shifted significantly enough to
re-open the matter of religious experience as an enriching potential
without rejecting the gift of intellect and the power of revelation
(Moltmann, 1996). Defenders also admit that Barth was con-
strained by the political threat to the church. Supporters of Nazism
deployed natural theology in the defense. Barth rejected this and
opened a debate that has endured. But a certain irony characterized the period because Schleiermacher opposed Barth without
accepting the Nazist rhetoric. Rather, he articulated the awakening
of the Spirit, re-appropriating the spirit of the Evangelical Revival
that emphasized the New Birth through which Germany initiated the modern global missionary enterprise. The true heritage of
African churches was a child of the recovery of spiritual experience
that ran like a strand through church history. However, many of
the early evangelicals did not emphasize the manifestation of the
charismata. Some took refuge under the cessationist idea while
others pandered to rationalism that was an equally potent force in
an environment suffused with scienticism. These constituted the
intellectual environment of the modern missionary movement.

Africa was a victim of this environment because racism was
given a scientific veneer as Darwin's theory was turned into an
instrument for social analysis. Scientific racism tangoed with
Manifest Destiny to produce a jaundiced cultural perception of
African religion. Iconoclasm became the hallmark of the entry of
the gospel. As usual counter forces intervened. Bible translation by
the same missionaries unleashed the forces of indigenization that
de-stigmatized the indigenous cultures (Sanneh, 1989). The contention here is that scientific racism informed the attempt to draw
a distinction between the spirits in indigenous contexts and the
biblical understanding of the Holy Spirit. This effort led further to
the diminution of the role of the Holy Spirit in missionary theology and practice. Missionaries did not want the people to mistake
the Holy Spirit for those spirits that suffused indigenous cosmology. In one such distinction, the Holy Spirit was translated as 'clean
breath' while the spirit that abounds in the indigenous map of the
universe was translated as 'foul breath' (Meyer, 1994: 45-68). In the

Efik Bible that was a high achievement by the Presbyterians, the Holy Spirit is translated as 'Nsasan Spirit' (Clean Spirit) for avoidance of confusion with *ndem, inyang, ekpo* and other such spirits in the Efik cosmology. Besides bible translation, another counterforce to missionary bias was a plurality of voices among the Protestant band. Missionary history is so fragmented that any assertion can be countered with an example from the many individuals and societies operating in the eco-theatre. For instance, the Qua Iboe Mission that originated from the Welsh Revival looked for a spiritual revival and gave much more emphasis to the role of the Holy Spirit. Ironically, when the Spirit poured on the Ibibio converts in 1927, the same missionaries sought the assistance of the District Officer to quench what could lead to excesses.

The Reformed Tradition left an ambiguous tradition over the role of the Holy Spirit less from a deliberate attempt to diminish but more from the pursuit of order in the face of threatening disorderliness and lack of control. The individualistic strain in Protestantism came to roost when advocates of charismatic experience 'dislocate' control into centrifugal nodes by arguing that the spirit of the prophet is under the control of the prophet. Sense of order spilled into the sedate liturgy and the interpretation of the sacraments as 'outward sign of an inward grace'. Limited to two (Baptism and Eucharist) instead of the prevailing seven among Catholics, the Lord's Table was hedged with catechetical requirements and other moral and financial hurdles. Dues must be paid and evidence of good standing provided before one could eat the bread. As an outward symbol, the sense of awe was removed. It diminished Luther's image of Christ's presence being in the bread as fire is a hot iron. The Westernization was completed with imported wafers and silver chalice. Repentance and guilt replaced celebration, feast and commensality. Similarly, Baptism was celebrated by sprinkling and infant baptism was practiced as a means of incorporation into membership. These major doctrinal stances became the contested grounds when charismatic youth and Pentecostals took a very high view of Eucharist as eating the body of Christ and drinking his blood to effect healing and experience transformation. They moved beyond Luther's notion of consubstantiation towards the Roman Catholic assertion that Christ is *ac verelier ac realiter in membrum sensum continetur*. Pentecostals do not see the act as mere signification but as real participation in the life of Christ. So a praying band fasts and prays for days on the elements before the actual celebration. Instead of wafers, they share the baked bread as a meal event. The hurdles mounted around the table are removed: no communion dues, no exclusion clauses.

The celebration is a feast with locally-made bread and unfermented wine. Alcohol intake in puritanical Pentecostal ethics is a very sensitive matter. Anointing and fellowship are key aspects that challenge the tradition. As in the early church, baptism among Pentecostals is by immersion after the teaching on the matter. It is accompanied with spirit baptism. Repentance is a pre-requisite and infant baptism is rejected. Jesus, they argue, laid hands on children and blessed them. Outdooring of children is, therefore, performed in church by a service of thanksgiving for safe delivery and blessing of the infant. Like a creeping plant, the challenge on one doctrine leads to another creating an atmosphere of deliberate attempt to subvert an inherited tradition bequeathed by white ancestors.

The celebrative atmosphere of Pentecostal worship brought further innovations. As is the case among the Aladura, orality became more pronounced. A certain ambiguity exists because Pentecostal foster anti-intellectualism by privileging spiritual experience but the emphasis on the Bible induces the need for literacy. Concern for the youth whose problems include the examinations and certificates for entering the job market has led to the establishment of tutorial facilities for those seeking entry in to Universities or taking professional examinations. Commentators have laid much emphasis on the liturgical innovations. For instance, they use choruses in local languages to bring the messages home to people. While they use native instruments, they also use orchestral bands imported from overseas for what is dubbed as 'praise-co' instead of 'disco'. People bring their offerings as they do in villages by dancing and waving handkerchiefs in joyful mood with indigenous rhythm.

The liturgical challenge is more disruptive than the debate over polity. This is because presbyterial polity is closer to the Ephesian hallmark, except that some Pentecostals would claim 'anointing and call' to the offices of apostles and prophets which the Reformed Tradition would rather leave for the early period of the Jesus movement. Both organizations share a liberal gender ideology in which women play enlarged roles. Perhaps the most disturbing aspect is the puritan ethics of the born again. It is not that they are saying anything that would merit objection from the Presbyterians, scions of puritan John Knox tradition; rather, ethical compromises and the confusion in cultural policy took their tolls through the years. Perhaps Pentecostal tendency to be Manichean, dividing the world between the saved born again and the rest of the lukewarm and dammed church-goers appears judgmental and disconcerting. Allegation of pharasaism follows apace. On the whole, the debate ranges over doctrine, liturgy, polity and ethics. Much of the ethical bile flows around cultural policy to which the Pentecostals have woven a new transforming structure.

COSMOLOGY AND APPROPRIATION OF THE TEXT

Another dimension to the doctrinal conflict is the differing patterns of appropriating the gospel text. This is clear in the response to the enduring conflict between culture and gospel. How do the Pentecostal and charismatic devotees negotiate the culture-gospel interface that has been a contested issue?[2] They challenge the compromise that the church and communities reached in the past. First generation African converts preserved an epicenter in which their indigenous spirituality was preserved while designing an epicycle in which interaction with the gospel occurred. But the new Christianity broke through the design and tried to confront the two spheres. It failed to pay attention to a theology of dialogue between religions, postured Christ as the only way and answer, and demanded a clean break with the past. Then comes the irony. The subtlety of charismatic attitude to culture is that it accepts culture as a redemptive gift but one capable of being high-jacked by the, 'prince of the world'. Christ is in all cultures but judges all cultures. So, the spirit behind every form of culture must be tested. To illustrate with art, this leads to iconoclasm as the plastic arts are seen as imbued with power; they are not museum pieces to be brought into homes. This would open a door for the enemy's attack. Hugging the aniconic passages in the bible, the charismatic would rather use photographs that shared the beauty of nature. Instead of dismissing the reality of indigenous worldview, it engages and identifies the kindred atmosphere and resonance between African and Biblical worldviews (Friesen, 1996; Engelke, 2004: 82-109). To mention only eight of such points of congruence: at the structural level, the Bible and many local stories of Creation share the triumph of creation and order over chaos and a three-dimensional perception of space. Thus, at the name of Jesus, every knee bows whether in the heavenlies (sky), or earth (land and water) or earth-beneath (ancestral world). At the interior and dynamic level, both agree that events at the manifest world are determined by what had already been determined in the unseen world. As Paul would say, things that are seen are made of things that are not seen. This aeon is subjected to the 'not-yet' period.

This cosmology influences the role of the supernatural in the explanation of causality in everyday life. Critics point to the diminution of human responsibility and the lack of a political activism because people are looking for miracles. Both are spiritualized worldviews in which angels and principalities and powers are involved in human affairs; therefore, the inexplicable is a valid part of reality; miracles can still happen. The Jewish world of Jesus placed heaven and earth in much closer proximity than Enlightenment world did. This blurs the boundaries of the sacred and profane. Life is always precarious because of the activities of evil forces just as Jews were keenly aware of the machinations of demons. The African understanding of evil resonates with the biblical. At the political level, it was accepted that people could be given power from evil sources just as Satan offered Christ. Dictators were, therefore, perceived as 'possessed'. In both, the reality of divination, witchcraft and sorcery appear indubitable. The power of the spoken Word and name, 'onoma' is acknowledged. Thus, at the name of Jesus, things could be spoken into being. Finally, both share the covenantal nature of human-divine relationship; hence there are rituals and festivals that re-enact and re-energize the covenants to ensure well-being. The entry of the gospel into a community triggers off a clash of covenants as the covenant with the gods is embattled by the offer of a new covenant with Jesus. This dynamic renegotiation of gospel and culture contests the inherited traditions and exacerbates the conflict.

The list could continue but suffice it to say that charismatics take the Bible as real, powerful and virtually as a tribal history; they read their cultural roots into it. It is as if the soil on which Abraham or Jesus walked had the same texture as the Presbyterian youth walks. In this reading of the bible, Abram came from a similar cult-ridden culture before he became a new person. Abraham and Jesus were born where the Magi still rode around on decorated horses. Thus, the hermeneutical principle mines the interior of primal worldview, and designs a spiritual map of the powers that govern a community. The next step is to translate the biblical contents into local idiom. Paul's principalities and powers and the entire range of evil forces are given their local names. They are declared to be the enemies of human beings and communities, hindering them from achieving their life goals and accessing the good things of life. People are, therefore, encouraged to renounce and reject these cultures which hinder progress in the modem world. The past is portrayed as a burden. Salvation, achieved through deliverance rituals, frees the person and community for victorious life.

A new covenant with Jesus replaces the old covenant with ancestors and other deities that failed to perform. Efficacy is the litmus test. As a votary told a deity, 'if you do not perform, the path to your shrine will become overgrown with grass'. People patronize powerful forms of Christianity to get the same things which they expected their ancestral deities to provide for them but which these failed to do. Charismatic movements build on this and invite people to be born again and receive the power of the Holy Spirit, manifest the charismata and come under the cover of the blood of Jesus which protects from witchcraft attacks and empowers one to gain the rich promises in the Scriptures. To be born again is a bridge-burning experience that deconstructs and repackages with a new identity. Testimonies are encouraged as narratives of biographical reconstruction. To be born again has many benefits including the insertion into a new network of the 'brethren' that nurtures, protects and provides access to resources in the midst of collapsed economies. Young people find spouses and are saved from being unequally yoked with unbelievers, one of the causes of divorce. For young girls it is a security base from the scourge of sexual harassment that is endemic in the corrupt social system.[3] It replaces the old network of extended family without disengaging the person from the mandate of ensuring that the person's family becomes born again. Indeed, mission to family and village is the first or Judean component of the Great Commission.

To further illustrate their reconstruction of the primal worldview, four examples will suffice: rites of passage, community and land, language of God and ritual (music, dance and offering). Africans celebrate each stage of life from birth to death with rituals. Outdooring and naming ceremony for a child is crucial for identity and incorporation into a particular family and community. Pentecostals avoid the covenanting of the child performed by the paterfamilias. Similarly, since Africans put a premium on land and community, those ethics are taken over into Christianity with rituals of land deliverance and covenanting to Jesus. Instead of blood, they sprinkle olive oil. New symbols replace old ones. The recovery of land from ancestral spirits is a crucial aspect of the lives of members because unless old covenants are broken, the individual and the community will continue to be under bondage. Satan is legalistic and would require continued allegiance because of the iniquities of the fathers. They argue that much of the hindrances suffered by individuals and communities could be explained by curses and covenants that have not been blotted by the blood of Jesus. 'God has promised, through Jesus, to blot out all handwritings on any ordinances contrary and against us' Land deliverance and intercessory ministries take over the traditional rituals to empower individuals and communities in the pursuit of well-being.

RE-IMAGINED CHRISTIAN LIVING

Missionaries often despaired about the impact of the gospel on the real lives of African communities. The conflict, therefore, could be probed through the strategies for domesticating the message. Recently, social science researches have focused on the use of media in Africa's new Christianity (De Witte, 2003: 172-202; see also Gifford, 2004). The hidden agenda is to demonstrate that this spirituality is an aspect of the cultural global flow from the West to the Third world, and, therefore, conversion could be explained with the modernity discourse. It follows that Christianity in the south is a replica of that in the north; externality dominates; there is little creativity in African Christianity because the Pentecostals adopt the ingredients of Western media with avidity- television, print, radio, audio and video cassettes and all. Closer analysis indicates that there are large areas of local appropriation and creative energy. Large quantities of literature, posters, handbills, car stickers, bullhorns, street evangelism, house-to-house visits, home cells are all pressed into the good cause (see Gifford, 1998). The proper concept is 'dislocation' as the church is moved out of the building into the entire community space-buses, taxis, offices, motor-parks, hospitals, prisons, military barracks, are turned into preaching points. The strategy of total immersion is supplemented by a 'reverse flow' missionary energy as African preachers travel to the northern and southern hemispheres.

Recent studies of immigrant religion indicate that many African churches have opened branches in Europe.[4] Others have expanded their foreign-based ministries to their homelands. The most prolific form of immigrant religion is the house cell, prayer groups that enhance the sustenance and coping capacity of migrants. Commentators, especially sociologists, have argued that African churches deliberately stimulate a feeling of belonging to a vast network of an international community of believers. The profile of an urban religion does not equate with reality precisely because many believers conduct land deliverance and evangelical outreaches in their villages and create vibrant evangelical bands. The appeal has shifted from the urban to rural sectors thereby nullifying the class-content analyses of earlier studies of the phenomenon. This is not a religion of the oppressed or the upwardly-mobile, but a new religious stream that washes all. Significantly, the youth have created a religious space for themselves in the quest to access a spirituality that sustains and is faithful to the mandate of the scriptures. It may not be a simple case of accessing the resources of modernity; rather, it is about the hermeneutics and appropriation of the gospel message within a certain worldview and socio-economic context. Some may query whether the move from narrative to application in real life situations shows enough fidelity to the scriptures, whether there is an adequate balance between private, conversionist emphasis and social engagement in the public space, whether this spirituality could confront the unjust social structures or challenge the rulers.

There is definitely a great need for research in African charismatic hermeneutics. African charismatic movements have taken over the praise names which traditionalists use for God and ancestors. They claim that these praise names are meant for the real God. This is akin to 'spoiling the Egyptians', a hermeneutic that the early church fathers used with great effect, though some like Tertullian would imply that it was very academic. It soon yielded a method of allegorization that has endured in popular preaching. As an example, when the Greek took over the word, *soter*, to describe Christ's salvatory role, they appropriated a word for deities and heroes who rescued the community. The intense form of vernacularization in the music, dance and praise is a form of creative inculturation. As God is praised and invoked in native idiom, the worship becomes very meaningful and no longer foreign. An indigenous Christology is crafted. From this perspective, the charismatic movements serve as a tool for decolonizing the church: in doctrine, they have challenged much of the missionary heritage, reinvented the evangelical certitude that the bible is true and real. The hermeneutic may be perceived as literalist and anti-intellectual because there is a diatribe against philosophical and systematic theology, a strand that goes back to the early church. They claim that the 'letter' kills and the rhema gives life. They reject the hermeneutics of suspicion by re-affirming the hermeneutics of trust. The 'homiletics of conscientization' spurs people to face the difficulties of the times with confidence as overcomers (Johns, 1993).

ENGAGING THE PUBLIC SPACE

Finally, it is a movement with many varieties and internal debates on doctrine and strategies abound. This has hindered the level of unity or ecumenism. The Pentecostal Fellowship of Nigeria (PFN) has been formed as an umbrella association that controls the integrity of the movement, and serves as the link with ecumenical bodies such as the Christian Association of Nigeria. The current President of PFN is the Vice Chairman of CAN. Still, the challenge of discipline remains real. The fear of wolves in sheep's clothing clouds the reputation of the movement and gives the mainline churches the stick to use against their enemies in the competitive religious market. Religious entrepreneurs could perfect learned techniques from American videos. A dimension of the conflict is the theology that engages the public space. On the political front, there have been an enlarged political space for Christianity and charismatic leaders compete for relevance and run the risk of playing into the hands of rulers. Stories abound about politicians who use the charismatic leaders as covers in their chicanery. It was imagined that charismatic ethics is conversionist and may avoid engagement of the political space. Some argue that the mainline churches have borne the brunt of building civil society and responding to both the state and enormous social service burdens. However, the complicity of the mainline churches in the colonial enterprise is forgotten; their theology of two kingdoms is forgotten; their collusion in the politics of independence as they waltzed with nationalists and served as pressure groups are forgotten. All churches have been forced by the collapse of economies and legitimacy crises to assume greater visibility in the public space. There are covert and overt forms of political participation as the purview of the political field widens. Some charismatic leaders are not only prophetic voices in the market place but encourage saints to vie for office.

Recently the import of the new Christianity has shown in the scrambling of the models of ministerial formation. Admittedly all churches that have been driven away from primary and secondary school systems have now founded Universities offering Theology and Business Studies. At one level, it indicates that the particular church is important and has enough resources for the cost-intensive adventure. At another level, it is a form of social engagement because of the failures of government-owned institutions that are bedeviled with serious moral problems such as cultism (Kalu, 2001). Beyond the challenge to inherited traditions, the aggressive advocacy of born again spirituality has clashed with Presbyterianism because of generational factor. Many of the older generation, educated and urbanized are averse to rapid changes. A generational approach to church history indicates different responses to the gospel and missionary control. The first generation experienced the full impact of missionary control and many through tutelage became very committed. A second generation treasured the memory and respect for the tradition. By the third generation, they had lost much of the memory and respect. This appears to be the fate of the younger generation. The matter is complicated by another factor. Some are also venerable members of Freemasonry lodges and Rosicrucianism. Lodges became popular on the West African coast as means of social mobility in the 19th Century. Scottish ministers were the vanguards of freemasonry in Nigeria. This adds a clash of spiritual orientation into the conflict. People who were comfortable to be Christians and Masons felt threatened by young people denouncing the secret society as unchristian and demonic. The high profile given to the Holy Spirit by the charismatics, compel a conflict with the compromisers among the older generation. The debate on cultism within the churches causes much internal strain. Similarly, ministerial for-

mation bred a corps of loyalists who were trained under missionaries to accept the tradition as canonical. Until quite recently few of
them were exposed to University education. Their utter dependence
on the mission for livelihood and entire career prospects hindered
ability to review the traditions. Missionary control was iron-clad.
But among younger generation of ministers, who imbibed charismatism in Secondary Schools or in the Universities, there is less
feeling of vulnerability; they can enter into secular careers, they are
more critical, and tend to empathize with the charismatism of the
youth. Some are more like youth leaders than as pastors.

CHARISMATIZATION PROCESS

Presbyterian responses have shifted through time. As mentioned, hostility characterized the 1970's but by the end of the
decade as the movement enlarged it became necessary to change
tack so as to retain the young people. The Presbyterian Young
People's Association of Nigeria was created. As a charismatic
movement it caused many conflicts in parishes but did much good.
More poignant is the authoritarian mode of power relations. Using
a set of patriarchal symbols derived from indigenous society, elders
and congregational sessions used top-down power flows to curb
religious fervor among the youth. This often produced mayhem as
the rebellion against the rulers of the synagogue thickened. The
Board of Faith and Order that understudies doctrinal matters for
the Synods and General Assembly prepared guidelines on the biblical teaching on the Holy Spirit and charismata. It sought to guide
pastors on how to handle the youth with sensitivity. By the 1980s,
the church created a Ministry for Church Revival under a former
Moderator of General Assembly who had undergone training at
the Haggai Institute in Singapore. It later redesigned this unit into
the Evangelism Ministry comprising a board of young graduate
pastors working to re-evangelize the whole church. Among Presbyterian University students, a charismatic body known as Presbyterian Students' Fellowship is expanding through many Nigerian
universities. Their Annual Conferences are now major events.

Why and how did so much change occur within the decades
of the 1980's and 1990's? First of all, this is the trend among all
the mission-instituted churches. It is an encapsulating strategy.
The heart-beat is survival. Many are not opening up willingly but

forced by the impact of the 'wind of God'. They essay to mount controls with varying degrees of success. Secondly, beyond the youth, women have been crucial in the change. Female patronage of hot religiosity is another matter. But the role of women is related to the laicization of the post Independent churches in Nigeria. The informal power of women is enormous because of their numbers, resources, commitment and mobilization. The number of graduate pastors in the church has increased rapidly in the 1990s. They have borne the brunt of the collapse of the economy and implosion of praetorian state. They find much solace in prayer retreats, fasting and the exhortations to believe that God can, in His faithfulness, change their circumstances. Pentecostal spirituality helps the individual to mobilize against the harsh realities of the day.

Thirdly, there is a relationship between the growth of charismatism and the socio-economic and political changes of recent years. This backdrop should not detract from the spiritual dimension but is crucial. Fourthly, the rapid expansion of Pentecostalism and its appeal to both urban and rural population means that many Presbyterians are members of fellowships such as Full Gospel Business Mens' Fellowship International, Womens' Aglow, Gideon Bible, Prayer for the Nation, Intercessors for Africa and Children Evangelism Ministry, all of which are interdenominational. The impact of Pentecostal propaganda, their books, videos and television programs barrage many churches. Mission churches are intrigued by the abilities of Pentecostals to raise money through tithing, and build large projects. They are compelled to re-examine the doctrine on tithes and are forced to imitate. Indeed, there is very little difference in the liturgy of some churches. Despite the adaptive strategies, there is still much rivalry, a habit of misrepresentation, and hostile attitude in the relationships between churches and Pentecostals. Allegations about pride and false doctrine abound.

Glossolalia and prophesy have been divisive issues since the doctrine of initial evidence was propounded. They are disruptive, break down decorum and order, and exclude. Paul's strictures on Corinthian churches arm the opponents of charismatism with contrary argument. The faith-claim-receive emphasis of prosperity preachers appears as cheap grace and crossless Christianity. Opponents argue that it does not allow God to be God. Of course, a balanced gospel must recognize the promises, their availability and conditions for receiving them. The Bible is clear that the promises are predicated on obedience. Admittedly, missionary rigor had virtually extolled poverty, but in the midst of the collapse of the economy, people are not excited to hear about the relationship between poverty and humility. Others find the large space given to demons and deliverance as disconcerting. Karl Barth had warned that looking too closely at the demons does not impress them and could make the onlooker a little demonic. However, the fascination with demonology responds to the challenges of the worldview. Balance and strong Bible studies are antidotes. The challenges posed by the charismatic movements force the churches to review authority patterns, seek ways to protect their heritage, and yet be sensitive to the possibility of quenching the spirit. Misrepresentations heighten conflict levels and produce schism.

CONCLUSION

Perhaps, Pentecostalism has picked up the core elements of Evangelicalism and imbued them with new life. As William Klempa concluded in a report prepared for the World Alliance of Reformed Churches in 1972,

> for those who wrote the New Testament, the Spirit was not primarily a doctrine but an experience, they did not speak of believing in the Holy Spirit but of receiving and experiencing the power of the Spirit when they believed. This experience of the Holy Spirit, was as Ernst Kasselmann has said, the real hallmark of post-Easter Christianity. The emphasis of the Pentecostal movement on the experience, the fullness of life in the Spirit, and the exercise of the diverse charisms, is therefore of unassailable validity. Pentecostalism has rediscovered the actuality of the Spirit as experienced by the apostolic community in a way that is often lacking in the mainline churches (Klempa, 1972: 101-121).

If the Presbyterian Church that came to Nigeria in 1846 will grow and be an instrument of God's grace, it must allow the 'Wind of God' to blow over it and bring freshness without compromising the core of it heritage.

Bibliography

Achunike, Hilary, 'The Roman Catholic Renewal Movement in Igboland, 1970-2000', PhD Diss, Religion, University of Nigeria, Nsukka, 2001.

Amucheazi, E.C., *Church and Politics in Eastern Nigeria, 1945-1966.* Lagos: Macmillan, 1986.

Richard Burgess, 'The Civil War Revival and Its Pentecostal Progeny: A Religious Movement among the Igbo People of Eastern Nigeria, 1967-2002', PhD Dissertation, School of Historical Studies, The University of Birmingham, June, 2004.

Buxton, Fowell, *African Slave Trade and Its Remedy*, 1841.

De Witte, Marken,'Altar Media's Living Word: televised charismatic Christianity in Ghana', *Journal of Religion in Africa*, 33, 2, 2003, pp. 172-202.

Ekechi, F.K., *Rivalry and Scramble in the Missionary Enterprise in Igboland, 1841-1914*, London: Frank Cass, 1971.

Engelke, Matthew,'Discontinuity and the discourse of conversion', *Journal of Religion in Africa*, 34, 1, 2, 2004, pp. 82-109.

Exchange, 29, 3, 2000, pp. 213-229.

Friesen, J. Stanley, *Missionary Responses to Tribal Religions at Edinburgh 1910*, New York: Peter Lang, 1996.

Gifford, Paul, *Ghana's New Christianity*, Bloomington IN: Indiana University Press, 2004.

Gifford, Paul, *African Christianity: Its Public Role*, Bloomington IN: Indiana University Press, 1998.

Johns, C.B., *Pentecostal Formation*, Sheffield: Academic Press, 1993.

Kalu, U. Ogbu, *Embattled Gods: Christianization of Igboland, 1841-1991*, Lagos/London: Minaj Publishers, 1996; Trenton, NJ: Africa World Press, (1996) 2003.

Kalu, U. Ogbu,'Preserving a Worldview: Pentecostalism in the African Map of the Universe', *Pneuma*, 24, 2, Fall, 2002, pp. 110-137.

Kalu, U. Ogbu, *The Scourge of the Vandals: the nature and control of secret cults in Nigerian Universities*, Enugu: University of Nigeria Press, 2001.

Kalu, U. Ogbu, *A Century and Half of Presbyterian Witness in Nigeria, 1846-1996*, Enugu: Presbyterian Church in Nigeria, 1996.

Kalu, U. Ogbu, *Divided People of God: Church Union Movement in Nigeria, 1875-1966*, New York: NOK Publishers, 1978.

Kendall, E., *The End of an Era: Africa and the Missionary*, London: SPCK, 1978.

Klempa, W., 'Ecstasy and the experience of the Holy Spirit', in *Reformed World*, 32, 1972, pp. 101-121.

Marshall-Fratani, Ruth, 'Power in the Name of Jesus', *Review of African Political Economy*, 52, Nov, 1991, pp. 21-37.

Meyer, Birgit, 'Beyond Syncretism' in Charles Stewart and R. Shaw, (eds.) *Syncretism / Anti-Syncretism: the politics of religious synthesis*, London: Routledge, 1994, pp: 45-68.

Moltmann, J., *Pentecostal Movement as an Ecumenical Challenge*, London: SCM Press, 1996.

Olorunfemi, D.A., 'The Impact of Charismatic Movement on the Nigerian Baptist Convention', M.Div. Project, Church History, West African Theological Seminary, Lagos, 2004.

Omenyo, Cephas N., *Pentecost Outside Pentecostalism: A Study of the Development of Charismatic Renewal of the Mainline Churches in Ghana*, Boekencentrum: Uitgeverij Boekencentrum Zoetermeer, 2002.

Sanneh, Lamin, *Translating the Message*, Maryknoll, NY: Orbis Books, 1989.

Stark, Rodney, *The Rise of Christianity*, Princeton University Press, 1997.

Turner, P., 'The wisdom of the fathers and the gospel of Christ', *Journal of Religion in Africa*, 4, 1, 1971, pp. 45-68.

Notes

1. See, for instance, Exchange, 29, 3, 2000: 213-229.

2. Kalu (2002: 110-137) examines the many areas of resonance between the biblical and African worldviews.

3. *Journal of Religion in Africa*, 28, 3, 1998 contains a number of articles dealing with Pentecostal response to modernity.

4. As one example of the burgeoning literature, see Afe Adogame, 'Engaging the Rhetoric of Spiritual Warfare: the public face of Aladura in diaspora', *Journal of Religion in Africa*, 34, 4, 2004, pp. 493-522.

Is Satan Local or Global?
Reflections on a Nigerian
Deliverance Movement

Rosalind I. J. Hackett

African Pentecostalism and the Global
Network Society[1]

Once Pentecostalism started assuming global proportions in the latter part of the twentieth century, scholarly analyses were soon forthcoming (Cox, 1996; Poewe, 1994; Hackett, 1996; Martin, 1990; Anderson, 1991, 1992, 1993; Gifford, 1991, 1998; Ojo, 1996; Dempster, Klaus and Petersen, 1999). For the main part, these contributions are multi-sited in orientation in that they examine the efflorescence of Pentecostal and charismatic movements in a variety of national or regional settings. Some of the more recent publications begin to address the global dynamics and interconnections of the larger 'family' of Pentecostal and charismatic movements (Freston, 2001; Martin, 2002; Corten and Marshall-Fratani, 2001). It is hoped that this expanding body of scholarship on Christianity's fastest growing wing will redress the failure of some globalization theorists to take Pentecostalism more seriously (cf. Freston, 2001, 2002; Gifford, 2001: 78; Droogers, 2001).

Given the vastly expanded channels of information and com-munication in today's global network society (Appadurai, 1996; Castells, 1996; Herzfeld, 2001; Vries and Weber, 2001), and the 'complex connectivity that defines our times' (Tomlinson, 1999: 31), more work remains to be done on examining Pentecostal-ism's formal and informal transnationalism. The more culturalist approach adopted in this essay can elucidate the circulation of ideas and images issuing from Pentecostal sources and how these get appropriated and translated into local contexts. I am fascinated (and concerned) both by the expansion of discourses of demonism, occultism, and satanism in the African context, and the key role played by Pentecostalism in facilitating these developments.[2] So, responding to the call for more cross-cultural and multi-disciplin-ary investigation of the global flows of ideas about the demonic 'Other' and symbolic interpretations of everyday misfortune and sickness (Corten and Marshall-Fratani, 2001), and the need for more studies of the local knowledges and practices that mediate global forces (Robertson, 1992; Urry, 2000: 46-47), this essay con-siders the case of one particular Nigerian deliverance ministry, the Mountain of Fire and Miracles Ministries (MFM). This rapidly growing religious organization is located just behind the back gate of the University of Lagos, where I was visiting in the summer of 2001. Each Sunday many thousands of people flock to MFM's cramped site amidst the already crowded buildings and congested streets. Before examining the significance of this group and its loca-tion in one of the most 'feared' cities in the world for interpreting the relationship between Pentecostalism and globalization, some general background is required on the resurgence of demonology in theology and popular culture in present-day Africa.

THE BUSINESS OF DELIVERANCE

The development of African Pentecostalism, notably its newer formations, has been accompanied by a significant preoccupation with demonology.[3] A growing number of authors have addressed this phenomenon (see especially Meyer, 1999; Faure, 2000). In the 1990s, specialized deliverance ministries grew up in Ghana and Nigeria, for example, to respond to this need (Gifford, 2001). The roots of this contemporary manifestation must be seen in the local efforts by Christians, and some Muslims, from the 1950s onwards to preach against secret societies and occult organizations.[4] In Nigeria their work received an impetus in 1976 from the moral campaign by the government of Murtala Muhammed, which banned secret society membership among government officials. Several churches took their cue from this. For example, from 1977 onwards, Nigerian Baptists incorporated a public declaration for members to state openly that they had no association with any 'secret society'. A major initiative was provided by the Christian Students' Social Movement (CSSM) which began looking for evidence of 'occult powers' in public life. An early target was FESTAC (the major black arts festival held in Nigeria in January/February 1977), with its emphasis on traditional cultural performance. Also during this period, two prominent religious figures added their own anti-satanic rhetoric. Ajagbemonkeferi (the one who makes noise against unbelievers) was a well-known Muslim preacher in Ibadan, renowned for physically attacking traditional masquerades. W. F. Kumuyi, the founder of the Deeper Life Bible Church in Lagos who, as part of his holiness and anti-worldliness message, demonized television as 'Satan's box', and also had strong words against fashionable dressing. Pa Elton's influential *Demon Manifestations in the Last Days*, published in the early 1980s, together with the popular CSSM prayer bulletins, gave a strong local flavor and agency to the Christian campaign against 'satanic dealings'.[5]

The continuing emphasis on evil is nurtured and sustained by the abundance of texts dealing with 'spiritual warfare' which can be found these days in many (particularly West) African Christian bookstores. The works of popular American deliverance specialists, such as Derek Prince, Rebecca Brown, Marilyn Hickey and Lester Sumrall are widely available.[6] Despite the popularity of American works, there is also a growing indigenous textual production. *The Last Outcast*, by the former music celebrity, Chris Okotie, founder/leader of the Household of God Church in Lagos, Nigeria, on the subject of the future anti-Christ (who will be cloned and European), is an example of contemporary output on this subject.[7] Many of these texts go further than conventional evangelical teachings on the powers of evil, they engage in 'spiritual mapping and strategic high-level warfare' (Meer, 2001). This growing phenomenon involves the identification of strongholds of opposing spiritual forces and their attempted destruction by groups of 'prayer warriors'. Some of these texts might also be classified as anti-cult literature in that they are concerned about alerting Christians against 'dangerous' organizations, whether 'dead churches' or 'occult' organizations (such as the Rosicrucians or local secret societies). American anti-cult organizations are known to operate in Africa. They were active following the massacre of several hundred members of the Ugandan, apocalyptic Marian community, known as the Movement for the Restoration of the Ten Commandments of God (Hackett, 2001).[8] It is as yet unclear as to how many African governments have been (or may yet be) influenced by these types of organizations or by former colonial powers in the management of religious pluralism. Belgium, Germany and France, for example, have all taken measures in recent years to restrict the activities of minority religious groups.[9]

One pertinent example is the Presidential Commission of Inquiry into Devil Worship established by the Kenyan government in 1994 in response to public concern, mainly voiced by Christian clergy. Its report was presented to Parliament in August 1999.[10] According to the U.S. State Department's 2000 *Annual Report for International Religious Freedom*, the Kenyan report alleged that 'Satanists' had infiltrated non-indigenous religious groups such as Jehovah's Witnesses, Mormons and Christian Scientists, as well as the Freemasons and the Theosophical Society. The State Department report notes pointedly that most members of the Commission were 'senior members of mainline Christian churches'.[11] A local journalist wryly commented that '[t]he commissioners overlooked the fact that Kenya is a secular state and went on to prescribe standards that only Moses the Lawmaker could think of recommending to the Jews'.[12] In a trenchant and humorous piece, *The Nation* journalist, G. K. Waruhiu wrote, 'It is also highly defamatory, scandalous, and poorly presented, full of clichés and empty statements which were not properly researched, and which in the final analysis amount to a new-fangled Kenyan Spanish Inquisition, or simple witch-hunting'.[13] He calls on the government to apologize for wasting taxpayers' time and money, and putting minority religions at risk.

So the demonological strain in African Pentecostal Christianity is sustained both by local understandings of human misfortune and spiritual agency (see for instance, Idowu, 1970) but also by the teachings of foreign evangelists, nowadays usually American, Korean and Brazilian (cf. Gifford, 2001). For example, the demonology of Korean Pentecostal churches, an intriguing blend of American deliverance theology and shamanic exorcism, is highly developed (cf. Cox, 1996: 225). Prominent church leaders such as Paul Yongghi Cho and Kim Ki Dong receive invitations to speak not just because of their successful church growth techniques but also because of the central place they accord to ritual practices of exorcism and aggressive prayer. Recent publicity in Ghanaian newspapers anticipating their August 2001 visits described their work as 'depopulating the kingdom of Satan'. The powerful Brazilian Pentecostal church, the Universal Church of the Kingdom of God, has branches in several African countries, with over fifty in South Africa (Freston, 2001; Kramer, 2002). It is known for its high media profile, aggressive proselytizing techniques and exorcizing practices.

In Ghana there has been criticism of these new generation churches for the centrality they accord to Satan, as well as the conspicuous consumption and personality cults which often develop around them (van Dijk 2001: 231-232). In Nigeria, there seems to be no holds barred in this area, notably in Lagos which is now estimated to have a population of around 14 million. The reasons for the prevalence of discourses of demonism and satanism in the Nigerian context will be analyzed in more detail below. First, I wish to explore how the forces of evil are interpreted, and mediated, both locally and globally in the case of the aforementioned Mountain of Fire and Miracles Ministries (MFM). I am interested in how these discourses constitute a powerful social and symbolic mechanism for helping people negotiate who they are, how they should live their lives in the complex, chaotic urban space which is Lagos – officially publicized by the Lagos State Government as the 'Center of Excellence'.[14] I am also concerned to examine how this rhetoric of power and evil also translates into strategies of exclusion and discrimination. I will conclude with some reflections on the social and cultural consequences of this type of religious orientation for inter-religious relations in Nigeria's competitive public sphere.

MOUNTAIN OF FIRE AND MIRACLES MINISTRIES

Members of MFM are very keen to point out to their various visitors, learned or otherwise, that their founder and General

Overseer Dr D.K. Olukoya obtained a First Class Honors Degree in Microbiology from the University of Lagos, and a Ph.D. in Molecular Genetics from the University of Reading in Britain. He purportedly has over 70 (religious) publications to his credit. Members like to discuss the rapid expansion of the movement which is keenly experienced by anyone who attends the sole Sunday morning service when around 100,000 people flock to the Akoka-Yaba site of the ministry. It seems hard to calculate the figures given that there is no large auditorium as in some of the other Pentecostal mega-churches, but rather a series of interconnected covered areas which radiate out from hall no. 1 where the altar and pulpit are located. There is closed circuit television to link the various areas, which are densely packed with wooden benches (I was told that they calculate the number of worshippers by the number of benches that get added weekly). The cramped and ramshackle environment is made more difficult by the numerous stalls vending MFM paraphernalia whether books or holy oil, or general merchandise and refreshments.

However, as suggested above, the MFM leaders take a positive view of the challenges arising from the overwhelming numbers of people who attend their services. In addition to the Yaba site there is also their Prayer City ground on the outskirts of Lagos where many thousands, if not millions, of supplicants attend crusades and prayer rallies. They emphasize that theirs is a ministry specialized in delivering people from the manifold evil forces that thwart well-being and success. This emphasis is well-evidenced in the abundant literature available for purchase on the subject, most of it written by the founder and leader, Dr. Olukoya. It can also be seen in the aggressive forms of prayer that take place within the main service or immediately following, among small, informal prayer groups. Furthermore, the graphic imagery of the books and magazines is a vivid indicator of the demonic preoccupations of this religious organization. Perhaps the most helpful way to address issues of globality and locality within MFM is to follow Olukoya's own model in his talks and sermons. I have culled this from sermon texts, church publications, and the official MFM website. Drawing on his scientific background, Dr Olukoya likes to identify the main problems in people's lives and then proceed to analyzing their causes, before prescribing appropriate remedies and projecting expected results.

Symptoms

The range of symptoms attributed to those in need of deliverance centers around lack of success and various forms of sickness. Olukoya writes frequently of the inability to reap due rewards in life in relation to one's job, family, marital instability, sexual problems, and poverty. He asks people whether they suffer from uncontrollable anger, unrestrained talking, or depression, or whether they find it difficult to stay in one church or concentrate on the Bible. He lists other symptoms such as visions of dark strangers and hearing strange noises. However it is the area of dreams that seems to command the most attention in Olukoya's teachings: 'dreaming is a natural way that the spirit world breaks out into our lives.'[15] He asks his readers if they dream about 'accidents, attacks, carrying loads, closed doors, youths growing old, chains in the neck, closed Bibles' for this is symbolic of a 'satanic attack.' Furthermore, dreams of 'snakes, water, dead relatives,' 'spirit husbands,' 'spirit children' and 'masquerades' are 'points of contact' used by the devil.[16] He also lists 'sweating profusely in the dream, laboring as in pregnancy, serving food to people you do not know, attending strange meetings in the dreams, being attacked by crocodiles, cats, dogs and lions and other strange occurrences in dreams are all part of satan's method of enslaving and destroying people.'[17] There are in fact several pages of dream symbol analysis pertaining to poverty, frustration, backsliding, spiritual weakness, marital problems, etc.[18]

Diagnosis

A good summary of Olukoya's teachings on suffering is as follows: 'a person could decide to waste his own life, a person could inherit wastage, a person can be wasted by powers of darkness.'[19] So while there is strong emphasis on the vulnerability of the individual in relation to a 'polluted background' and nefarious powers, Olukoya advocates human agency in terms of leading a life of morality and devotion, actively seeking to understand the relationship between problems and 'foundation', and engaging in regular prayer. The main thrust of his arguments concerning the 'human condition' centers around the dangers of 'bad foundations,' 'destructive linkages' and 'wrong connections'. These may either be known or unknown to the sufferer. But it is his/her responsibility to know and to see these 'evil links' whether between people, or between people and spirits, 'family idols', 'family curses', 'family taboos', and take the appropriate remedial action. Problems can stem from the fact that members of one's family were witches, traditional priests, polygamists, 'missionary-killers' or 'idol-worshipers'. A family curse may also cause problems as may chieftaincy titles and (ethnic) body markings. More broadly, Olukoya also links the 'revival of witchcraft and Satanism' to the resurgence of cultism in Nigeria's universities. He notes that witches and wizards, or their spouses, now brazenly appear on television.[20] In fact, he complains that 'the television has become [the] Sodom and Gomorrah of many people's sitting rooms.'[21]

CURE OR 'POWER AGAINST POWER'

Olukoya is at pains to argue that confession alone is insufficient. Violent, aggressive prayer or 'high voltage prayer' is called for on a regular basis, often at night when dream spirits are at their height. To avoid 'contamination' and attack by evil spirits the Christian must be 'spiritual' not 'religious', and express 'righteous anger.'[22] 'Absolute holiness within and without is "the spiritual insecticide" required for entry into heaven.'[23] Central to the ritual action recommended by Olukoya for those needing deliverance are 'prayer points'. These are prayer formulae for dealing with particular problems. Here are some selections from the (68) prayer points in response to 'satanic dreams.'[24]

> I claim all the good things which God has revealed to me through dreams. I reject all bad and satanic dreams in the name of Jesus.
>
> O Lord, perform the necessary surgical operation in my life and change all that had gone wrong in the spirit world.
>
> I claim back all the good things which I have lost as a result of defeat and attacks in my dreams in Jesus' name.
>
> Lord Jesus, replace all satanic dreams with heavenly visions and divinely-inspired dreams.

The above examples indicate the importance of invoking the name of Jesus. In fact, Olukoya calls it the 'most powerful weapon which is available for our use against satanic dreams.'[25] He also lists as spiritual weapons, the blood of Jesus, the Fire of God, and the Angels of God.[26] There is considerable use of militaristic language and imagery in the battle against Satan and his troops. For example, the sub-heading to the book, *Power against Local Wickedness* (1997), informs readers that it '[c]ontains over 1,000 Prayer Points to enable you to disgrace your Goliath and destroy local satanic military technology.'

MFM is described as a 'do-it-yourself Gospel Ministry, where your hands are trained to wage war and your fingers to fight'.[27] But Olukoya also wants Christians to look beyond the physical and human side of their problems to see the real, spiritual, causes. For example, he commands: '[e]xamine that family house very well, reject the images there, dissociate yourself from it, disown it, force the spirit behind them to disown you too'.[28] In some cases this may entail the physical destruction of objects, plants or animals that have evil ancestral connections, or spiritual destruction in the form of 'fire prayer'. It may also involve changing a family name that includes reference to a particular deity or ancestor. Based on the biblical doctrine of restitution, Olukoya advocates that all wrongfully acquired goods, or gifts from many lovers, should be returned to the givers.

PROGNOSIS

The prognosis offered by Olukoya is aptly captured by the subtitle of the weekly magazine: *Power must change hands.* In one of his sermons he also utilizes the metaphor of gardening and planting to explain the right outcomes in this life. Using the right tools and conditions will provide protection, success and self-realization. The cover to the *Victory Over Satanic Dreams* booklet shows a man asleep, dreaming of warding off with a sword various maleficent agents from his 'modern' bungalow, neat garden, sack of millions of dollars, and fancy new car. The projected outcome for the individual is freedom from oppressive spiritual forces. So a common image in MFM literature is the breaking of chains and of someone being released from 'family captivity' or enslavement to 'spirit-spouses', for example. It is unclear whether this liberation will be lasting; at very least it seems that the individual must be constantly vigilant and proactive with regard to the machinations of the Devil and his agents. It is, of course, this point that comes up for perhaps the most trenchant criticism from other African Pentecostalists who see it as a denial of the sufficiency of Christian salvation.[29]

A LOCAL ONTOLOGY OF ENGAGEMENT

Significantly, Olukoya's writings do not target or even allude to political questions and policy issues, as we might find in the sermons and writings of such Pentecostal pastors as Matthew Ashimolowo (Nigerian pastor based in London) and Mensa Otabil, who regularly addresses Ghana's (and Africa's) national problems (see Gifford 1998).[30] In fact, in keeping with his scientific training, he seems to articulate a more microcosmic view of the world with his emphasis on the familial/ancestral roots of personal problems. However, it is also possible to view his teaching as providing the lens of an exotic, yet culturally meaningful, underworld/underwater imaginary with which to interpret and debate social and political problems. Similarly, he provides a *local* theory of supernatural agency which can plausibly account for deviance and misfortune in the lives of individuals, families, communities, nations, nay even the global community. Some may see this as a form of externalization, of not assuming responsibility for problems, while others may deem it a cogent rhetorical device for communicating the gravity of Nigeria's predicament, in the hope of eliciting more effective responses. Given the predominance and distinctiveness of Dr. Olukoya's demonology, it hardly seems to be a ploy to stimulate church growth and revival. Consider, in this regard, the widely publicized opinion of Pastor Matthew Ashimolowo, General Overseer of the London-based Kingsway International Christian Center, that Nigeria's ethnic clashes and problems of development were attributable to satanic forces and its present state of 'demon-cracy', and that, consequently, Nigerians needed to turn to Christ.[31]

As all those who have spent time in Lagos will appreciate, quotidian existence is characterized by a constant battle for survival against traffic, pollution, crime, corruption, and violence. People feel insecure and very vulnerable. They frequently voice frustration with the unreliability, if not outright failure, of public services, security forces, and political leaders. In addition, Lagos is described as 'very hot' or supernaturally charged because it is a crossroads of people and commodities, from around the country and the world. It is a node for drug-traffickers and smugglers, and for rural migrants seeking jobs and education. Despite the relocation of many government and diplomatic institutions to the federal capital in Abuja, Lagos still attracts those seeking the 'big time' in their careers and professions.[32] In light of this, Olukoya's narratives and depictions of nefarious spiritual powers (e.g. 'dream criminals' and 'satanic night-raiders'), causing suffering and preventing self-realization in this modernizing world, appear as powerful metaphorical representations of living conditions for the majority of Lagosians in this 'contact zone' (Herzfeld 2001: 141). They express cogently the dangers of human interactions in this notorious, unknowable urban space. Stories of mysterious abductions from taxis and buses, traffic in body parts and demonic spirits posing as humans are in everyone's narrative repertoire.[33]

Once 'personified' and cognitively identified as 'marine agents' or witches, these satanic forces can be 'practically' treated via ritual exorcism and prayer.[34] In ways similar to that of the traditional diviner or *babalawo*, modern scientist Dr. Olukoya, speaking with the authority of well-honed scientific knowledge as well as spiritual insight, diagnoses and prescribes the causes of suffering, offering enough flexibility for people to draw on their own 'knowledges' and construct their own courses of action. Of course, the emphasis on self-deliverance can be somewhat contradicted, or at least diminished, by the dependency on his interpretative powers, and the adulations expressed by grateful supplicants. That notwithstanding, it should be noted that Olukoya's status is that of General Overseer, and not Bishop or Sole Spiritual Leader, as in equivalent religious organizations. Moreover, MFM's website and literature carry no images of him or his wife and very little information on them. There is far more emphasis on what might be called Olukoya's 'technologies of deliverance'.

Just as the vibrant, teeming city of Lagos defies categorization with its intersections of the local and the global, the traditional and the modern, the rural and the urban, the boundaries defined by MFM are similarly 'porous', to use Michael Herzfeld's felicitous term (Herzfeld 2001). Olukoya's discursive strategies also reflect some of the powerlessness and inequalities experienced by individuals in the face of national and global trends.[35] Bewitchment, marital and sexual problems, educational failure, unemployment and poverty feature commonly in his sermons. The theme of deception, the devil's main strategy, is paramount – wives may be water spirits, children may be ritual killers, attractive women may be snakes, university students may be cult members or prostitutes, television personalities may be witches, neighbours may be armed robbers, and family homes may conceal occult artifacts.[36] His references to the 'local' (village and family) are interpolated with allusions to his encounters with people in other locations – 'a sister in London', 'a brother in the north', and brief cameos of their problems and cures. Purportedly, the effects of the 'local' can be experienced both at home and abroad. But the expanding 'global' presence of MFM as a counteractive force is regularly documented at the back of the weekly newsletter and the website.[37] A few of MFM's publications are translated into French, including one for business professionals, *Prières de Perce pour les Hommes d'Affaires*. There are also translations of some of his works into Yoruba, Hausa, and Igbo – the main languages of Nigeria.

As stated earlier, Olukoya's theories of affliction and healing are predicated on traditional systems of thought and practice, as well as earlier Christian initiatives to negotiate new boundaries and identities. The advocacy of forceful prayer conjoins both an existential recognition of the vagaries of the spirit world as well as Aladura/ Pentecostal convictions that prayer is a powerful weapon against the panoply of principalities and powers.[38] One could also argue that his techniques reflect traditional beliefs that the spirit forces are capricious and necessitate constant maintenance. But perhaps the distinctiveness of Dr Olukoya's message is that he is advocating a more proactive, than reactive, approach to human ills. It blends modern pop psychology and marriage counseling with tales of bewitchment and sorcery. It could perhaps be more appropriately categorized under the rubric of the 'security gospel' rather than the 'prosperity gospel' movement (England, 2001: 241). Furthermore, it extends the application of traditional ideas of witchcraft agency to modern urban problems, and enjoins supplicants to pray with 'scientific' precision. Moreover, it uses contemporary graphic design and communication technologies to disseminate powerful images of Satan and his agents. In contrast to some of his Pentecostal counterparts, Olukoya does not devote much time and energy to contesting the powers of his competitors.[39]

In sum, MFM's orientation reflects to some extent what Urry, citing Ingold's work on the concept of the 'globe' in environmentalist discourse, terms the 'the local ontology of engagement' as opposed to the 'global ontology of detachment' (Urry, 2000: 46). In this regard the local is not perceived as more narrowly focused or limited than the global but rather based on a contrasting mode of apprehension, 'one based on an active perceptual engagement with components of the dwelt-in world, in the practical business of life, rather than on the detached, disinterested observation of a world apart' (Ingold, 1993: 40).

'Satan Is Good To Think With'

Several of the scholars who have studied modern witchcraft and occult practices in West and South Africa take a slightly different, but arguably more relevant, approach to the local-global distinction. Rather than postulating this in polarized terms, they conclude that the persistence of such beliefs and practices indicates precisely their capacity to *mediate* between the local and the global. In particular, Birgit Meyer's work on Ghanaian Christianity (notably among the Ewe people) persuasively demonstrates that 'images of the Devil and demons are means by which to address the attractive and destructive aspects of Ewe's encounter with global economics, politics and culture' (Meyer, 1999: xxii).[40] In her conclusion, Meyer asserts that Christianity cannot displace beliefs about the Devil because people themselves have to live with contradictions and ambiguities at all levels of their existence (Meyer, 1999). In other words, a dualistic worldview allows for the apparent failure of good up until the end-time, and the call to arms for the faithful provides a means of empowerment (ritual, symbolic, eventually social) in the face of powerlessness and disorder, if not chaos. Moreover, in Meyer's words, 'Satan is "good to think with" about the ambivalence entailed by adopting the new ways and leaving the old' (ibid., p. 111). Taking this notion a little further, Satan is 'good to think with' about local malevolent forces such as witches and water spirits who are viewed as his agents, as well as global conspiratorial forces such as the United Nations, the American entertainment industries, the CIA, the World Bank, IMF, Christian missionaries, Western feminism, al Qaeda, or the Zionist-controlled mass media. Or, to extend Peter Geschiere's point about witchcraft bridging family and state (Geschiere, 1997: 24), and Bastian's about linking rural and urban spaces (Bastian, 1993: 154f.), we might say that satanism adds globalization to the formula. Bastian is reasonably sanguine about the capacity of witchcraft to continue to provide descriptions of deprivation and evil in a changing world.

Likewise, Geschiere writes of the 'incorporative faculty' of witchcraft discourses, and their ability to address, notably through personification, of new inequalities 'from below' (Geschiere, 1997: 24-25; see also Bongmba, 2001). In his extensive study of the ambiguous relationship between politics and the occult in Cameroon, and the 'accumulative' and 'leveling' effects of witchcraft, Geschiere observes that democratization from 1989 onwards did not result in a reduction in witchcraft notions (ibid. p. 205). Rather than countering the occultism of witchcraft, the new public space created uncertainties which allowed rumors about the involvement of witchcraft in politics to flourish. Interestingly, he suggests that the successful rise of the Pentecostal churches, which developed later in Cameroon than in Nigeria or Ghana, to be in part due to their ability to provide a public space where witchcraft was both existentially recognized and effectively dealt with using ritual techniques (Gifford, 2001: 324). Corten and Marshall-Fratani argue, somewhat enthusiastically, that the 'idiom of occult powers' is that aspect of contemporary Pentecostalism which has the greatest potential 'to forge a rapprochement between global and local, between new notions of selfhood and the public space' (Corten and Marshall-Fratani, 2001: 10). The very ambiguity and *bricolage* of such definitions of evil and affliction, in their estimation, permit greater flexibility in 'the creation of local forms of closure and opposition' (ibid. 10-11). Geschiere and Meyer lay particular emphasis on the paradox of 'cultural closure' which is a common response to the experience of 'open-ended global flows' (Geschiere and Meyer 1998). In that regard, MFM's efforts to help Christians purge their lives of nefarious forces can be seen as a defensive, protectionist strategy.

CONCLUSION

Because of the focus of this essay on demonism and deliverance in the context of a fragile nation-state, some readers may expect commentary on the problematic of this type of religious orientation. One might examine the social (family and local group over national or wider human community), psychological (generating rather than alleviating fears), and physiological (sleep deprivation, excessive noise levels), theological (privileging demonology over theology) and cultural (antipathy toward traditional cultural practices) consequences. Such pressing concerns deserve fuller treatment in another context. I have begun to do this elsewhere with a discussion of the negative impact of such demonic discourses on civil society, religious freedom and religious pluralism (Hackett, 2002). For, as Herzfeld insists, '[e]verything in social life is indeed political' (Herzfeld, 2001: 132). The overt or covert discrimination against particular religious communities is antithetical to the development of a human rights culture, which is predicated on non-discrimination and free exercise of religion. It is this consideration, coupled with my advocacy of the need for more informed analysis of the cultural conjunctures and disjunctures within Pentecostalism as they pertain to theories, as well as experiences, of evil and suffering, that I hope exonerates me from Michael Herzfeld's (apposite) criticism of undue scholarly emphasis on sensationalist or exoticized difference (Herzfeld, 2001: 148; cf. Meyer 1999).

Bibliography

Anderson, Allan, *Moya: The Holy Spirit in an African Context*, Pretoria: University of South Africa, 1991.

————, *Bazalwane: African Pentecostals in South Africa*. Pretoria: University of South Africa, 1992.

————, *Tumelo: The Faith of African Pentecostals in South Africa*, Pretoria: University of South Africa, 1993.

Appadurai, Arjun, *Modernity at Large: Cultural Dimensions of Globalization*. Minneapolis, MN: University of Minnesota Press, 1996.

Barbier, Jean-Claude, 'Entre Satan et Jesus-Christ: Le Temoignage d'un Jeune Citadin ou l'Introduction du Dualisme en Afrique Noire', *Societe d'Anthropologie du Sud-Ouest* 29, 1, 1994, 21-29.

Bastian, Misty, '"Bloodhounds Who Have No Friends": Witchcraft and Locality in the Nigerian Popular Press', In J. Comaroff and J. Comaroff (eds.), *Modernity and its Malcontents: Ritual and Power in Postcolonial Africa*, Chicago: University of Chicago, 1993.

Biaya, T. K., 'Postcolonial State Strategies, Sacralization of Power and Popular Proselytization in Congo-Zaire, 1960-1995', in A. A. An-Na'im. (eds.),

Proselytization and Communal Self-Determination in Africa, Maryknoll, NY: Orbis.

Bongmba, Elias Kifon, *African Witchcraft and Otherness: A Philosophical and Theological Critique of Intersubjective Relations*, Albany, NY: State University of New York Press, 2001.

Castells, Manuell, *The Information Age: Economy, Society and Culture*, Vol. I: The Rise of the Nework Society; Vol. II The Power of Identity; Vol. III End of Millennium. Oxford: Blackwell, 1996.

Corten, André, and Ruth Marshall-Fratani, *Introduction*, In A. Corten and R. Marshall-Fratani (eds.), *Between Babel and Pentecost: Transnational Pentecostalism in Africa and Latin America*, 2001.

Corten, A. and R. Marshall-Fratani (eds.), *Between Babel and Pentecost: Transnational Pentecostalism in Africa and Latin America*. Bloomington, IN: Indiana, 2001.

Cox, Harvey, *Fire from Heaven: the Rise of Pentecostal Spirituality and the Reshaping of Religion in the Twenty-first Century*. London: Cassell, 1996.

Dempster, M., B. Klaus, and D. Petersen, (eds.), *The Globalization of Pentecostalism: A Religion Made to Travel*. Oxford and Irvine, CA: Regnum, 1999.

Droogers, André, 'Globalization and Pentecostal Success', In A. Corten and R. Marshall-Fratani *(eds.)*, *Between Babel and Pentecost: Transnational Pentecostalism in Africa and Latin America*, Bloomington, Indiana University Press, 2001.

Englund, Harri, 'The Quest for Missionaries: Transnationalism and Township Pentecostalism in Malawi'. In A. Corten and R. Marshall-Fratani (eds.) *Between Babel and Pentecost: Transnational Pentecostalism in Africa and Latin America*, Bloomington, Indiana University Press, 2001.

Faure, Veronique, 'L'occulte et le politique en Afrique du Sud', In Faure, V., *Dynamiques religieuses en Afrique australe*, Paris: Karthala, 2000.

Freston, Paul, *Evangelicals and Politics in Asia, Africa, and Latin America*, New York: Cambridge University Press, 2001.

———, 'The Transnationalization of Brazilian Pentecostalism: the Universal Church of the Kingdom of God'. In A. Corten and R. Marshall-Fratani, *Between Babel and Pentecost: Transnational Pentecostalism in Africa and Latin America*, Bloomington, Indiana University Press, 2001.

———, 'Globalization, Religion and Evangelical Christianity: A Sociological Meditation from the Third World'. In *Currents in World Christianity*, Pretoria: UNISA Press, 2002.

Geschiere, Peter, *The Modernity of Witchcraft: Politics and the Occult in Postcolonial Africa*. Charlottesville: University Press of Virginia, 1997.

Geschiere, Peter, and Birgit Meyer (eds.) *Globalization and Identity: Dialectics of Flow and Closure.* Oxford: Blackwell, 1998.

Gifford, Paul. *The New Crusaders: Christianity and the New Right in Southern Africa.* London: Pluto, 1991.

———, *African Christianity. Its Public Role,* Bloomington: Indiana University Press, 1998.

———, 'The Complex Provenance of Some Elements of African Pentecostal Theology'. In A. Corten and R. Marshall-Fratani, *Between Babel and Pentecost: Transnational Pentecostalism in Africa and Latin America.* Bloomington: Indiana University Press, 2001.

Gordillo, Gaston, 'The Breath of the Devils: Memories and Places of Experience of Terror', *American Ethnologist* 29, 1, 2002, pp. 33-57.

Hackett, Rosalind I. J, 'New Directions and Connections for African and Asian Charismatics', *Pneuma* 18, 1, 1996, pp. 69-77.

———, 'Prophets', 'False Prophets' and the African State: Emergent Issues of Religious Freedom and Conflict', *Nova Religio* 4, 2, 2001, pp. 187-212.

———, 'Discourses of Demonization in Africa and Beyond', *Diogenes* 199, 2002.

Herzfeld, Michael, *Anthropology: Theoretical Practice in Culture and Society,* Oxford: Blackwell, 2001.

———, 'Media', In M. Herzfeld, *Anthropology: Theoretical Practice in Culture and Society,* Oxford: Blackwell, 2001.

Hunt, Stephen, 'Deliverance: The Evolution of a Doctrine', *Themelios* 21, 1, 1995, pp. 10-13.

———, 'Managing the Demonic: Some Aspects of the Neo-Pentecostal Deliverance Ministry', *Journal of Contemporary Religion* 13, 2, 1998, pp. 215-230.

Idowu, E. Bolaji, 'The Challenge of Witchcraft', *Orita* 4, 1, 1970.

Ingold, T., 'Globes and Spheres: the Topology of Environmentalism', In K. Milton, *Environmentalism,* London: Routledge, 1993.

Kramer, Eric, 'Making Global Faith Universal: Media and a Brazilian Prosperity Movement', *Culture and Religion* 3, 1, 2002, pp. 21-47.

Martin, David, *Tongues of Fire,* Oxford: Blackwell, 1990.

———, *Pentecostalism: The World Their Parish.* Oxford: Blackwell, 2002.

Meer, Erwin van der., 'Reflections on Spiritual Mapping', *Africa Journal of Evangelical Theology* 20, 1, 2001.

Meyer, Birgit, *Translating the Devil: Religion and Modernity among the Ewe in Ghana.* Edinburgh: Edinburgh University Press, 1999.

Ojo, Matthews A., 'Charismatic Movement in Africa', In C. Fyfe and A. F. Walls, *Christianity in Africa in the 1990s*, Edinburgh: Center for African Studies, 1996.

Poewe, Karla (ed.), *Charismatic Christianity as Global Culture*, Columbia, SC: University of South Carolina, 1994.

Robertson, Roland, *Globalization: Social Theory and Global Culture*. London: Sage, 1992.

Taussig, Michael T., *The Devil and Commodity Fetishism in South America*, Chapel Hill: University of North Carolina Press, 1980.

Tomlimson, John, *Globalization and Culture*, Oxford: Polity, 1999.

Urry, John, *Sociology Beyond Societies: Mobilities for the Twenty-first Century*, New York: Routledge, 2000.

van Dijk, Rijk, 'The Soul is the Stranger: Ghanaian Pentecostalism and the Diasporic Contestation of 'Flow' and 'Individuality', *Culture and Religion* 3, 1, 2002, pp. 49-65.

van Dijk, Rijk A., 'Time and Transcultural Technologies of the Self in the Ghanaian Pentecostal Diaspora' In A. Corten and R. Marshall-Fratani, *Between Babel and Pentecost: Transnational Pentecostalism in Africa and Latin America*, Bloomington, Indiana University Press, 2001.

Vries, Hent de, Samuel Weber (eds.), *Religion and Media*, Stanford: Stanford University Press, 2001.

Notes

1. An earlier version of this paper was presented to the African Studies Centre, University of Bayreuth, December 10, 2001. It benefited from the comments of the audience, and especially from Afe Adogame and Ulrich Berner. Portions of the current text have appeared in (Hackett, 2002). I am also grateful to Matthews A. Ojo for his critical insights and research support.

2. Droogers argues that the 'duality of worldview' has a certain universality and he lists it as one of the three principal characteristics of Pentecostalism that enable its global expansion (the other two being experience of the Spirit and the conversion experience) (Droogers, 2001: 56).

3. For a history of the concept, see Hunt (1995, 1998).

4. I am grateful to Matthews A. Ojo for this information. Personal communication, June 25, 2002.

5. A number of popular texts detailing conversion from satanic and occult societies circulated in the 1980s and early 1990s. See, e.g., Emmanuel Eni, *Delivered from the Powers of Darkness* and Kalu Abosi, *Born Twice: From Demonism to Christianity*. See (Barbier, 1994).

6. Paul Gifford has a more extensive list of sources used by Ghanaian pastors in (Gifford, 2001). Reports on the worldwide persecution of Christians are also available in some locations.

7. http://www.uhrc.org/publications/%5B1022501764%5DKanu ngu%20report-website.htm. See also the short report by Jean-Francois Mayer, http://www.religioscope.com/notes/2002/007_mrtcg.htm.

8. Olayiwola Adeniji, 'Parable of the Last Outcast', *This Day* (Lagos), March 19, 2002. Geoffrey Ekenna, 'Will Cloning Undermine Christianity?', *Newswatch* (Lagos), March 10, 2002.

9. For current and recent information on these developments, see www. hrwf.net and www.cesnur.org. For example, the Eritrean government closed all churches except the Orthodox, Catholic and Evangelical Lutheran churches in June 2002. This affected smaller evangelical/Pentecostal churches in particular. Information from the WEA Religious Liberty Commission/HRWF International Secretariat (03.06.2002). See Biaya (1999) for the history of Mobutu's efforts to regulate religious freedom in former Zaire from the 1970s onwards.

10. It was originally scheduled to remain under government wraps for four years but the report was leaked by the *Daily Nation* newspaper.

11. http://www.state.gov/www/global/human_rights/irf/irf_rpt/irf_index.html

12 Otsieno Namwaya, 'Dark Forces, Bloody Rituals under Probe'. *The East African* (Nairobi), August 17, 1999.

13. 'Devil Worship Report the Height of Naivete (Commentary)'. *The Nation*, August 13, 1999.

14. In contrast, the following description appeared in the *New Republic* (July 12, 1993, p. 11) '[i]mpoverished, filthy, steamy, overcrowded and corrupt, Lagos is the ultimate incarnation of the modern megalopolis gone to hell'.

15. D. K. Olukoya, *Power Against Dream Criminals*. Ikeja, Lagos: The Battle Cry Ministries, 2001, p. 153.

16. D. K. Olukoya, *Victory Over Satanic Dreams*. Onike, Yaba, Lagos: Mountain of Fire and Miracles Ministries, 1996, p. 14.

17. D. K. Olukoya, *Power Against Dream Criminals*. Ikeja, Lagos: The Battle Cry Ministries, 2001, p. 169.

18. Ibid., pp. 179-196.

19. 'Your Foundation and Your Problems', *Power Must Change Hands* 12, July-September 2001, p. 18.

20. 'Power against Power', *Fire in the Word*, July 22-28, 2001, p. 2.

21. 'Your Foundation and Your Problems', *Power Must Change Hands* 12, July-September 2001, p. 23.

22. 'Power against Power', *Fire in the Word*, July 22-28, 2001, p. 3.

23. D.K. Olukoya, *Power Against Destiny Catchers*, Onike, Yaba, Lagos: Mountain of Fire and Miracles Ministries, 1996, back cover.

24. D. K. Olukoya, *Victory over Satanic Dreams*, Onike, Yaba, Lagos: Mountain of Fire and Miracles Ministries, 1996, pp. 37-43.

25. D.K. Olukoya, *Power Against Dream Criminals*, Onike, Yaba, Lagos: The Battle Cry Christian Ministries, 2001, p. 170.

26. Ibid., pp. 171-174.

27. D.K. Olukoya, *Power Against Destiny Catchers*, Onike, Yaba, Lagos: Mountain of Fire and Miracles Ministries, 1996, back cover.

'28. Your Foundation and Your Problems'. *Power Must Change Hands* 12, July-September 2001, pp. 20-21.

29. I am grateful to Kingsley Larbi for elucidating this topic. Personal communication, August 5, 2001.

30. www.centralgospel.com

31. Babs Bello, 'Cause of Ethnic Crisis Identified', P.M. News, Lagos, October 30, 2000.

32. Cf. http://www.lagos-online.com

33. See, for example, Ogunsi, Temitope, Lekan Fadeyi and Emma Eke, 'The Ever Rising Case of Ritual Murders'. The Guardian Online (Nigeria), Sunday December 3, 2000. Writing on the experiences of terror among the Toba Indians working in the appalling conditions of Chaco, Argentina, Gaston Gordillo shows how these are inscribed and crystallized in the fear of devils (Gordillo, 2002). He notes also the strong spatial dimensions of these images which are linked in people's minds to capitalist forms of accumulating wealth.

34. While my woman friend who initiated my visit to MFM insisted that the leader was very concerned to treat men and women equally (she herself is a lawyer and runs the lawyers' group in MFM), there does seem to be special vilification of 'marine spirits'. They are generally visually represented as fancy mermaids, preening themselves in their mirrors, sometimes howling in pain as some huge knife lops off their tails or their heads. See, e.g. D. K. Olukoya, *Power Against Marine Spirits*, Onike, Yaba, Nigeria: The Battle Cry Ministries, 1999. The cover of *The 'Tongue Trap*, Onike, Yaba, Nigeria: The Battle Cry Ministries, 1999, seems to perpetuate the stereotype of women talking too much and not being able to keep secrets, it shows a woman being asphyxiated by her own tongue as it wraps itself around her body.

35. Cf. Michael Taussig's study of the significance of the devil in the folk-lore of contemporary plantation workers and miners in South America (Taussig 1980). He finds that the fetishization of evil, in the image of the devil, is an image which mediates between the conflict between pre-capitalist and capitalist modes of objectifying the human condition.

36. Ogbu Kalu refers to this as the 'villageization' of Nigeria. Personal communication, July 14, 1999.

37. For beliefs of Ghanaian Pentecostal migrants in Europe about the demonic and moral threats of the Western world, see (van Dijk 2002).

38. In fact, Olukoya is an admirer of Babalola, founder of the Christ Apostolic Church, and has authored a couple of books on him.

39. See for example the recriminations and accusations which fly between several leading Pentecostalists on the pages of Lagos-based publications such as *The New Treasure* and *National Encomium*.

40. Cf. Veronique Faure's work on South Africa (Faure 2000).

GLOBALIZATION AND INDEPENDENT PENTECOSTALS IN AFRICA FROM A SOUTH AFRICAN PERSPECTIVE

Allan Anderson

THE 'GLOBALIZATION' OF PENTECOSTALISM?

Pentecostalism has become a form of Christianity found in almost every country on earth, and is now one of the dominant Christian expressions in Africa. If this current buzz-word 'globalization' refers to geographical extent, then Pentecostalism is certainly 'globalized'. But if we are talking about some 'supra-cultural' quality of Pentecostalism, that is, its dominant feature, then 'globalization' may not be taken for granted. The Salvadorian Pentecostal anthropologist Ronald Bueno prefers to speak of 'Pentecostalisms' and questions whether talking about the 'globalization' of Pentecostalism is even appropriate:

> Aside from questioning whether there is a perspective shared by all Pentecostals globally, do we run the risk of under-emphasizing to the fatal degree of erasing these sets of historically and politically constructed distinctions? Is 'routinization' or 'globalization' the same thing as imperialism or hegemony of one set of voices over others?[1]

Bueno says that the 'dynamic intersections between the local and global' should be examined in order to explain the 'specific formations of Pentecostalisms'.[2] Pentecostalism has taken many different shapes and sizes in various parts of the world, and in Africa itself there are many widely differing forms, from African initiated churches with a Pentecostal emphasis, to European founded 'classical Pentecostal' churches and most recently, the new Pentecostals and Charismatics. Within these different 'types' there are a bewildering variety of 'sub-types' that complicate the issues even further.

Pentecostalism's strengths lie especially in its ability to adjust itself and 'incarnate' in any culture, and so the particular, local expressions of Pentecostalism (the 'Pentecostalisms') are more important than any 'global' or 'supra-cultural' quality of 'Pentecostalism'. It is 'the quintessential indigenous religion, adapting readily to a variety of cultures', says Byron Klaus.[3] Its emphasis on the 'freedom of the Spirit' militates against any homogenizing or dispassionate standardizing tendencies. Nevertheless, there is a sense in which access to modern electronic media, communications and rapid travel, and the consequential interdependence of Pentecostals and Charismatics the world over, have resulted in certain commonalities within the Pentecostal and Charismatic movements themselves that have affected any local character. This is particularly true of the emphasis on the power and gifts of the Spirit and the sense and experience of the immediacy of God that pervades Pentecostalism throughout the globe, but also is found in such characteristics as an emphasis on prayer, a high view of the Bible, participation of all believers in Christian service and witness, the use of an indigenous leadership, and a conservative Christian morality. Karla Poewe has suggested that Pentecostalism is a 'global culture' as a result of this.[4] But this is not a one-way street, an inexorable process of homogenization. In these discussions, not enough attention has been given to how the so-called 'global culture' is itself changed and formed by its encounter with a local context.

'Globalization' must not be construed to mean an overarching hegemony of an 'international culture' that neatly separates the 'global' from the 'local' and, in the African context, is often seen as the 'Americanization' of African Christianity. In fact, 'globalization' is both defined and limited by the local context. All the common features of Pentecostalism like those mentioned above are reinterpreted and conditioned by the social and religio-cultural context. This chapter will look at how this occurs in the changing phenomenon of Pentecostalism in the African Sub-Sahara, with a focus on South Africa. After looking at the characteristics of the new Pentecostalism in Africa and its expressions in South Africa, the paper will conclude with a discussion of the challenges posed by this form of Christianity for the church throughout the world and for our understanding of Christianity today.

A New Factor in African Christianity

Recognition is being given to the increasingly significant role of a rapidly growing form of African Christianity,[5] that of independent Pentecostal and Charismatic churches.[6] This movement, which emerged in about 1970, is becoming one of the most significant expressions of Christianity on the continent, especially in African cities. We cannot understand African Christianity today without also understanding this latest movement of revival and renewal. Nigerian historian Ogbu Kalu calls it the 'third response' to white cultural domination and power in the church, the former two responses being Ethiopianism at the beginning of the 20th Century and the Aladura/Zionist churches some twenty years later.[7] I consider that this newer Pentecostal and Charismatic movement is not fundamentally different from the Holy Spirit movements and so-called 'prophet-healing' and 'spiritual churches' that preceded it in the African Initiated Churches (AICs),[8] but it is a continuation of them in a different context. The older 'prophet-healing' AICs, the 'classical' Pentecostals and the newer Pentecostal churches have all responded to the existential needs of the African worldview. They have all offered a personal encounter with God through the power of the Spirit, healing from sickness and deliverance from evil in all its manifestations, spiritual, social and structural. This is not to say that there are no tensions or differences between the 'new' and the 'old' AICs, which will be obvious in this chapter.

The entrance and pervading influence of these new churches on the African Christian scene and in the African Diaspora in other continents now make it difficult, if not impossible, to put African churches into types and categories. It is becoming increasingly difficult to define 'Pentecostal' precisely, and narrow perceptions of the term escape reality. In the West, a limited, rather stereotyped and dogmatic understanding of 'Pentecostal' (as those churches that hold that speaking in tongues is the 'initial evidence' of Spirit baptism) fails to recognize the great variety of different Pentecostal movements in most of the rest of the world, many of which arose quite independently of western Pentecostalism. Rather than a precise theological definition, Pentecostal and Charismatic movements are better understood as concerned primarily with the *experience* of the working of the Holy Spirit and the *practice* of spiritual gifts. In this sense, in Africa the term would include the majority of older AICs, those 'classical' Pentecostals originating in western Pentecostal missions, and those newer independent churches, 'fellowships' and 'ministries' in Africa which are the focus of this paper. The 'classical' or 'denominational' Pentecostals (like the Assemblies of God and the Church of God) are also a very active and growing phenomenon throughout Africa, and undoubtedly played a significant role in the emergence of some of the new groups. But as the denominational Pentecostals were founded by missionaries mostly from Britain and North America, although with more African involvement in leadership and financial independence than was the case in most of the older missionary founded churches, they cannot be regarded primarily as African *initiated* movements, even though most of their proliferation was due to the untiring efforts of African preachers.

Pentecostal churches of western origins have operated in Africa for most of the twentieth century. Most of these churches trace their historical origins to the impetus generated by the Azusa Street Revival, which sent out missionaries to fifty nations within two years.[9] The connections between this 'classical' Pentecostal movement and AICs throughout Africa have been amply demonstrated.[10] Some of these 'classical' Pentecostal churches have become vibrant and rapidly expanding African churches throughout the continent, in particular the Assemblies of God, which operates in most countries of the Sub-Sahara. Throughout the history of AICs there has been a predominance of Pentecostal features and phenomena. Although Paul Gifford correctly questions whether the older AICs can be regarded as *paradigmatic* of the Pentecostal movement in Africa,[11] Harvey Cox is at least partly correct to refer to Apostolic/Zionist, Lumpa and Kimbanguist churches as 'the African expression of the worldwide Pentecostal movement'. These churches do not usually define themselves in this way, but not enough attention has been given to the resonance between the 'Spirit' AICs and Pentecostalism.

THE DEVELOPMENT OF NEW CHURCHES

In the 1970s, new independent Pentecostal and Charismatic churches began to emerge all over Africa, especially in West Africa, partly as a reaction to the bureaucratization process in established churches. These vigorous new churches have many similarities all over the continent. Many of them were influenced by the Pentecostal and Charismatic movements in Europe and North America and by established Pentecostal mission churches in Africa. However, it must be remembered that the new churches were largely independent of foreign organizations and had an African foundation. Many arose in the context of interdenominational and evangelical campus and school Christian organizations, from which young charismatic leaders emerged with significant followings, and often the new churches eventually, replaced the former interdenominational movements.[12] At first they were 'nondenominational' churches, but in recent years, as they have expanded, many have developed denominational structures, several prominent leaders have been 'episcopized', and some are now international churches. The process of 'ageing' and the proliferation of these new movements now continue as their founders die or approach old age. The African Charismatic churches or 'ministries' initially tended to have a younger, more formally educated and consequently more westernized leadership and membership, including young professionals and middle class urban Africans. In leadership structures, theology and liturgy, these churches differ quite markedly from the older AICs and the western mission-founded churches, Pentecostal and non-Pentecostal. Their services are usually emotional and enthusiastic, and many churches use electronic musical instruments, publish their own literature and run their own Bible training centers for preachers, both men and women, to further propagate their message. These movements encourage the planting of new independent churches and make use of schoolrooms, cinemas, community halls and even hotel conference rooms for their revival meetings. Church leaders sometimes travel the continent and abroad, and some produce glossy booklets and broadcast radio and television programs. They are often linked to wider international networks of independent

Charismatic preachers, some of which, but by no means all, are dominated by North Americans. The question of North American involvement in the new churches of Africa will be discussed below.

It is argued that these churches are, like the older AICs before them, an African phenomenon, churches that for the most part have been instituted by Africans for Africans. If the 'three-self' formula is applied to determine indigeneity, they are also self-governing, self-propagating and (in some cases to a lesser extent) self-supporting; and usually they have no organizational links with any outside church or denomination. Although they differ from the older AICs in that they do not try as much to offer solutions for traditional problems, yet they do address the type of problems faced by AICs, offering a radical reorientation to a modern and industrial, global society. Kwabena Asamoah-Gyadu makes the interesting point that one of the basic differences between the older AICs and the new churches lies in the fact that in the spiritual churches, 'members are the clients of the prophets who may be the custodians of powers to overcome the ills of life'. In the new churches, however, he says that 'each believer is empowered through the baptism of the Holy Spirit to overcome them.'[13] It may be argued that in the spiritual churches too, provision is made for any person to become a prophet and therefore to be a custodian of spiritual power, and that the difference might not be as great as imagined.

Some of the main methods employed by the new churches are very similar to those used by most Pentecostals – including door-to-door evangelism, meetings held in homes of interested inquirers, preaching in trains, buses, on street corners and at places of public concourse, and 'tent crusades' held all over the continent.[14] Access to modern communications has resulted in the popularizing of western (especially North American) independent Pentecostal 'televangelists', several of whom make regular visits to Africa and broadcast their own television programs there, public scandals notwithstanding. The strategies employed by these evangelists have been subject to criticism,[15] but have had the effect of promoting a form of Christianity that has appealed especially to the urbanized and significantly westernized new generation of Africans. Theologically, these churches are Christocentric but share an emphasis on the power of the Spirit with other Pentecostals, including many AICs. A particular focus on personal encounter with Christ (being 'born again'), long periods of individual and communal prayer, prayer for healing and problems like unemployment and poverty, deliverance from demons and 'the occult' (this term often means traditional beliefs and witchcraft), the use of spiritual gifts like speaking in tongues and (to a lesser extent) prophecy, these features more or less characterize all the independent Pentecostals.

The growth of new churches has been most dramatic in West Africa, especially in Nigeria and Ghana, where many churches arose in interdenominational university student groups, notably the Scripture Union and the Christian Union. These groups later became 'fellowships' that grew into full-blown denominations often led by lecturers and teachers.[16] New churches in West Africa have begun to move from loose associations of 'ministries' to more institutionalized denominations, and in this transition many seem to be moving away from the earlier emphasis on 'prosperity' that resulted from an imitation of the North American televangelists.[17] The new churches tend to be more enthusiastic in their services than the older Pentecostals are, and they usually emphasize miracles and healings more than personal holiness and ethical legalism. A particular emphasis in West African new churches is a stress on the need for deliverance from a whole host of demonic forces, most of which are identified with traditional deities and 'ancestral curses'.[18] These churches have now a great influence, particularly in Nigeria. In 1986 the Pentecostal Fellowship of Nigeria (PFN) was formed, an ecumenical association incorporating most of the various 'born again' movements and one of the most influential ecumenical organizations in Nigeria. By 1995 the PFN was considered the most powerful voice in the national Christian Association of Nigeria of which it is now a part. There were more than 700 churches registered as members of PFN in 1991 in Lagos State alone.[19]

Among the African Diaspora in Europe, the latest churches are these independent Pentecostal and Charismatic churches. They have taken Western Europe by storm since the 1980s and now form the majority of African churches there.[20] A particularly prominent case is the Kingsway International Christian Center in London. This church was founded in 1992 by a Nigerian, Matthew Ashimolowo, formerly a minister in the North American classical Pentecostal church, the International Church of the Foursquare Gospel. The London congregation had over 5,000 members in

2001 and had become the largest congregation in Britain, attracting national media attention. The majority of the members are West Africans, predominantly Nigerians. Large Ghanaian churches like the Church of Pentecost, or other Nigerian ones like the Redeemed Christian Church of God of Pastor Adeboye and the Deeper Life Bible Church of William Kimuyi now have congregations all over Western Europe and North America, and even in places as far afield as Tel Aviv, Israel and Vancouver, Canada. The congregations of the Church of Pentecost are directed from its central headquarters in Accra, through its International Missions Director.

Elsewhere in Africa, new independent Pentecostals were sometimes seen as a threat by older churches, from whom they often gained members. Some of these new churches were directly affected by the phenomenon in West Africa. Preachers like Nigerian Archbishop Benson Idahosa (1938-98), perhaps the most influential African Charismatic preacher and founder (1972) of the Church of God Mission International based in Benin City, Ghanaian Bishop Nicholas Duncan-Williams of the Christian Action Faith Ministries in Accra (1980), and Mensa Otabil of the International Central Gospel Church in Accra (1984) have traveled extensively in several African countries. New churches are active throughout Africa and in some countries they consist of many different smaller groups. For instance, young preachers in Blantyre, Malawi in the 1970s propagated a 'born again' message in their revival meetings that at first did not always result in the formation of new churches. By the 1980s however, the pattern of new churches elsewhere in Africa was emerging. These revival meetings had developed into 'ministries' and 'fellowships', and inevitably some were further institutionalized into new churches. As elsewhere, the Malawian movements focused on young people in schools, colleges and university.[21]

President Frederick Chiluba, a 'born again' Christian with a Pentecostal experience, declared Zambia a 'Christian nation' two months after his landslide election victory in 1991. He appointed 'born-again' Christians to government posts, and regularly promotes Pentecostal evangelistic crusades and conventions, where he is sometimes featured as a preacher. Vice-President Godfrey Miyanda attends a new Pentcostal church, the Jesus Worship Center led by Ernest Chelelwa. New churches are now in abundance in Zambia and the Charismatic movement has split some 'mainline' churches.[22] One of the largest denominations in Zimbabwe is the Zimbabwe Assemblies of God Africa (popularly called ZAOGA), a Pentecostal church with roots in South African Pentecostalism. ZAOGA commenced in urban areas of Zimbabwe in 1967 and is led by Archbishop Ezekiel Guti. Guti went to Christ for the Nations Institute in 1971 just as Benson Idahosa of Nigeria had done, and he too received financial and other resources from the USA. But Guti, like many new church leaders, resists any attempts to identify his church with the 'religious right' of the USA or to be controlled by 'neo-colonial' interests. David Maxwell describes a very pertinent development in 1986, when leaders of twelve of the largest Pentecostal churches in Zimbabwe, including Guti, wrote a 'blistering rebuttal' to a right-wing attack on the Zimbabwean state by a North American Charismatic preacher.[23] Since 1986, ZAOGA has also had churches in Britain, Zimbabwean ZAOGA missionaries went to South Africa to plant churches there in 1989, and the church also has branches in seventeen other African countries called 'Forward in Faith'. ZAOGA is now organized as a full-fledged denomination with complex administrative structures headed by Guti. By 1999 ZAOGA had an estimated 600,000 affiliated members, which made it the third largest denomination in Zimbabwe after the Marange Apostles and the Roman Catholics, with over 10% of the total number of Christians in the country. ZAOGA itself claimed to be the largest, with one and a half million members in 1995, but this figure is disputed. Guti's leadership style and expensive overseas trips became contentious issues in the 1990s. ZAOGA has already experienced various splits, one of the most significant led by Guti's co-founder, Abel Sande.[24] There are several rapidly expanding new Pentecostal churches with branches throughout Zimbabwe.

Indirectly related to the phenomenon of new churches is a growing 'charismatic movement' in many of the older mission-founded churches in Africa, having a profound effect on all forms of Christianity in the continent. Some of the leaders of this Holy Spirit movement in older churches have seceded in the past to form AICs and more recently, new churches. But there are still a considerable number of people who have remained in the older churches with a charismatic form of Christianity, expressed in fellowship and prayer groups, Sunday services and 'renewal' conferences to some extent inspired and encouraged by similar movements in other parts of the world. The older churches have responded to the new churches with innovations that can be described as 'charismatic', where a place is given to gifts of the Holy Spirit in the church. There are many examples of this throughout Africa. One of the best known was the controversial healing ministry of Zambian Roman Catholic Archbishop Emmanuel Milingo, who was removed to Rome thereafter. Other examples are a popular Anglican healing center in Zimbabwe; the Charismatic 'Legion of Christ's Witnesses' (*Iviyo*) association within South African Anglicanism led by Bishop Alpheus Zulu long before the Charismatic movement began in America; a thriving Charismatic movement among Catholics in Uganda; one among Lutherans and in the inter-denominational 'Big November' Crusade' in Tanzania; multitudes of Ghanaian Catholic, Methodist and Presbyterian Charismatics; and the Charismatic movement in Nigerian Anglicanism led by Professor Simeon Onibere.[25] The list could go on.

PENTECOSTALS IN SOUTH AFRICA

In South Africa, new churches may not be quite as prominent as in other parts of Africa, but are nevertheless very significant. Today, some three-quarters of the Black population are members of many 'Protestant' churches, but this figure includes a majority of African initiated/independent churches (AICs), most of which are of a Pentecostal type. South Africa was one of the first countries on the continent to receive Pentecostalism, in 1908. In less than a century, between 10-40% of the population have become Pentecostals, depending on how 'Pentecostal' is defined. The 10% includes 'classical Pentecostals' of several denominations, the largest being the Apostolic Faith Mission, the South African Assemblies of God and the Full Gospel Church of God. It also includes various new Pentecostals and 'Charismatics', and many non-aligned churches. These together would be accepted as 'Pentecostal/Charismatic' by their fellow Pentecostals and Charismatics in the West, with whom they have great affinity, and most of these churches have both Blacks and Whites as members. But the other 30% of the population consists of the almost entirely Black 'Zionist' and 'Apostolic' churches, including the largest denomination in South Africa, the Zion Christian Church (ZCC), and other significant churches like the St Engenas Zion Christian Church, the St John Apostolic

Faith Mission, and the Nazareth Baptist Church (*amaNazaretha*).[26] There are between 4,000 and 7,000 smaller church organizations of a similar type, many being house-churches which form socially meaningful groups both in rural villages and especially in urban sprawls. Almost all of these churches, like all Pentecostal churches, emphasize the power of the Spirit in the church, especially manifested through healing, prophecy, exorcism and speaking in tongues. These are African forms of worldwide Pentecostalism with their genesis in the western Pentecostal movement,[27] which have maintained both historical and theological affinities while developing in quite different and distinctive directions.[28] The Pentecostal movement, including the many African churches that have emanated from it, is not a North American imposition but collectively one of the most significant African expressions of Christianity in South Africa today, where at least ten million people can be identified with a form of Pentecostalism.

The largest Christian congregation here is a white-led Charismatic church, the Rhema Ministries (1980) of Ray McCauley based in Randburg, near Johannesburg, and one of the few multi-ethnic churches in South Africa. McCauley's original inspiration and training came from the father of the 'faith message', Kenneth Hagin of Tulsa, Oklahoma. McCauley attended the Rhema Bible Training Center in Tulsa in 1979. For many years, however, he has cut contact with the Tulsa organization and has toned down his earlier emphasis on the 'prosperity gospel'.[29] Within South Africa, McCauley is President of the International Fellowship of Christian Churches, the largest association of Charismatic churches in the country, and as such he is one of the most significant Christian leaders. During the run-up to the 1994 democratic elections, he was involved in high profile discussions with political leaders, and was part of the 'Rustenburg Declaration' of 1990, a broad church-based document that called for political change, the creation of a democratic society and the end of apartheid. A significant number of Pentecostals were involved in this event.[30] A member of parliament, Kenneth Meshoe, is leader of the African Christian Democratic Party, which polled enough votes in the 1999 elections to gain seven seats in parliament. Meshoe is pastor of the independent Hope of Glory Tabernacle and was formerly an evangelist in German mass evangelist Reinhard Bonnke's Christ for the Nations organization, which was formerly based in South Africa.

Secretary General of the ANC turned business magnate, Cyril Ramaphosa, who headed the ANC negotiation team in the period leading to the 1994 elections, was formerly a Pentecostal, and at the University of the North near Pietersburg in the early 1970s was chair of the local Student Christian Movement (SCM), but his political activities were seen as inconsistent with his Christian faith by most Pentecostals. His fellow student at university and successor to the chair of the SCM was Frank Chikane. Now Director General of President Thabo Mbeki's 'Office of the President', Chikane, is a 'classical' Pentecostal and was still Vice-President of South Africa's largest Pentecostal denomination, the Apostolic Faith Mission, in 2001. Chikane is a person of considerable influence, having one of the most powerful executive positions in the ANC government and being well placed to speak on behalf of South Africa's large Christian constituency. He maintains personal relationships with the ruling ANC hierarchy and church leaders across the denominational board from new churches to ecumenical 'mainline' churches. He has the unique distinction of having been General Secretary of the South African Council of Churches during apartheid's final years, the only Pentecostal to occupy that position, and he also spent some time in Bonnke's organization.

The largest single Christian congregation in Soweto, South Africa is the Grace Bible Church led by Mosa Sono, with over 6,000 members in 2001. This church has planted new congregations in some major urban areas, including the poverty-stricken 'informal settlement' (slum) area of Orange Farm, outside Soweto. Sono, born in Soweto in 1961, grew up in the Dutch Reformed Church, and attended the AFM Bible College in Soshanguve before leaving to attend McCauley's Rhema Bible Training Center in Randburg. He formed Grace Bible Church in 1984, and in 1996 he became Vice-President of the International Fellowship of Christian Churches (IFCC). Although the connection between some of these new churches and North American 'prosperity' preachers is apparent, Sono, and increasingly, McCauley too, are cautious regarding the 'Word of Faith' teaching. Sono has repeatedly sought to distance himself from 'prosperity theology' and western, white domination, and there are signs that his stance is having a positive influence on McCauley.[31]

The historic Truth and Reconciliation Commission (TRC), held between 1996 and 1998, was chaired by Anglican Archbishop Desmond Tutu. This unique event was also a watershed for the Pentecostal and Charismatic churches, especially as their national significance was recognized by an invitation to address the TRC in November 1997. Both the IFCC and the AFM made representations to the TRC on behalf of Pentecostal and Charismatic churches. Ray McCauley, representing the IFCC, confessed the 'shortcomings' of White Charismatics who 'hid behind their so-called spirituality while closing their eyes to the dark events of the apartheid years'. The AFM was represented by its President Isak Burger and Vice-President Frank Chikane. After showing a videotape of the historic unity celebration the previous year, they confessed that they 'jointly accepted responsibility for the past' and had 'helped maintain the system of apartheid and prolong the agony'.[32] The representations of the IFCC and the AFM indicate that a significant change of view had taken place, and that the apartheid government was now seen as part of the invisible evil forces that had been overcome by good forces of reconciliation and truth.

The Challenge of the Newer Churches

A consequence of the globalization debate is that one of the main criticisms levelled against new Pentecostal churches is that they propagate a 'prosperity gospel', the 'Faith' or 'Word' movement originating in North American independent Charismatic movements, particularly found in the preaching and writings of Kenneth Hagin and Kenneth Copeland. This 'health and wealth' gospel seems to reproduce some of the worst forms of capitalism in Christian guise. Paul Gifford has become a leading exponent on this subject. He suggests that the biggest single factor in the emergence of these new churches is the collapse of African economies by the 1980s and the subsequent increasing dependence of new churches on the USA. He proposes that it is 'Americanization' rather than any 'African quality' that is responsible for the growth of these churches. He sees this new phenomenon as a type of neo-colonialism propagated by American 'prosperity preachers', a sort of 'conspiracy theory'.[33] But there is another side to this scenario. Gifford's analysis, which he has modified to some extent more recently,[34] has been accepted in many church and academic circles. However, it seems to ignore some fun-

damental features of the globalization of Pentecostalism. As Pentecostalism is now predominantly a Third World phenomenon, their
experience and practice are more important than formal ideology
or even theology. As Kalu points out, the relationship between the
African new church pastor and his or her 'western patron' is entirely
eclectic, and the 'dependency' in fact has been mutual. The western
supporter often needs the African pastor to bolster his own international image and increase his own financial resources. Kalu observes
that in the 1990s, since the public disgracing of American 'televangelists', the mood in Africa has changed, and new churches are now
'characterized by independence and an emphasis on the Africanist
roots of the ministries'.[35] With reference to AICs, Daneel points out
that in traditional Africa, 'wealth and success are naturally signs of
the blessing of God', so it is no wonder that such a message should
be uncritically accepted there – and this is as true for the newer
AICs as it is for the older ones.[36] There *are* connections between
some of the new churches and the American 'health and wealth'
movement, and it is also true that some of the new African churches
reproduce and promote 'health and wealth' teaching and literature.
But identifying new churches with the American 'prosperity gospel'
is a generalization that particularly fails to appreciate the recon-
structions and innovations made by these new African movements
in adapting to a radically different context, just as the older AICs did
some years before. This is a case where outside observers' emphasis
on 'globalization' or 'Americanization' has obscured the local, African
nature of these new movements.

The new churches form a new challenge to the whole Christian
church in Africa. To the European mission-founded churches, they
are demonstrations of a form of Christianity that appeals to a new
generation of Africans, and from which older churches can learn.
There are indications that the new churches increase at the expense
of all types of older churches, including the prophet-healing AICs.[37]
To these older AICs, with whom they actually have much in
common, they are consequently often a source of tension. The new
churches preach against 'tribalism' and parochial denominationalism. They are often sharply critical of the older AICs, particularly in
what they perceive as the African traditional religious component
of AIC practices, which are sometimes seen as manifestations of
demons needing 'deliverance'.[38] As a result, older AICs feel hurt and
threatened by them. In addition, the new churches have, to some

extent, embraced and externalized western notions of a 'nuclear family' and individualized, urban lifestyles. This brings them into further tension with African traditional culture and ethnic ties, thereby enabling members to escape the onerous commitments to the extended family and to achieve success and accumulate possessions independently.[39] The new churches also sometimes castigate 'mainline' churches for their dead formalism and traditionalism, so the 'mainline' churches also feel threatened by them. Commenting on this, Ogbu Kalu makes the salient point:

> The established churches usually react in three stages: hostility, apologetics and adaptation. Institutionalisation breeds late adoption of innovations. We witnessed this pattern in the response to the Aladura challenge. It is being repeated without any lessons learnt from history.[40]

Gifford himself is aware of the problems inherent in a too simplistic interpretation of the newer African Pentecostalism. After discussing Christian fundamentalism in the USA and the 'rapidly growing sector of African Christianity' closely related to it, he says that the American groups operating in Africa 'find themselves functioning in a context considerably different from that in the United States.'[41] Perhaps Gifford has not taken this 'considerably different' context seriously enough in his substantial analyses of the newer Pentecostals in Africa. The oversimplified and patronizing idea that 'prosperity' churches in Africa are led by unscrupulous manipulators greedy for wealth and power does not account for the increasing popularity of these new churches with educated and responsible people, who continue to give financial support and feel their needs are met there.[42] Often, those who are 'anti-charismatic' and resent or are threatened by the growth and influence of the newer churches are the source of these criticisms. Kalu says that in the decade after 1985, the new churches 'blossomed into complex varieties' and that in their development, 'European influence became more pronounced'. But he points out that in spite of this, 'the originators continued to be African, imitating foreigners, eclectically producing foreign theologies but transforming these for immediate contextual purposes.'[43] Matthews Ojo, who writes extensively on Nigerian new churches, says that they 'are increasingly responding to the needs and aspirations of Nigerians amid the uncertainty of their political life and the pain of their constant and unending economic adjustments.'[44] It is clear, then, that new churches are not simply an 'Americanization' of African Christianity.

Like the churches before them, the new churches have a sense of identity as a separated and egalitarian community with democratic access to spiritual power, whose primary purpose is to promote their cause to those outside. These churches see themselves as the 'born again' people of God, with a strong sense of belonging to the community of God's people, those chosen from out of the world to witness to the new life they experience in the power of the Spirit. The cornerstone of their message is this 'born again' conversion experience through repentance of sin and submission to Christ and this is what identifies them, even to outsiders.[45] Unlike the older AICs, where there tends to be an emphasis on the prophet figure or principal leader as the one dispensing God's gifts to his or her followers, the new churches usually emphasize the availability and encourage the practice of gifts of the Holy Spirit by all of their members. The emergence of these churches at the end of the twentieth century indicates that there are unresolved questions facing the church in Africa, such as the role of 'success' and 'prosperity' in God's economy, enjoying God *and* his gifts, including healing and material provision, and the holistic dimension of 'salvation' which is always meaningful in an African context. Asamoah-Gyadu believes that the 'greatest virtue' of the 'health and wealth' gospel of the new churches lies in 'the indomitable spirit that believers develop in the face of life's odds... In essence, misfortune becomes only temporary.'[46] The 'here-and-now' problems being addressed by new churches in modern Africa are not unlike those faced by the older AICs decades before, and these problems still challenge the church as a whole today. They remind the church of the age-old conviction of Africa that for any faith to be relevant and enduring, it must also be experienced.

Bibliography

Anderson, Allan, 'The Prosperity Message in the Eschatology of Some New Charismatic Churches in South Africa', *Missionalia* 15, 2, 1987, pp. 72-83.

Anderson, Allan, *Bazalwane: African Pentecostals in South Africa*, Pretoria: University of South Africa Press, 1992.

Anderson, Allan, 'Dangerous Memories for South African Pentecostals', In Allan Anderson and Walter J Hollenweger (eds), *Pentecostals After a*

Century: *Global Perspectives on a Movement in Transition.* Sheffield: Sheffield Academic Press, 1999, pp. 89-107.

Anderson, Allan, *Zion and Pentecost: The Spirituality and Experience of Pentecostal and Zionist/ Apostolic Churches in South Africa.* Pretoria: University of South Africa Press, 2000.

Anderson, Allan, *African Reformation: African Initiated Christianity in the Twentieth Century.* Trenton, NJ: Africa World Press, 2001.

Anderson, Allan and Samuel Otwang, *Tumelo: The Faith of African Pentecostals in South Africa,* Pretoria: University of South Africa Press, 1993.

Anderson, Allan and Gerald J. Pillay, 'The Segregated Spirit: The Pentecostals', Richard Elphick & Rodney Davenport (eds.), *Christianity in South Africa: A Political, Social & Cultural History,* Oxford: James Currey & Cape Town: David Philip, 1997, pp. 227-241.

Asamoah-Gyadu, Kwabena J., 'Traditional missionary Christianity and new religious movements in Ghana', MTh thesis, Accra: University of Ghana, 1996.

Asamoah-Gyadu, Kwabena J., 'The Church in the African State: The Pentecostal/Charismatic Experience in Ghana', *Journal of African Christian Thought,* 1, 2, 1998, pp. 51-57.

Bueno, Ronald N. 'Listening to the Margins: Re-historicizing Pentecostal Experiences and Identities', In Murray W Dempster, Byron D Klaus & Douglas Petersen (eds), *The Globalization of Pentecostalism: A Religion Made to Travel,* Oxford: Regnum Books, 1999, pp. 268-288.

Cox, Harvey, *Fire from Heaven: the Rise of Pentecostal Spirituality and the Reshaping of Religion in the Twentieth-First Century,* London: Cassell, 1996.

Daneel, Inus, *Quest for Belonging,* Gweru, Zimbabwe: Mambo Press, 1987.

Gifford, Paul, 'Reinhard Bonnke's mission to Africa, and his 1991 Nairobi crusade', in Gifford, Paul (ed.), *New Dimensions in African Christianity,* Nairobi: All Africa Conference of Churches, 1992.

Gifford, Paul, *Christianity and Politics in Doe's Liberia,* Cambridge: Cambridge University Press, 1993.

Gifford, Paul (ed), *The Christian Churches and the Democratization of Africa,* Leiden: E.J. Brill, 1995.

Gifford, Paul, *African Christianity: Its Public Role.* London: Hurst, 1998.

Hayes, Stephen, *Black Charismatic Anglicans: The Iviyo loFakazi bakaKristu and its relations with other renewal movements,* Pretoria: University of South Africa Press, 1990.

Hollenweger, Walter J, *The Pentecostals,* London: SCM, 1972.

Johnstone, Patrick, *Operation World.* Carlisle, UK: OM Publishing, 1993.

Kalu, Ogbu U, 'The Third Response: Pentecostalism and the Reconstruction of Christian Experience in Africa, 1970-1995', *Journal of African Christian Thought,* 1, 2, 1998, pp. 3-16.

Klaus, Byron D, 'Pentecostalism as a Global Culture: An Introductory Overview', in Murray W Dempster, Byron D Klaus & Douglas Petersen (eds), *The Globalization of Pentecostalism: A Religion Made to Travel,* Oxford: Regnum Books, 1999, pp. 127-130.

Marshall, Ruth, 'Pentecostalism in Southern Nigeria: an overview', Gifford, Paul (ed.), *New Dimensions in African Christianity,* Nairobi: All Africa Conference of Churches, 1992, pp. 7-32.

Maxwell, David, 'Witches, Prophets and Avenging Spirits: The Second Christian Movement in North-East Zimbabwe', *Journal of Religion in Africa* 25, 3, 1995, pp. 309-335.

Maxwell, David, '"Delivered from the Spirit of Poverty": Pentecostalism, Prosperity and Modernity in Zimbabwe'. *Journal of Religion in Africa* 28, 4, 1998, pp. 350-373

Meiring, Piet, *Chronicle of the Truth Commission,* Vanderbijlpark: Carpe Diem Books, 1999.

Meyer, Birgit,'"Make a Complete Break with the Past": Memory and Post-Colonial Modernity in Ghanaian Pentecostalist Discourse', *Journal of Religion in Africa* 28, 4, 1998, pp. 316-349.

Milingo, Emmanuel, *The World in Between: Christian Healing and the Struggle for Spiritual Survival,* London: Hurst, 1984.

Mlahagwa, Josiah R.'Contending for the Faith: Spiritual Revival & the Fellowship Church in Tanzania', in Thomas Spear & Isaria N. Kimambo (eds), *East African Expressions of Christianity,* Oxford: James Currey, 1999, pp. 296-306.

Ojo, Matthews A.'The Church in the African State: The Charismatic/Pentecostal Experience in Nigeria', *Journal of African Christian Thought,* 1, 2, 1998, pp. 25-32.

Poewe, Karla (ed.), *Charismatic Christianity as a Global Culture,* Columbia: University of South Carolina Press, 1994.

Synan, Vinson, *The Holiness-Pentecostal Tradition: Charismatic Movements in the Twentieth Century,* Grand Rapids & Cambridge: Eerdmans, 1997.

Ter Haar, Gerrie, *Halfway to Paradise: African Christians in Europe,* Cardiff: Cardiff Academic Press, 1998.

Van Dijk, Richard, 'Young Born-Again Preachers in post-independence Malawi: the significance of an extraneous identity', in Gifford, Paul (ed.), *New Dimensions in African Christianity,* Nairobi: All Africa Conference of Churches, 1992, pp. 55-65.

Notes

1. Ronald N Bueno,'Listening to the Margins: Re-historicizing Pentecostal Experiences and Identities, in Murray, Dempster, Byron, Klaus & Douglas, Petersen (eds), *The Globalization of Pentecostalism: A Religion Made to Travel*, Oxford: Regnum Books, 1999, p. 269.

2. Bueno,'Listening, p. 271.

3. Byron, Klaus, 'Pentecostalism as a Global Culture: An Introductory Overview, Murray, Dempster, Byron, Klaus & Douglas, Petersen (eds), *The Globalization of Pentecostalism: A Religion Made to Travel*, Oxford: Regnum Books, 1999, 127.

4. Poewe, Karla (ed), *Charismatic Christianity as a Global Culture*. Columbia: University of South Carolina Press, 1994.

5. For more details on New Pentecostals throughout Africa, see Allan Anderson, *African Reformation: African Initiated Christianity in the Twentieth Century*, Trenton, NJ: Africa World Press, 2001, pp. 167-186.

6. David Maxwell,'Witches, Prophets and Avenging Spirits: The Second Christian Movement in North-East Zimbabwe, *Journal of Religion in Africa* 25, 3, 1995, p. 313; Paul Gifford, *African Christianity: Its Public Role*, London: Hurst, 1998, p. 31; Allan Anderson, *Zion and Pentecost: The Spirituality and Experience of Pentecostal and Zionist/Apostolic Churches in South Africa*, Pretoria: University of South Africa Press, 2000, pp. 237-55.

7. Ogbu U. Kalu, 'The Third Response: Pentecostalism and the Reconstruction of Christian Experience in Africa, 1970-1995, *Journal of African Christian Thought*, 1, 2, 1998, p. 3.

8. The terms 'African Independent Church' and 'African Indigenous Church' have been substituted more recently with 'African Initiated Church' or 'African Instituted Church, all using the now familiar acronym 'AIC'.

9. Walter J. Hollenweger, *The Pentecostals*, London: SCM, 1972, pp. 22-4; Vinson Synan, *The Holiness-Pentecostal Tradition: Charismatic Movements in the Twentieth Century*, Grand Rapids & Cambridge, 1997, pp. 84-106.

10. Anderson, *African Reformation*, 69-163; Allan H. Anderson & Gerald J. Pillay, 'The Segregated Spirit: The Pentecostals, Elphick, Richard & Davenport, Rodney (eds.), *Christianity in South Africa: A Political, Social & Cultural History*, Oxford: James Currey & Cape Town: David Philip, 1997, pp. 228-9; Allan H. Anderson, 'Dangerous Memories for South African Pentecostals, Anderson, Allan H. & Hollenweger, Walter J. (eds.), *Pentecostals After a Century: Global Perspectives on a*

Movement in Transition. Sheffield: Sheffield Academic Press, 1999, pp. 88-92; Allan Anderson, *Bazalwane: African Pentecostals in South Africa,* Pretoria: University of South Africa Press, pp. 22-4; Allan Anderson, *Zion and Pentecost,* pp. 56-74.

11. Harvey Cox, *Fire from Heaven: the Rise of Pentecostal Spirituality and the Reshaping of Religion in the Twentieth-First Century,* London: Cassell, 1996, p. 246; Gifford, *African Christianity,* p. 33.

12. Kwabena J. Asamoah-Gyadu, 'Traditional missionary Christianity and new religious movements in Ghana', MTh thesis, Accra: University of Ghana, 1996; Kalu, 'Third Response', p. 7.

13. Kwabena J. Asamoah-Gyadu, 'The Church in the African State: The Pentecostal/Charismatic Experience in Ghana', *Journal of African Christian Thought,* 1, 2, 1998, p. 56.

14. This latest expression of African Pentecostalism is to some extent the result of the popular method of tent evangelism pioneered mainly by North Americans in the 1940s and 1950s (with roots in the nineteenth century revivals). This was continued with considerable effect by popular South African black Pentecostals Nicholas Bhengu and Richard Ngidi, and more recently by Nigerian Benson Idahosa and German evangelist Reinhard Bonnke.

15. For example, see Paul Gifford, 'Reinhard Bonnke's mission to Africa, and his 1991 Nairobi crusade', Gifford, Paul (ed.), *New Dimensions in African Christianity,* Nairobi: All Africa Conference of Churches, 1992, p. 157.

16. Ruth Marshall, 'Pentecostalism in Southern Nigeria: An overview', Gifford, *New Dimensions,* p. 9; Paul Gifford (ed.), *The Christian Churches and the Democratization of Africa,* Leiden: E.J. Brill, 1995, p. 244.

17. Marshall, pp. 15-16, 25.

18. Birgit Meyer,'"Make a Complete Break with the Past": Memory and Post-Colonial Modernity in Ghanaian Pentecostalist Discourse', *Journal of Religion in Africa* 28, 4, 1998, pp. 323-4; Gifford, *African Christianity,* pp. 97-109.

19. Gifford, *Christian Churches,* p. 256; Marshall, pp. 23-9.

20. Gerrie ter Haar, *Halfway to Paradise: African Christians in Europe,* Cardiff: Cardiff Academic Press, 1998, p. 97.

21. Richard van Dijk,'Young Born-Again Preachers in post-independence Malawi: the significance of an extraneous identity', in Gifford, *New Dimensions,* pp. 55-65.

22. Gifford, *African Christianity,* pp. 197-205, 220, 230, 233.

23. David Maxwell, "'Delivered from the Spirit of Poverty": Pentecostalism, Prosperity and Modernity in Zimbabwe', in *Journal of Religion in Africa* 28, 4, 1998, p. 357; Gifford, *Christian Churches*, p. 123.

24. Maxwell, 'Delivered', pp. 351-2, 366-8, 372, n. 8; Johnstone, p. 598; Gifford, *Christian Churches*, p. 121.

25. Emmanuel Milingo, *The World in Between: Christian Healing and the Struggle for Spiritual Survival*, London: Hurst, 1984; Stephen Hayes, *Black Charismatic Anglicans: The Iviyo loFakazi bakaKristu and its relations with other renewal movements*, Pretoria: University of South Africa Press, 1990; Josiah R. Mlahagwa, 'Contending for the Faith: Spiritual Revival and the Fellowship Church in Tanzania', in Spear, Thomas, & Kimambo, Isaria N. (eds.), *East African Expressions of Christianity*, Oxford: James Currey, 1999, pp. 296-306; Gifford, *African Christianity*, pp. 95-6, 154, 227-8, 330.

26. Another 30% of the population belonged to Protestant churches and 12% were Catholics. Percentages given are very approximate estimates, based on available statistics, and do not include the numbers of people in Protestant and Catholic churches who would be 'Charismatic'. See Allan Anderson and Samuel Otwang, *Tumelo: The Faith of African Pentecostals in South Africa*, Pretoria: University of South Africa Press, 1993, pp. 3-9, 14-5.

27. Hollenweger, *The Pentecostals*, p. 120; Cox, *Fire from Heaven*, p. 246; Anderson, *Zion and Pentecost*, pp. 56-63.

28. For recent information on South African Pentecostalism as well as historical detail, see Anderson, *Zion and Pentecost*.

29. Allan Anderson, 'The prosperity message in the eschatology of some new Charismatic churches in South Africa', *Missionalia* 15, 2, 1987, pp. 72-83.

30. *Rustenburg Declaration: National Conference of Churches in South Africa*, Pretoria: National Initiative for Reconciliation, 1990.

31. Anderson, *Bazalwane*, pp. 52-5; Anderson, *Zion and Pentecost*, pp. 201-17, 237-55; Gifford, *African Christianity*, pp. 236-7.

32. Piet Meiring, *Chronicle of the Truth Commission*. Vanderbijlpark: Carpe Diem Books, 1999, pp. 275-7.

33. Gifford, *Christianity and Politics*, pp. 196-9, 294, 314-5.

34. See for example Gifford, *African Christianity*, pp. 236-44.

35. Kalu, 'Third Response', p. 8.

36. Inus Daneel, *Quest for Belonging*, Gweru, Zimbabwe: Mambo Press, 1987, p. 46; Gifford, *Christianity and Politics*, p. 188.

37. Ter Haar, 'Standing Up', p. 224; Marshall, p. 5; Meyer, p. 319; Gifford, *African Christianity*, pp. 62-3, 95, 233.

38. Asamoah-Gyadu, 'The church', p. 56; Marshall, p. 11; Kalu, 'Third Reponse', p. 8.

39. Meyer, p. 320; Maxwell, p. 354; Marshall, pp. 21-2.

40. Kalu, 'Third Response', p. 3.

41. Gifford, *African Christianity*, p. 43.

42. Marshall, p. 8, 24.

43. Kalu, 'Third Response', p. 7.

44. Matthews A.Ojo, 'The Church in the African State: The Charismatic/ Pentecostal Experience in Nigeria', *Journal of African Christian Thought*, 1, 2, 1998, p. 25.

45. Marshall, p. 9; Gifford, *Christian Churches*, p. 244.

46. Asamoah-Gyadu, 'The church', p. 55.

New Pentecostal Churches and Prosperity Theology in Nigeria

Deji Ayegboyin

Introduction

It is important to mention here that wealth is not evil. Rather, it provides answers to your social needs. There is a natural demand for money in daily life. From the scriptures, it is clear that wisdom is what begets wealth. Wealth will come as a result of your acquisition and utilization of covenant sense... Keep at it! Keep at your tithing and kingdom investments. Do it delightfully... No matter how angry the devil is, when your cloud is full, your rainfall is sure.[1]

This kind of teaching emphasizing 'covenant access to a world of financial fortune' has gained much currency in most new generation churches in Nigeria. In these churches, prosperity, not only in things spiritual but also in the secular realm, is accentuated. Poverty is no longer seen as an ideal to be striven for; rather pauperism, destitution and slender means are simply interpreted as God's chastisement.

This teaching seems a clear departure from the pre-occupation of the mainstream Christian organizations, which regarded material wealth as possible impediments in the path of the Christian's journey towards heaven. Before the 1970's the main-line or historic churches demonstrated that they were more concerned about 'saving souls' than other things including 'nurturing of the body' which were given secondary importance. Besides, the world was painted as a wicked place of darkness that militates against the aspirations of the children of light who are bound for the celestial city. In a sense they preached 'poverty theology' which contends that possessions are a curse and condemn materialism in every form.'[2] Consequently, they advocated that there must be as little attachment to this world as possible.[3]

The above thinking has characterized the religious divide between the new- Pentecostals and the mainline churches; prosperity teaching being the major factor. This situation has persisted until recently when new common grounds for interaction are emerging between the two. There is now a genuine need for re-thinking prosperity theology in relation to spirituality in the emergent globalization process. This chapter begins with some introductory remarks on the background to the new Pentecostal churches, most of which emphasize prosperity teaching. It situates these movements within their historical context and examines briefly their primary characteristics. The case study of Bishop Oyedepo's Living Faith Church Worldwide Inc. (Winners' Chapel) is a choice made from a rich variety of prosperity preaching churches in Nigeria. It is suggested that David Oyedepo is the most communicative among this variety. An evaluation of prosperity teaching is made in order to demonstrate that there is the need for a rethinking in the formulation and dissemination of prosperity theology in Nigeria.

Situating the New-Pentecostals

As Ogbu Kalu has rightly cautioned, it is necessary to pay close attention to periodization.[4] In Nigeria as well as in some other African countries, the Pentecostal wind blew strongly from the 1970's. This new wave evidently assumed a different disposition from 'classical Pentecostalism,'[5] which held sway from the 1920's. From the 1980's a new form of Pentecostalism grew at a tremendous speed and flourished in complex varieties. This phenomenon is probably not unconnected with the country's adoption of a structural adjustment program and its attendant problems. One of the obvious effects of the implementation of the program was the massive devaluation of the national currency by more than one thousand percent. The corollary of it all was that the quality of life of the majority of Nigerians was altered for the worse, by the very high level of inflation that followed the successive devaluation of the Nigerian currency *Naira*. With these came high levels of unemployment and stagnant wages.[6] Ingenious Nigerians employed a variety of survival mechanisms during these hard times. These included multiple job holdings, illegal activities, begging, 'child labor'[7] and so on. It was at this time more than ever before that many seemed to have found in religious institutions, especially, in the charismatics, an oasis in the midst of the economic turmoil and spiritual drought that seemed to prevail everywhere. Indeed, there was a rich variety of voices in the emergent movement but in spite of the complexities, two types of Pentecostal movements are discernible. The first is the group that has 'holiness' and 'righteousness' as its hallmark. In adopting these values, this group was evidently influenced by the classical Pentecostals. We reserve the term Charismatic Pentecostals for them.[8] In this category are The Deeper Life Bible Church, the Holiness Evangelical Mission and Holiness Bible Church. These stress baptism in the Holy Spirit, holiness of life ethics leading to perfection and the mandate to mission. The second group, on which we shall focus, is known for its emphasis on the faith message for healing and prosperity.

PROSPERITY CHURCHES

As we have done elsewhere,[9] we would like to classify these churches as new Pentecostals. All churches in this category date from the 1980's.[10] Some draw their structural and operational inspiration from American Pentecostalism,[11] as they embark on an aggressive drive for membership and accentuate the theology of affluence. A number of these 'prosperity preachers' as some prefer to call them, have written several books, tracts and handbills and made hundreds of audio and videocassette tapes all giving scriptural principles for prosperity, health and happiness. Indeed, there are varieties of prosperity preachers. They develop different versions of the message, making the Gospel to suit them and encourage their adherents to give generously in order to 'reap a bountiful harvest'. Because of their unprecedented emphasis on material prosperity, they have been given epithets such as: 'Give and Prosper Churches', 'Jesus Trading Company', 'Prosperity Liability International Incorporation'. Examples of prosperity churches abound in Nigeria. They include the Church of God Mission in Benin, which was founded by the Late Archbishop Benson Idahosa. He is often referred to as the prime celebrity of material prosperity preaching in Nigeria. He reasoned that the divine boom of the 1970's was to provide believers with material, physical and financial needs and to enhance the furtherance of the course of the gospel. His catch phrase is '*Expect a miracle...you are made for success and not for failure*'. Archbishop Idahosa is reputed to be mentor to a multitude of prosperity preachers. Quite a number of these ministers were ordained by Archbishop Idahosa.[12] Another prominent prosperity preacher is Gabriel Oduyemi of the Bethel Ministry situated in the *nouveau riche* Lekki Peninsula, Epe. He, like Archbishop Idahosa, has a bold inscription in his church '*the God we serve is not a poor God*'.

One of the most recent in the catalogue is Pastor Patrick Ngozi Anwuzia, a food technologist turned pastor. He is the founder of Zoe Ministry International in Lagos. He stresses that anyone 'who would receive God's abundant blessings must first of all give abundantly to God'.[13] He has an ally in Rev Mensa Otabil who decreed 'If you haven't deposited anything, you have no right to ask for anything'[14] A few others in the list include Francis Wale Oke, a land and engineering surveyor, the president and presiding Bishop of the Sword of the Spirit Ministries; Tunde Joda of Christ Chapel. Ruth Marshall describes him as an articulate pastor who leads highly emotional and charismatic service.[15] He has opened several churches like the Household of God Fellowship and Powerline Bible Church which have similar doctrinal approaches.[16] The list is inexhaustible but we must include the amiable brothers, George Adewale Adegboye of the Ever Increasing Word Ministries (a.k.a Rhema Chapel founded in 1987) and Alex Adegboye, senior pastor of the World Alive Ministries: The Stone Church (founded in 1993). One of the most popular is David Oyedepo, founder and presiding bishop of the Living Faith Church Worldwide Inc. (a.k.a.Winners Chapel).

CHARACTERISTICS AND EMPHASIS OF THE 'PROSPERITY CHURCHES'

As Paul Gifford observed concerning Mensa Otabil, the founder of International Central Gospel Church, prosperity preachers present themselves as entrepreneurs who have developed a successful enterprise and thus should serve as models for enterprising businessmen.'[17] First, in their bid to stress the teaching of victorious, prosperous and healthy living in the spiritual as well as in the physical realm, they start from the premise that *Jehovah Jireh* 'our provider', is a God of abundance. He owns the silver and the gold. He has placed us in the world of abundance and it is His perfect will for Christians to prosper. They emphasise that because of centuries of misinformation, the Holy Spirit is now striving to bring the body of Christ to a new faith level and a greater revelation of truth so that the material things needed could be brought in to communicate the gospel and make the church prosper.

Secondly, they teach and demonstrate that Christians should excel both spiritually and materially. In consequence of this they dispute the views of mainline Christians and Holiness movements who hold that it is worldly or carnal to have wealth or modern conveniences or to wear the best clothes and drive the latest cars. Consequently, a good number of the ministers exhibit flamboyance and high social taste. Quite a number possess and drive in a convoy and in exotic cars with a few boasting that they own private jets,[18] have assets both in Nigeria and abroad and patronize big banks.

Thirdly, in the midst of the competitive religious landscape of Christian Ministries, Churches and para-churches, 'enlisting' new members into these churches has come to require and involve all the subtleties of modern marketing strategies. As Ukah rightly observes, in order to mobilize the public for patronage, the new Pentecostals employ 'marketing drives and strategies in the range of their advertisements in both print and electronic media.'[19] They sell their 'wares and products'. These products are not only tangible things like books, tapes (audio and video) and stickers but also ideas and services[20] like deliverance sessions, retreats for 'singles' (spinsters and bachelors), marriage seminars, counseling sessions, assembly for 'those waiting on the Lord for the fruit of the womb', 'Rebecca' retreats for 'those waiting on the Lord for partners', monthly crusades, and annual conventions at big stadia. In their bid to do these effectively, the churches 'mobilize the public for patronage through the mass media and regular revival rallies in public places.'[21] They appropriate and make effective use of modern media technologies and facilities. They buy airtime on local radios, especially those with wide coverage, and they feature prominently on television stations. Reporting the recent 'exploits' of the 'flamboyant' Nigeria pastor, Mathew Ashimolowo in Ghana, *The Sunday Times* said:

> Ashimolowo, the General Overseer of the Kingsway International Christian Center organized a six-day crusade and Conference entitled Winning Ways Crusade 2001 held in Kumasi... The Ashimolowo Crusade which received *heavy air time especially in television advertisement* (emphasis mine) pooled a number of renowned international motivational speakers...[22]

Another feature that portrays new-Pentecostal pastors as high-class religious entrepreneurs has to do with their exhibition of signboards and posters. These compete favorably in magnitude, caliber and decoration with signboards of commercial enterprises and firms. Some of these large and attractive signboards and posters are re-designed often to reflect the themes of current conventions, seminars and crusades. The designs and appeal of these signboards portray the ministers as professionals who are fashionable, modish and current in 'their acquisition of the latest technology necessary for services, healing, deliverance, prosperity and total successful living'. Not a few maintain regular columns in weekly newspapers under various titles such as 'Divine Message,' 'Wisdom from Above', 'Prophetic utterance' among others. Most have also shown increased use of posters, banners and hand bills as forms of advertisement. Some of these posters usually carry blaring headlines such as 'Signs and Miracles', 'Divine Favour', 'Enthronement to Prosperity', 'Total deliverance from Poverty', 'This same Jesus', and 'Open Heavens'.

The new-Pentecostal churches are growing at a fantastic rate at home and abroad. One of the reasons for this is because they have domesticated the culture of 'dealing with demons.' They call it deliverance: which includes human, town, state, national and continental 'deliverance' exercises. Bishop Wale Oke once expressed the view jokingly that 'the demons in Africans are "deadlier" than those in Europe and America'. Of course, the new Pentecostals like the African Indigenous Churches are pragmatic in contextualizing Christianity in African culture. The African cosmos, it is believed, is saturated with wicked spirits who are the causes of all misfortunes and failures.[23] The new Pentecostal churches are believed to provide a way out for all those 'wallowing helplessly under poverty and all kinds of satanic harassments.'[24] Quite a number of deliverance ministers all over the continent were trained in Nigeria.[25] They tend to insist that 'conversion and the consequent spiritual gifts would ensure one's right to progress and prosper in all areas of life'. This contentious opinion has, to all intents and purposes, found fertile ground among the poor and lower income masses not only in Africa but also in Latin America and Asia.[26] It is well known that since the arrival of Prosperity preachers in Brazil from early 1990's with their message of 'empowerment and emphasis on health and wealth for Christians the new Pentecostal movements have flourished tremendously in poor communities.'[27]

Like churches in South America and Korea, quite a number have cultivated the habit of having one large church congregation with numerous cell group meetings in the homes of church members. With all these ministries firmly under their control, the leadership becomes domineering and makes virtually all decisions. Ultimately, the funding and management of the churches are portrayed in some circles as business concerns. In recent years calendars and posters advertising conventions and big rallies carry the photographs of 'host pastors' standing by their wives. To the credit of new-Pentecostal preachers, this phenomenon has been interpreted by some to imply that women have been accorded elevated position in these churches. Kalu holds that Pentecostalism (in Nigeria) 'exudes a liberating gender ideology.'[28] However, some critics see this as 'a ploy to keep the church estate in the firm grips of the founder's family'.[29] The poster is used therefore to build the public image of the wife as an accomplished partner. While the senior pastor serves as the President and Chief Executive, the wife serves as the Co-founder, Deputy President and Treasurer.[30] However, this is not a general feature as many of these churches already have complex hierarchical and administrative structures in place.

The new Pentecostal churches emphasize the seed-faith principle of sowing and reaping. The preachers have various ways of persuading people to give. They admonish their adherents to give a variety of offerings – seed offerings, covenant offerings, breakthrough offerings, success offerings and the like. Apart from the 'give and prosper messages' in some of these ministries, there appears what may be regarded as a full scale 'commercialization' of the Gospel through the sale of 'break-through handkerchiefs' (called mantles), anointing oil, prayer books and vow-making. Most stress, like T.L Osborn, that 'the financial boom for God's people must begin here and now, not in the sweet bye and bye'.[31]

Some of the pastors make deliberate efforts to enter into relationships with overseas churches and ministries. Through these international contacts, they may obtain funds, scholarships and 'exchange of pulpits' and seize the opportunity to open branches especially in Europe and America. An example of this was reported recently under the caption 'Taiwo Adelakun – Minister of no mean repute'.[32] Bishop Taiwo Adelakun is the General Overseer of Victory International Church in Ibadan. The church has branches located in over twenty states in Nigeria. He is working assiduously to have representatives in all continents of the world. He was very close to Late Archbishop Idahosa. In fact, the late Archbishop was his mentor who frequently attended his church's annual conventions. Bishop (Mrs.) Idahosa, Bishop Francis Wale Oke, Rev Dr. Uma Ukpai, Bishop Oyedepo are other Pentecostal leaders that are close to Adelakun. In 1999 Adelakun was invited to Holland where he opened a branch of his church. As he later commented,

> my recent trip to Holland has opened the whole of Europe for us. I discovered that God just took us to Holland to open more doors for us. More than thirteen different nations were brought together for us to meet and they are now set to open branches of Victory International Church in their different countries spread over all continents of the world.[33]

Apparently, in order to entice young students and accommodate professionals, businessmen and businesswomen, new-Pentecostals support a variety of sports, amusements and current fashions. Unlike the Holiness movements, they allow women to expose their hair, having it 'jerry-curled' or 'permed'. They hardly frown at women putting on expensive jewelry and gorgeous adornment. They declare that 'grace gives license for all things', and that 'to the pure all things are pure'. In addition to the religious and spiritual significance attached, choreographed dance, symbolic hand movements in worship and 'gospel music' are also encouraged to entertain members as well as for commercial purposes. In institutions of higher learning and commercial/entertainment centers, their artistes are allowed to use their gifts and talents to motivate people to support their ministries financially just as it serves as an alternative strategy of evangelization.

Finally, what appears like an imitation of Robert Schueller's ministry of positive living and success principles, several prosperity preachers introduce a formula for prosperity. The prescriptions include,

'Run after your prosperity'
'Seed into our ministry regularly'
'Give a giant offering'
'Have an encounter with men/women of God'
'Press the success buttons'
'Affirm three times: "I am breaking financial hardship"'
'Work on your mind'.[34]

A good number of people testify that following the observance of the prosperity principles in which they implemented the law of 'covenant giving' or 'sowing', they had good fortune in return. One of such testimonies reads:

Ever since, I have been going against everything they said about prosperity until the last two months when I decided to do exactly all that our Pastor said and God responded immediately by embarrassing me with blessings. One, I became a bus owner. Two, I became a truck controller and thirdly, somebody blessed me financially.[35]

Another testimony reveals:

God laid it upon my heart to give most of the money we had in the family account. Behold God returned it hundred-fold. Also God asked me to give a table for the church office, which costs eighty-five percent of the money I had while I was preparing for my wedding in 1998. With about a month to go the Lord supplied all my needs for the wedding.[36]

DAVID OYEDEPO'S LIVING FAITH CHURCH WORLDWIDE INC. (WINNERS' CHAPEL)

There are varieties of prosperity preaching in Nigeria. Chris and Gordon Oanuoha described 'the kind of confusion' generated by the teachings on prosperity as 'a babel of voices'.[37] Each preacher seems to have his own version. Of all the above named preachers the most revealing and helpful in our evaluation is Bishop David Oyedepo, the founder and presiding bishop of the Living Faith Church. Although full church operation of the Winners' Chapel started in Kaduna in 1984, growth and development really started after the takeoff of the Word of Faith Bible Institute (WOFBI) in September 1986.[38] In 1988, Dr Oyedepo became the first Pentecostal bishop in Northern Nigeria and within a span of fifteen years the Living Faith Church has become one of the fastest growing ministries in Africa through its African Gospel Invasion Program (AGIP).[39] The recently dedicated Faith Tabernacle which seats 50,000 worshippers has been described as the largest church auditorium in the world.[40] Built within a year, the building is perhaps 'the fastest construction endeavor in the building industry if magnitude is matched with the time frame.'[41]

OYEDEPO'S TEACHING ON PROSPERITY

Definition

Oyedepo defines prosperity as 'a condition of being successful, in which you enjoy abundant peace, and experience fulfillment in every area of life.'[42] He underlines further that 'it is a state of wellbeing which you enter into through the covenant of abundance.'[43] He stresses that prosperity is not the availability of cash but encounter with light.[44]

Origin of Prosperity

Oyedepo maintains that God is the originator of prosperity contrary to some ministers' teaching that 'poverty is a virtue'. Oyedepo contends that God is the source of good things including spiritual and material riches. He argues that since heaven is the epitome of affluence, wealth must be acknowledged to be more heavenly than worldly. He insists that 'since the buildings in heaven are mansions and the streets there are paved with gold, if being prosperous is sinful, then God is the worst sinner.'[45] Oyedepo teaches that just as a seed will not multiply until it is sown, prosperity has laws that guide its acquisition. He argues that if one activates the laws of prosperity one will reap a handsome reward. The laws are encapsulated in his book, 'Fundamentals and Pillars of Prosperity'.

Fundamentals and Pillars

According to Oyedepo, prosperity has fundamentals and pillars.[46] He stresses that only appropriate and adequate insights into these principles can help one to prosper. His first fundamental note is that 'prosperity is not a promise one claims in prayers or with fasting and confessions, rather it is a covenant which one practices'. That means God has set a stage upon which one only needs to understand one's own part and then the power to realize the promise will be delivered to him. All that a Christian needs is a good understanding of what the covenant entails and then one will be catapulted into the realms of abundance. Oyedepo makes a claim to the fact that the understanding of prosperity in Christianity is unique. He argues that what the world calls prosperity is determined by 'how much one has' but in the kingdom of God, prosperity is determined by 'how much one gives'. He equates giving (tithes, offerings and love offerings) to sowing seeds, which is necessary for anyone who wants to reap a bountiful harvest. He contends that verbal confession is a 'key factor' in the realm of prosperity. The reason is that prosperity is produced on the ticket of faith and faith is given expression through verbal confession. As he puts it succinctly, 'one cannot enter into the land flowing with milk and honey by talking poverty'. He claims that if one follows all other principles but misses out at the talking state, 'he wipes off everything'. Unlike the mainline churches and the 'holiness' Pentecostals who, for a long time were sceptical or rather reluctant to seize the opportunities offered by electronic communications over the past years, Oyedepo has made effective use of radio and television. Within the last three years, the Internet has become a major medium of publishing success stories of the Winner's family worldwide. What the *Winner's World* on the Internet calls: *Winner's Profile* – 'happenings, book-excerpts, success motives, classified ads, and global letters' focus on the secrets behind the success and transformations that members of the church have had.[47]

Oyedepo makes copious use of his personal testimonies and those of members of his congregation. He points out that what enhances successful, cheerful and related giving is 'trusting'. Putting absolute trust in God is the highway to giving which ultimately leads to the realms of prosperity. He recalls:

> I gave God something one day and He said to me 'my son David, even if you don't want to be rich it's too late'. Today, the summary of my story is that I am highly favoured.[48]

Finally, gratitude, according to Oyedepo, is the last unshakable strategy for unlimited prosperity. Oyedepo believes that until one becomes thankful one cannot be fruitful. He even admonishes that one should not wait for the manifestations of the blessings before one shows gratitude for, according to him, 'it is praise that provokes the increase'.

OYEDEPO'S INFLUENCE

Gifford says emphatically that:

> This Gospel of Prosperity does not belong in Africa's revival. It did not originate in Africa, it started off with the media evangelists of the United States...The fact that it is so commonly preached in Africa shows the degree to which this current revival is direct from the U.S.A.[49]

It is often canvassed by scholars such as Gifford that most of the new Pentecostal Churches are fashioned after American media evangelists' ministries. As controversial as this claim is, we must emphasise that in spite of some levels of external influence, there has been remarkably ample evidence of indigenous creativity in the larger new Pentecostal churches in Nigeria. As a matter of fact, globalization has increased the opportunity for shared ideas. These African movements claim with good reasons that they have more to give than they have taken from the global village. Using the Living Faith Church as a model we can see that new Pentecostalism is increasingly seen as a formidable force not only in Nigeria but all over the globe.[50]

Oyedepo is involved in vigorous global evangelism. As the President of World Mission Agency, he has major missionary activities in over thirty nations of Africa and vibrant churches outside the continent of Africa.[51] The genesis of the African Gospel Invasion Program (AGIP) was presented in a dramatic and moving scene.

On 8th May 1994, four giant maps of Africa were lifted up while prayers and prophecies into each of the nations were made to illuminate the hitherto dark continent of Africa.[52] The WMA claims to have carried out relief operations in the Koma Hills (Nigeria) where foodstuffs, clothing and much needed basic materials were made available in container loads in 1997. It also declares that it has provided 80 water bore holes with portable drinking water to improve the sanitary conditions in some localities. Also, at the International level in 1996, WMA avers that it has airlifted 2 separate shipments of assorted relief materials to war torn Liberia. In addition, Oyedepo's Word of Faith Bible Institute has a network of about 60 campuses scattered all over Africa.[53] Apart from these, the Winners' profile on the Internet discloses that 'he is a counsellor and consultant to world leaders and ministers at various levels.'[54] Oyedepo is also interested in circular education. He is the founder of the Faith Academy, a model Christian college and Chancellor of the Covenant University. The University which was inaugurated on October 21, 2002 aims 'to embark on raising a new generation of leaders in various fields of human endeavors by a training methodology that emphasises skill and character'.[55] The Living Faith Church also owns the Gilead Medical Center which is the scientific medical arm of the LFC. It is aimed at alleviating and resolving medical conditions by relying both on divine and medical expertise. The website recounts many amazing medical records, reports and testimonies of patients who claim to have been healed at the Center.[56]

A RETHINKING OF PROSPERITY TEACHING

First, there may perhaps be some truth in the claim that some prosperity ministers manage their ministries as private and special businesses. They develop a Christian leadership pyramid whereby the 'Senior Pastor' or 'Presiding Bishop' becomes virtually a *Papa* (father) to those under them. Most of them have developed the concept of running multiple ministries (big educational institutions, mission training schools, literacy and medical missions, publishing, ministry, secretariat services and of course, pasturing). Ukah argues that 'the authentic raison d'être for all these is proselytization which would ensure a replenished financial base.'[57] While this assertion may be valid in some cases, it may be difficult to generalize on this point on the complex diversity of the pentecostal phenomenon. Secondly, some have questioned the validity of the practice of giving money to the preacher in order to win God's blessings or rather, what is called 'prophesying into the spirit of one's businesses and projects.'[58] Most critics suppose that there is a form of exploitation, which is attendant on this practice. Of course, even the suggested 'abuse' is as ancient as Balaam's who tried to prophesy for his own personal gain. It is commonplace to hear statements such as:

> Thus says the Lord, there are ten people here whose hearts have been touched by God to support this Ministry, with "a one-time gift of N100.000 each". God has promised hundred-fold in return. If you have not started a project now ... start it.

Some members may in actual fact rush into business situations based on such personal prophecy because they believe such prophecies would cause them to prosper. In some cases, quite a number end up giving out the little they have only to wait endlessly for a hundred-fold multiplication of what they have given. There are also hundreds of testimonies of members who claim that such prophecies manifested in their existential lives.

Third, in recent years the 'hundred-fold returns' rhetoric common among most 'apostles' of prosperity has come under severe scrutiny both from outside and within the Pentecostal fold, sometimes by some leading Pentecostal evengelists. Bruce Barron quotes Kenneth Hagin as 'doubting its validity in all cases.'[59] An outstanding charismatic, faith preacher Rev. Benny Hinn repined in an interview:

> It promotes greed when we tell people that if they give $10 they'll get back $1,000. I feel terrible that I once put too much emphasis on material prosperity and now I am saying Lord, please forgive me.[60]

Hector Avalos, a former faith healer, also says preachers are basically playing on people's greed when they assert that an abundant giver will 'enjoy a life free of sickness, stress and vices, such as alcohol and will be flushed with material goods – a new car, a fine house, a big account...'[61] Stephen Buckley relates the experience of a worshipper:

> Maria dos Santos who lived in a Rio slum complained
> that the pastor always told the worshippers "The more
> you give the more God will bless you". She believed the
> pastor and started giving half of her income. In spite of
> this sacrificial giving more than a year later her marriage
> was still in pieces, her business remained feeble and she
> was still depressed. She became so disillusioned she had
> to leave the church.[62]

Buckey recalls that Maria who no longer goes to church said: 'I still believe in God, but I don't believe in any church and I don't believe in pastors. Now, when I have problems I solve them myself'.[63]

Fourth, other critics have argued that the concept of 'a hundred-fold returns' entails false *exegesis* or interpretation of scriptures. It merely asserts the literal meaning of Jesus' promise to his disciples:

> I tell you the truth Jesus replied, no one who has left home
> ...or fields for me and the sake of the gospel who will fail
> to receive a hundred times as much in this present age ...
> and in the age to come, eternal life. (Mk.10:29-30)

This attitude to biblical interpretation only leads to the fallacy of proof-texting. Of course, proof-texting is probably the worst form of biblical *exegesis* because with it one can find biblical support for anything. Technically, this kind of interpretation is rather *eisegesis* or reading predetermined beliefs into the Bible. Besides, some critics point out that the insistence of prosperity teachers that Christian faith guarantees absolute prosperity and progress is unsustainable. It is plainly irreconcilable with scores of passages in the New Testament. For instance, Saint Luke recounts God's option for the poor in Jesus' life (See Lk. 4:18; 6:20-23; 6:24-25; 16:19-31; 18:18-23). Also, there are some passages which express the dimension of what is termed the 'theology of suffering' or the 'theology of the cross' (Lk. 9:23, 14:27; Mk.8:34) without which Christianity would become artificial, shallow and superficial. Also, in the early church those who had possessions sold them and shared out the proceeds (Acts 2:42-47; 4:32-37). This, in a sense, denotes the fact that the church cannot but have the poor (Rom.15:26; 2 Cor.8-9). In this way, the churches expressed their special concern for the poor.[64] Paul also demonstrates that in Christ, God shows solidarity with an intrinsically poor humanity. Contrary to the prosperity teaching, therefore, it is clear that the recognition and solidarity with the poor is not 'absolute novelty, nor a discovery made completely *ex novo*, it has a substantial continuity with the tradition of our faith'.[65]

Fifth, it is certain that there is much tendency for the teachings of prosperity gospel to make its proponents become conceited and egocentric. This is the tendency to be self-centered, viewing every situation in relation to one's welfare. Most of the televangelists make egocentric proclamations now and again. For example, Tilton boasts: 'Your pastor is healthy and prosperous having an annual income of $80 million and I am not ashamed of it.'[66] And so Oyedepo can also say: 'Today, I am swimming in plenty as a result of an encounter with a woman of God (Gloria Copeland) through her books.'[67] Elsewhere, he says:

> For the first time in my life, I knew that God deals with people on covenant terms. From that time the yoke of poverty was broken in my life and I knew I can never be poor. I am not in any trade, neither have I ever invested any dime into any business; yet I will never beg till my time on earth is over. Why? Because I favour His kingdom.[68]

Sixth, some critics also submit that prosperity teaching accentuates selective theology. As they would argue, coming from a context where the majority of people live below the poverty line, some African preachers do not acknowledge that prosperity preaching cannot be applied universally. Benny Hinn in his 'reflections' with Stephen Strang narrated the moving experience he had in Manila. He confessed that he could not preach 'prosperity nor teach seed sowing' in Manila as was his custom in America because there: 'God opened my eyes to see the poor suffering saints of the Word…those saints who were destitute and afflicted.'[69] If prosperity and 'seed sowing' cannot be preached everywhere, then it is very unlikely universal. Africa is in dire need of a theology of hope. In Nigeria, in particular, the public role and social relevance of these churches needs a further investigation.

Moreover, in some circles, prosperity theology emphasizes principles or a blueprint that may appear controversial. Oyedepo maintains that God 'enlarges your room in proportion to your gift'[70] and also that the discovery of the principles gives instant results:

I define knowledge as discovery and wisdom as the application of knowledge. That is, discovery applied, which
equals recovery. When there is discovery, and it is correctly applied, it brings instant reward, that is, automatic
recovery.[71]

Testimonies are published to underscore the authenticity of the
principles. Oyedepo remarks:

You can have God's favour with your gifts. A brother testi-
fied in church recently, how when the offering was being
taken he had no money to give. He said he was, however,
led to give the shirt he was wearing. He did this reluctantly
in September, and in November, he was blessed with the
sum of 150,000 Naira! He provoked God's favour with his
gift.

Elsewhere he quotes the testimony of a couple:

Before we started attending this church, we had financial
problems. When we started worshipping here, we heard
about giving, and we started giving. But there was no
result. I then went to one of the pastors, for counseling.
He told me to read one of the Bishop's books, *Covenant
Wealth*. My husband and I read the book and we discov-
ered why we had not been seeing results in our giving.
The reason was that we had been giving towards our own
need, not to the kingdom of God. We then asked for for-
giveness from God. That same week, miracles started in
our lives! My husband was on a salary of 1,200 Naira per
month. But after reading the book, he had to leave that
job. Immediately, God gave him another job. Someone
called him to interpret English for him. My husband is
a Frenchman and can't speak English very well. But this
man called him to interpret English. The man gave him
9,400 Naira for his efforts that week. The man also said,
'You are a good man, you are a Christian. You will now
represent our company here in Nigeria.' That is not all!
God now made way for us to get money without struggling. God showed my husband the way to get money
without serving under anybody. He now gets a minimum
of 1,000 Naira per day! Also, since we got married, we
had been looking for a house, because we had been living
in my father's house. But the following week, a brother
called my husband and told him to go and look for a

house, that he would give him the money to pay for three
years rent. Another person called him again and told him
to look for a house, that the money to pay for it was ready.
Now, about three different people want to pay for a house
for us! They are the ones now hastening us up to go and
get a house![72]

Some of these testimonies raise critical questions about the sources
of the monies these believers claimed 'they were blessed with'.
Ample evidence suggests that the prosperity discourse does not
place emphasis mainly on biblical theology of money and possession. Some of the principles canvassed by Oyedepo are carried over
from pseudo-religious literature. As he admits:

> I came in contact with a book titled, *The Power of Posi-
> tive Thinking* by Norman Vincent Pearl. This book has
> influenced so many lives through a process of mental
> revolution. It teaches us about the ability we have to use
> our minds to knock down mountains. Friends, books are
> destiny moulders![73]

Against this backdrop, some theologians even hold that prosperity
teaching is a 'non-Christian way of thinking'.[74] They would adduce
some reasons to this. First, they take issue do with their concept of
prayer,'God is bound by spiritual regulations which it is up to human
beings to understand and exploit- that in a sense does not give much
room left for God's sovereignty.[75] Second, it concerns the leaders'
claim to revealed knowledge which those outside do not have. Lastly,
they even argue that some of the principles stressed by prosperity
preachers are similar to those emphasized by secular counselors.[76]

Oyedepo makes clear that his guiding principle is integrity.
According to him 'prightness is richer than smartness'. As he warns:
'When I say wisdom, I am not talking about craftiness or dirty
games. By wisdom I mean insight, illumination and application of
facts'.[77] Elsewhere, he emphasized the need for financial integrity:

> When you lack financial integrity, you are eternally dis-
> qualified from having fortune. There is therefore no point
> in wasting your money in giving, because it won't be cred-
> ited to your account in heaven.[78]

While the compliance with the guiding principles of integrity is believed by members to result in financial prosperity, a feature which is often voiced in the form of testimonies, such emphasis in tithes has attained a controversial stance in the public sphere, where many criticize charlatans who pose as pastors to extort tithes and monies for their own selfish gains. The fact that the source of member's tithes is largely unknown may raise other critical issues especially as money may sometimes be obtained through dubious and fraudulent means.

CONCLUSION

This chapter has been concerned with the emphasis by some Pentecostal leaders on aspects of the prosperity theology. It argues for a rethinking of prosperity teaching in such a way that focuses on all aspects of the doctrine so that its impact become visible at both the official and popular levels of religiosity. The chapter shows how local theological reflections on aspects of the prosperity theology have strong foreign influence and philosophical underpinnings inspite of attempts to contextualize and localize it. While the socio-economic, political and religious realities of the local Nigerian context will continue to provide ample space for the Pentecostal discourse on prosperity to thrive, it is rather uncertain whether the critical, negative stance emanating from the public domain and even some segments of the Pentecostal churches against the prevalence and (abuses) of prosperity theology would disappear at least in the near future. It is also a matter of guess how, whether and to what extent the adherence to this doctrine will change the social-economic well-being of members and the society at large in the long run.

Bibliography

Ayegboyin, Deji and Ishola, Ademola, *African Indigenous Churches: an Historical Perspective*, Lagos Greater Heights, 1999.

Ayegboyin, Deji and Ukah, Asonzeh, 'Taxonomy of Churches in Nigeria: A Historical Perspective', *Orita: Ibadan Journal of Religious Studies*, 33, 1&2, 2002, pp. 68-86.

Bruce Barron, *The Health and Wealth Gospel*, Downers Grove: Intervarsity Press, 1987.

Fatokun, S., 'Prosperity Theology in the Colonial Nigeria Christianity', *Castalia: Ibadan Journal of Multicultural/Multidisciplinary Studies*, 3, 1, March, 1999.

Gifford, Paul, 'Prosperity: A New and Foreign Element in African Christianity', *Religion*, 20, 1990, pp. 373-388.

Gifford, Paul, *African Christianity: Its Public Role*. Indiana: Inidana University Press, 1998.

Isamah, A.N., 'Family Life under economic adjustment: The rise of children bread-winners' Paper read at workshop on Devaluation and the Popular Economy 1986-1996 at the Development Policy Center, Ibadan, August, 1997.

Kalu, U. Ogbu, 'The Third Response: Pentecostalism and the Reconstruction of Christian Experience in Africa, 1970-1995', *Journal of African Christian Thought*, 1, 2, December 1998, pp. 3-16.

Marshall, Ruth, 'Pentecostalism in Southern Nigeria: an Overview', in Paul Gifford (ed) *New Dimensions in African Christianity*, Ibadan: Sefer, 1993, pp. 10-16.

Neuman, Terris, 'Cultic Origin of Word – Faith Theology within the Charismatic Movement', *Pneuma* 12, 1, 1990, pp. 32-55.

Ojo, Matthews, 'The Deeper Life Bible Church', *Journal of Religion in Africa* 18, 1988; and *Africa*, 58, 1987, pp.175-192.

Olukoya, D.K., *Prayer Rain: The most powerful and practical prayer manual ever written*, Lagos: MFMM, 1999.

Onuoha, Chris and Onuoha, Gordon (eds.) *Prosperity: What The Word Of God Says About It*, Aba: V.I. Pub. 1996.

Onyendi, M.E, 'The Prosperity Theology of the New Religious Movements in Nigeria', M.A. dissertation, Religious Studies Dept., University of Ibadan, 1998.

Osborn, T.L., *The Good Life*, Tulsa: Osborn Int'l, 1977.

Oyedepo, David, *Bible sense for Financial Fortune*, Lagos: Dominion Publication House, 1999.

Oyedepo, David, *Success Buttons*, Lagos: Dominion Press, 1998.

Oyedepo, David, *Understanding Financial Prosperity*, Lagos: Dominion Press, 1997.

Oyedepo, David, *The Vision*, Lagos: Dominion Press, 1997.

Oyedepo, David, *The Force of Freedom*, Lagos: Dominion Press, 1996.

Pixley, Jorge and Boff, Clodovis, *The Bible, The Church And The Poor*, Kent: Burns and Oates, 1989.

Tweneboa-Kodua, Maxwell, *The Man and His Ministry: Five Years of Miracle Ministry of Bishop David Oyedepo*, Lagos: Lantern Press 1988.

Ukah, Asonzeh and Ayegboyin, Deji, 'Media Publicity and Neo-Pentecostal Strategies: Conversion or Proselytization?', *Castalia* (forthcoming).

Ukah, Asonzeh. 'Religion and Mass Media: A Sociological Perspective,' M.A Dissertation, Department of Religious Studies, University of Ibadan, 1997.

Notes

1. Graham Thomson, 'Introduction: Situating Globalization', *International Social Science Journal*, 51, 1999, p.139.

2. Akin Jimoh, 'The Problem with Globalization', *The Guardian*, February 1, 2001, p.15.

3. Anthony Giddens, *Ruth/BBC Lecture*, London, 1999, p.1.

4. *European Commission*, 1997, p.45.

5. Konrad Raiser, '*Oikumene* and Globalization', *Echoes*, WCC, 12, 1997, p.3.

6. Roland Robertson, 'Globalization, Politics and Religion', in J. A. Beckford and Thomas Luckmann (ed.) *Sage Studies in International Sociology*, 1989, p.12.

7. Robertson, p. 12.

8. Robertson, p. 12.

9. D. F. Asaju, 'Politicization of Religion in Nigeria', in Segun Johnson (ed.) *Studies in Selected Nigeria problems*, Lagos: Okanlawon Press, 1990, p. 112.

10. M. Darol Bryant 'Can there be a Muslim-Christian Dialogue concerning Jesus/Isah?', in M. D. Bryant and S. Ali (eds.) *Muslim-Christian Dialogue*, Minnesota: Paragon House, 1998.

11. The governments of Saudi Arabia, Iran and Libya were outspoken, through their respective Ambassadors in supporting the implementation of *Sharia* as State religion. Muammar Gaddafi of Libya advocated same during his visit to Nigeria in 1998.

12. *The Constitution of the Federal Republic of Nigeria*, 1979, Section 10.

13. I. L. Akintola, *Sharia in Nigeria*, Ijebu Ode: Shebiotimo Press, 2001, p. 200.

14. Gifford, *African Christianity*, p .80

15. Marshall, Pentecostalism in Southern Nigeria', p. 21.

16. Marshall, Pentecostalism in Southern Nigeria', p. 22.

17. Gifford, *African Christianity*, p. 91.

18. Rev. Timothy Omotosho (fondly called Tim Tosh 'boasted on several occasions that his Church has acquired 37 jets including a Boeing 777' (sic). See 'The face of a 419 Pastor' *Focus: Nigeria's International Society Magazine*, 17, 2000.

19. Ukah, Asonzeh. 'Religion and Mass Media: A Sociological Perspective,' M.A Dissertation, Department of Religious Studies, University of Ibadan, 1997, p.128.

20. Ukah, Asonzeh and Deji Ayegboyin 'Media Publicity and Neo-Pentecostal Strategies: Conversion or Proselytization?', *Castalia* (forthcoming).

21. Ukah, 'Religion and Mass Media', Chpt. 4.

22. *The Sunday Times*, 18th March, 2001, pp. 1-2

23. See for example, Deji Ayegboyin and Ademola Ishola, *African Indigenous Churches: an Historical Perspective*, Lagos Greater Heights, 1999, pp. 28-31. Internet edition, www.irr.org/african-indigenous-churches-intro.html

24. *See* Editors' comment on D.K Olukoya, *Prayer Rain: The most powerful and practical prayer manual ever written*, Lagos: MFMM, 1999.

25. See For example, Gifford, *African Christianity*, pp. 97-109.

26. See Word of Life or Prosperity Theology, available at: www.dci.dk/en/mtr/word_life.html.

27. Stephen Buckley, 'Prosperity Theology Pulls On Purse', available at: www.rickross.com/ref.univ

28. Kalu, 'The Third Response', p. 13.

29. See for example Ukah, 'Religion and Media'.

30. On the Winners World website, Bishop Oyedepo and his wife's photograph is displayed. In the *Winner's Profile* on the said Internet, Bishop Oyedepo says, 'I am among the most successful married people on the earth today because of the covenant steps I've been taking in my home. I respect my wife because if I don't know no one else will. I do not care what people give to my wife, I still owe her a covenant responsibility to provide for her out of the blessings God has given me'. After the death of Archbishop Idahosa, his co-founder and wife, Bishop (Mrs) Idahosa was enthroned as the next presiding bishop of the Church of God Missions International.

31. T.L. Osborn, *The Good Life*, Tulsa: Osborn Int'l, 1977, p. 193.

32. See 'Taiwo Adelakun – 'Minister of no mean repute', *Sunday Times*, 18 March, 2001, p.14.

33. Adelakun, *Sunday Times.*

34. See the following by David Oyedepo: *The Force of Freedom*, Lagos: Dominion Press, 1996; *Success Buttons*, 1998; *Understanding Financial Prosperity*, 1997; *The Vision*, Lagos: Dominion Press, 1997.

35. See Testimonies, 'The God of Covenants'– *Rhema Chapel Newsletter*, Surulere: Rhema Chapel Int., Sept. 2000. pp. 3-6.

36. Testimonies, 'The God of Covenants'.

37. Chris and Gordon Onuoha, (eds.) *Prosperity: What The Word Of God Says About It*, Aba: V.I. Pub. 1996, p. 23.

38. See Maxwell Tweneboa-Kodua, *The Man and His Ministry: Five Years of Miracle Ministry of Bishop David Oyedepo*, Lagos: Lantern Press 1988, p. 6.

39. AGIP was commissioned on 8th May 1994 in a dramatic way. Four giant maps of Africa were lifted up while prayers and prophecies into each of the nations were made to illuminate the hitherto dark continent of Africa. See *The Visions*, Lagos: Dominion Publishing House, 1997, p. 7.

40. The Editor, 'Heroes of the Church' – Bishop David Oyedepo in *Triumphant March*, 1, 2, April, 2000, p. 16.

41. John Atala, *et al.*, 'Inside Bishop Oyedepo's ₦ bn Miracle', *Fame: A Nigerian Magazine*, Sept. 1999, pp. 10-11.

42. D. Oyedepo, *Understanding Financial Prosperity*, p. 17. See in particular, Onyendi, M.E, 'The Prosperity Theology of the New Religious Movements in Nigeria'. M.A. dissertation, Religious Studies Dept., University of Ibadan, 1998.

43. Oyedepo, *Understanding Financial Prosperity*, p. 17.

44. Oyedepo, *Financial Prosperity*, p. 19.

45. See Oyedepo, *Covenant Wealth*, p. 8; *Success Buttons*, p. 23.

46. He lists five fundamentals: covenant dimension, consecration, dedication, affection, and addiction. He mentions seven pillars: Giving, working, thinking, trusting, waiting, confessing, and showing gratitude. See M.O. Onyendi, 'The Prosperity Theology of the New Religious Movements'.

47. *Winners' World*, A Publication of the Living Faith Church Worldwide, Vol. 2, Oct. 2000.

48. *Financial Fortune*, A Publication of Living Faith Church Worldwide, p. 13.

49. Paul Gifford, 'Prosperity: A New and Foreign Element in African Christianity', *Religion*, 20, 1990, p. 382.

50. Ministries such as that of Bishop and Archbishop Idahosa's have also had a global effect through secondary means. Students trained in their institutions have become general overseers, bishops and presidents of sprawling churches in Europe, America, Asia and Australasia. These churches have served the needs of African immigrants resident in those continents. A case in point is Bishop Abraham Bediako of the Christian Church Outreach Mission in Germany.

51. See Winners Profile, available at: http://www.winners-chapel.com/profile/default.htm

52. Winners Profile.

53. Winners Profile.

54. Winners Profile.

55. See http://www.vanguardngr.com/articles/2002/features/educ

56. http://www.winnerscannanland.org/au.htm

57. Ukah, 'Religion and Mass Media', p. 128.

58. See e.g. See Stephen Buckley, 'Prosperity Theology Pulls On Purse' www.rickross.com/ref.univ

59. See Bruce Barron, *The Health and Wealth Gospel*, Downers Grove: Intervarsity Press, 1987, p. 93. Gloria Copeland's commentary on Mk.10.29-30 summarises it all.'You give $1.00 for the gospel's sake and $100 belongs to you. You give $10 and receive $1,000. Give $1,000 and receive $100,000. Give one aeroplane and receive an equivalence of ten aeroplanes.

60. Stephen Strang, 'Benny Hinn speaks out', in *Charisma*, August, 1993, pp.26-28.

61. See Stephen Buckley, 'Prosperity Theology Pulls On Purse', at: www.rickross.com/ref.univ

62. Buckley, 'Prosperity 'Promises of Riches entice Brazil's Poor' in *Washington Post Foreign Service*, February 13, 2001.

63. Buckley, 'Prosperity 'Promises of Riches entice Brazil's Poor', *ibid.*

64. See Jorge Pixley and Clodovis Boff, *The Bible, The Church And The Poor*, Kent: Burns & Oates, 1989, p. 66.

65. Pixley and Boff, *The Bible, The Church And The Poor*, p.117.

66. Strang, *Charisma*, Feb. 1992, p.31.

67. Oyedepo, *The Force of Freedom*, 1998, p. 95.

68. Oyedepo, *The Force of Freedom* p.83

69. Strang, *Charisma*, pp. 26-28.

70. Oyedepo, *Bible Sense for financial fortune*, p. 16.

71. Oyedepo, *The Force of Freedom*, p. 61.

72. Oyedepo, *The Force of Freedom*, pp. 83-84.

73. See Oyedepo, *The Force of Freedom*. The glaring fact is that some of the principles are similar to those emphasized by secular counselors. See The First Chapter 'The Major Requirements for becoming rich' in Charles Albert Puissant, *How to think like a Millionaire: Applying a Principle of Wealth*.

74. Neuman makes a case for the cultic foundation of faith theology. See Terris Neuman, 'Cultic Origin of Word – Faith Theology within the Charismatic Movement', *Pneuma* 12, 1, 1990, pp. 32-55. See also Scott Mc Mcmahan, 'Editorial: The Pitfalls of Prosperity Theology', available at: www.skwc/com/essent/cr_pitfall_prosperity.html. Buckley, 'Prosperity Theology Pulls on Purse,' and Dialogue Centre, The Word of Life or Prosperity, available at: www.dci.dk/en/mtrl/word_life.html.

75. Dialogue Centre 'Word of life'.

76. Puissant *How to Think like a Millionaire*, p. 56.

77. Oyedepo, *Financial Fortune*, p. 11.

78. Oyedepo, *Financial Fortune*, p. 40.

Globalization, Politicization of Religion and Religious Networking – The Case of the Pentecostal Fellowship of Nigeria

Dapo F. Asaju

Preamble

The common perception of *globalisierung* (globalization) has been dominantly political, economic and technological. But the global village does not exclusively consist of capital, politics and machines. Fundamental to this concept is religious ideology which evolved pre- and post-Christianity. Christian teachings contain ingredients that 'prophetically' anticipate the role of a super-mastermind behind the global concept and the ramifications of its implementation. In other words, the religious factor of globalization has been largely unexplored by scholars. This paper intends to do that, from the perspective of the 'Pentecostal Fellowship of Nigeria' (P.F.N.), a conglomeration of Pentecostal organizations in Nigeria, Black Africa's most populous nation.

Graham Thomson defines 'globalization' as just another word for the internationalization of economic activity, in terms of greater integration and interdependence.[1] A local Nigerian journalist sees it as 'a process that seeks to destroy trade barriers through unfettered integration and interaction of global capital and labor, thereby leading to an unhindered exchange of goods and services across borders....'[2] According to Giddens, 'globalization has something to do with the thesis that we now all live in one world'.[3] The European commission's definition agrees with Thomson's above:

> Globalization can be defined as the process by which markets and production in different countries are becoming increasingly interdependent due to the dynamics of trade in goods and services and flows of capital and technology. It is not a new phenomenon but the continuation of developments that have been in train for some considerable time.[4]

The prominence of the reduction of globalization to the confines of a global economy is due apparently to the fundamental impact of the economy to human life. It has been rightly observed that the impact of economic globalization is being felt even in the remote parts of the developing world. This is due to the growing disintegration of national and regional economies, replaced by the emergent global economy. In July 2001, the Organization of African Unity (OAU) approved the formation of the 'African Union', patterned after the 'European Union', indicating the regionalization and pro-globalization trend.

A cursory observer of a typical Nigerian market will find that goods from the international community have virtually flooded the market, whereas the local input in production and manufacture is comparatively very minimal. In the same vein, cherished African cultural values that were the African pride are rapidly giving way to foreign culture; thanks to the internet, telecommunication and the electronic mass media. In reality, there are many ways by which the world has become a global village. One of this is the religious. As mentioned earlier, the religious concept of globalization predates the contemporary estimation of the phenomenon. In a sense, we argue that the current trend is a consequence of initial religious frameworks. The concept of οικουμενε (referring either to the inhabited earth or in a more theological sense of eschatology) and the efforts of the ecumenical movement are fundamentally complimentary to the process of globalization. Konrad Raiser observes that 'the Christian community preserves the memory of the ancient Church to an earlier form of globalization in the Hellenistic empire. The very concept of οικουμενε was the expression of this global consciousness:'...one God, one Emperor, one empire, one language, one currency, one citizenship.'[5]

POLITICIZATION OF RELIGION AS PRECURSOR TO RELIGIOUS NETWORKING

Robertson identifies the factor of politicization of religion as being germane in the globalization process.[6] This is a relevant causative factor in the African globalization process. While recognizing that there is a globe-wide politicization of religion in recent years, he defines the phenomenon as an increase in concern on the part of ostensibly religious collectivities with governmental issues and, secondly, an inflation of interest among those with declared religious commitments in coordinating the latter with secular-ideological perspectives and program. He also identifies a more diffused strand of the politicization process as involving in effect,

> ...a denial of the autonomy of religious, as well as theological, commitment. For some, that denial veers in the direction of grounding religious doctrine and practice in secular ideology or experience; for others it moves toward claiming that religious doctrine and practice must have ideological consequences.[7]

In other words, there has been both 'emphasis upon the governmental relevance of religion and the close aligning or conflation of religion and ideology.'[8] Whereas this growing phenomenon is global, it has assumed a major proportion in contemporary Nigeria; a situation, which has engendered religions networking by Christian groups in the country. Elsewhere, the author identifies Islamic expansionism as the crux of politicization of religion in Nigeria, a situation which has also encouraged a reactionary Christian revivalism and networking in response to the Islamic 'offensives.'[9] In particular, several areas of the politicization process can be identified, such as religious representation in government cabinets, foreign policy/foreign influences, government's take-over of Christian Mission Schools, social and religious discrimination and outright persecution of Christians in areas that have large Muslim population.

Two incidents were fundamental, the registration of Nigeria as full member of Organization of Islamic Conference (OIC) and the full adoption of the *Sharia* (Islamic legal codes) by most States in the Muslim-dominated Northern Nigeria. In both cases, there was notable opposition by the Christian populace to what was seen as state-sponsored Islamic domination; all to no avail. In March 2000, the *Sharia* crisis led to Christian – Muslim clashes and civil disturbances which claimed the lives of more than 2000 persons in Kaduna metropolis with retaliatory killings in other parts of the country. A typical example of Christian networking in response to the above development, can be seen in the role of the (then) Archbishop of Canterbury, George Carey, who led all Christian denominations, including the Pentecostal Fellowship of Nigeria in a united voice against *Sharia*. He visited and dialogued with the Governor of Zamfara State, where the *Islamic* code was first fully introduced. Carey requested the protection of the rights of all Christians to freedom of religious worship. The implication of this symbolic action is that no local community is any longer an island unto itself. All local happenings are of interest for the international community.

Before the Kaduna riots and the official adoption of *Sharia*, there had been repeated violent clashes between Christians and Muslims. In most of the following cases, the Muslims initiated attacks. A Christian procession was assaulted and several Churches were destroyed by Muslim fanatics in Ilorin (1986); Muslim violent resistance to Christian Students' evangelism in Kafanchan (1987), anti-Christian riots in Kano to prevent the proposed evangelistic crusade of the German Reinhard Bonnke (1990), the clash between Christian-dominated *Zango Kataf* people and Muslim feudal lords who had officially oppressed the Northern minority of Zango Kataf people (1992); burning of Churches in Bauchi (1995), a repeated attack on Christians in Ilorin (1999), and one of the recent being the Muslims' attack on a peaceful Christian procession organized by both the Christian Association of Nigeria (CAN) and the Pentecostal Fellowship of Nigeria (PFN) in

Kaduna to protest the proposed imposition of the *Sharia* on the religiously plural state communities (2000). Persistent clashes like these may have led Bryant to ask whether there was the possibility of a Christian-Muslim networking.[10] No doubt, this dimension is a fall-out of the partial religious globalization process, which witnessed foreign influences and interaction from the Islamic Block.[11] This dimension was only brought to the recognition of the international community after the September 2001 terrorist attack against selected targets in the United States of America.

Whereas the Christian populace, speaking through the Churches and Church organizations: the Christian Association of Nigeria (CAN), and Pentecostal Fellowship of Nigeria (PFN), insist upon the governments' upholding the provision of the Constitution of the Federal Republic of Nigeria which stipulate the secularity of the country and that no religion shall be adopted as State religion,[12] the Muslim populace argue that for them, secularity is unacceptable because Nigeria is 'multi-religious' and there can be no distinction between religion and politics.[13] This is re-echoing a declaration by Muammar Gaddafi of Libya that there is no distinction between the State and Islam. Consequently, some Muslims are regularly incited to fight to assume control of government at all levels, wherever they are, and institute the Islamic mode of life. So undisguised is this resolution that Sokoto State government publicly inscribed on vehicle plate numbers the tag 'Born to rule'. In other words, the Muslim Jihadists regard governance as their birthright and have indeed provided the leadership of the country for most period of the nation's existence. Such a totalitarian adoption of the role and influence of religion in a religiously plural society like Nigeria can be problematic, breeding inevitable religious misunderstanding and physical clashes between adherents of contending faiths.

Stackhouse[14] tends to recognize the inevitability of a mutual relationship between religion and politics, against the widely argued need for distinction between the sacred and the profane. We argue that religion should better remain within the confines of an individual's private life without being brought into public policy and process of government, but not in the secular sense of total elimination or isolation. According to Stackhouse, 'religion must be reckoned with in politics...the ideas that religion is and should be "private" and "nonpolitical" and that the state is "public" and "secular" derive in large measure from the enormous impact that a specific religious tradition has had upon modern Western social life.[15] He attributes this influence to the old British Empire. Furthermore, he argues that,

> the constraint on modern states to be essentially secular has been complemented by globally diffused ideas concerning the category of religion on the one hand, and the individual, on the other... to a significant extent, even the idea of religion as being basically "privatized", is a socio-cultural "product" of the modern global circumstance, an aspect of the ordering involved in the rendering of the world as a single place.[16]

To Robertson, 'politicization' and 'religionization' are mutually amplifying processes, in that the more 'religious' the state becomes the more it provokes expansion of the activities of ostensibly religious actors along political lines.[17] We believe that for the diverse Nigerian ethnic nationalities, the viable approach to religious peace and justice is to maintain secularity of the state while religion is limited to the private space. It appears improper for a State to adopt one of existing major religions as state religion. Robertson rightly notes that,

> in Africa, leaving on one side predominantly Muslim North Africa, where Islamic fundamentalism has certainly made some political impact – it is clear that in recent years, there has been an acceleration of interest in political activity within and among religious collectivities (much of it along Catholic or Protestant "liberationist" lines) while in South Africa, politicization of religion has greatly increased as part of the turmoil attendant upon the problem of apartheid...[18]

This shows that the peculiarities of each community, society or nation determine the prevalence and mode of its use of religion in public space. There may be some common social problems that call for global collaboration or involving foreign influence, such as the maintenance of law and order, lack of meaningful leisure activities, the extent of organization, control and bureaucracy, loneliness and poverty.[19]

PFN AND INTRA-RELIGIOUS NETWORKING

The Pentecostal Fellowship of Nigeria at its National Conference in February 2001 issued the following statement:

> The Pentecostal Fellowship of Nigeria Conference acknowledged the present move of God in Nigeria and enjoined all Christian Ministers to keep contending earnestly for the precious (Christian) faith...PFN reminded Christians that the pendulum of Gospel explosion was swinging towards Africa and Nigeria is pivotal in God's plans and purposes for Africa and the world...PFN called on all Christians to regard soul winning as a major and most urgent task for every believer. Christians must not be afraid of the great risks involved in soul winning. The Conference firmly resolved to keep supporting the Federal Government...We have encouraged all members to be actively involved in politics for the purpose of righteous governance in the land. We shall continually make unity our pursuit in all essentials, through networking.[20]

The above communiqué reflects some undercurrents. First, the need for religious networking as a response to the prevalent politicization of religion in Nigeria. Second, the Christians' initiatives to get involved in partisan politics and third, the need for collaborative action to respond to the dynamics of the Nigeria religious system. This collaboration or networking is both intra-religious and inter-religious.

One of the remarkable trends of the last decade among the Christian population of Southern Nigeria has been the dramatic rise of the so-called "charismatic" or "Pentecostal" movement. Literally thousands of new Churches and evangelical groups have been established in cities and towns, forming a broad-based religious movement which is rapidly becoming a powerful new social and religious force.[21]

Ruth Marshall's description above of the growth and impact of the Pentecostal movement in Nigeria is apt. She is also partly right to have linked modern Pentecostalism to the Anglo-American revivalist charismatic movement particularly in the early part of the 20th century. Liardon's biographical documentation of champions of this movement (God's Generals)[22] reveals an internationalization of the ministries of Pentecostal preachers like William Seymour (the catalyst of the Azusa Pentecostal revival in America), Smith Wigglesorth, Aimée Semple Mcpherson, and Kathryn Kuhlman. Each of these persons has left a mark upon the face of modern Pentecostalism globally. Aimee Semple McPherson founded the Church of the Foursquare Gospel in July 1922 as well as the training institution for producing Pentecostal pastors, the Lighthouse of International Foursquare Evangelism (LIFE) Bible College in February 1923.[23] The Foursquare Gospel Church in Nigeria is one of the earliest modern Pentecostal Churches in the country. It has also played a leading role in the formation and running of the Pentecostal Fellowship of Nigeria. Indeed, some Churches which constitute the Pentecostal movement in Nigeria are international or global. Through the influence of Wigglesworth, the recourse to 'faith' as a doctrinal pivot in Christian living became pronounced, while the dynamic manifestation of the healing and deliverance phenomenon is traceable to Kathryn Kuhlman. Today, Pentecostalism is synonymous with the demonstration of the 'anointing'. These pioneer classical Pentecostal preachers were succeeded by equally prominent international preachers such as Oral Roberts, Kenneth Hagin, Billy Graham and T. L. Osborn. Whereas these figures have used literature and the electronic media to impact Nigeria, perhaps the most consistent impact in terms of personal contact – evangelism, has come from the German evangelist, Reinhard Bonnke, who has continued to draw the biggest crowd in each of his numerous crusades in various parts of the country. The influence of these Pentecostal leaders and their groups contribute to the globalization of Pentecostalism within the religious forum. Today, there is a rather worrisome proliferation of Pentecostal Churches, many of which have been characterized in many public circles as pseudo-churches characterized by 'questionable' doctrinal practices and syncretism.

In our view, the common exclusion by scholars, of the African Initiated Churches (AIC) as a branch of Pentecostals is a fundamental error. This is because, on a theological level, they are indeed Pentecostal and charismatic in doctrine and nature. Pentecostalism in Nigeria initially began as a reaction to the pronounced legalism and orthodoxy of the mainline mission churches (like the Catholic, Anglican and Methodist), especially their resistance to aspects of Pentecostal doctrines such as faith healing, exorcism, speaking in tongues, visions and prophecy, as well as charismatic expression in songs and worship. These qualities which have marked the Nigeria Pentecostal movement is no longer the exclusive preserve of so-called Pentecostal churches. The Mission/Evangelical churches in Nigeria, such as the Anglicans and Methodists are currently imbibing Pentecostalism by allowing divine healing, speaking in tongues and charismatic worship, a trend which has encouraged many of their members, which left for Pentecostal churches, to return. Many of these churches today are more 'Pentecostal' in practice than the Pentecostal churches themselves; therefore the term 'Pentecostalism' in present usage has transcended the limited boundary of a group of churches, but is more appropriately a universal phenomenon found in virtually every church group in this context. It appears that the very spread of the Pentecostal spirit in most churches is in itself a form of spiritual globalization. However, in discussing religious networking in relation to the Pentecostal Fellowship of Nigeria, we mean those group of churches which still lay claim to Pentecostal characterization as a sub-group identity within the umbrella of the general organized body of the Christian Association of Nigeria (CAN). Prior to the emergence of CAN, the Christian Council of Nigeria was founded on March 14th 1930, made up of Protestant and Evangelical Church groups affiliated to the World Council of Churches. It had the set objectives of 'Fostering Fellowship and unity of the Christian Church in Nigeria, *to further the realization of its oneness with the church throughout the world* (emphasis mine) and keep in touch with the International Missionary Council and the World Council of Churches in Geneva.'[24] In other words, CCN was set up to further pursue the goal of globalization, while CAN may be regarded as a regional arm in the realization of this goal.

Religious networking among Nigerian Churches was effectively enhanced by the formation at the National Catholic Secretariat in Lagos, of Christian Association of Nigeria on August 27, 1976. CAN objectives included the defense of the general interest of Christians in the nation, promoting understanding, peace and unity among the various people, particularly Christians (and church denominations) and serving as watchdog of the spiritual and moral welfare of the nation.[25] These aims imply networking between the following sub-groups which make up CAN[26]: the Catholic Secretariat of Nigeria (CSN); the Christian Council of Nigeria (CCN); the 'Christian' Pentecostal Fellowship of Nigeria (CPFN, which later evolved into PFN after a split of the initial

CPFN); Organization of African Instituted Churches (OAIC) and the Evangelical Church of West Africa (ECWA, and its close affiliate, the ethnic (Hausa) *Tarayya Ekklesiyoyin Kristi a Nigeria* (TEKAN). The broad composition of CAN is made up of strange bedfellows, different in many respects, but united by common goals; first by the common Christian profession and second, by the need to defend Christian interests. Oyalana posits that ecumenical witnessing through networking is the key to achieving positive impact of Christianity in Nigeria.[27]

The chief hindrances for PFN in achieving this aim is discernible from the following statement (published as advertorial), being outcome of its conference (attended by more than 5000 ministers throughout the country), which asserted thus:

> The conference decried the attitude of certain pretenders who merely lay claim to the Pentecostal faith, but lack Godly character and good reputation. It therefore condemned all forms of rebellion and breakaways... The PFN in unequivocal terms condemned every thing that gives even the most insignificant semblance of the practice of occultism, spiritism of necromancy among Christians...The PFN repudiated the practice of inadequately exposed, unqualified, insufficiently experienced, and partly matured ministers using the title of Bishop as a stepping stone to compelling unearned recognition. Discipline shall be strictly followed Biblically with no sacred cow. Honour must come back to the pulpit...[28]

The PFN remains a force to be reckoned with socially and politically as it has been playing complementary roles, to its mother body (CAN), in political intervention. Politically, the potency of CAN/PFN intervention has depended upon the vibrancy of their respective leadership at any point in time. When the President of CAN is politically potent, he speaks for all Christians in Nigeria including the PFN, but when the CAN leadership is complacent or compromising in response to urgent anti-Christian politics, the PFN often comes out to speak, not just for its members but for the entire Christians in the nation. A typical case is the role of Benson Idahosa (then president of PFN) during the 1993 electioneering campaigns when the PFN summoned presidential aspirants of the political parties to a public debate and scrutiny to declare their manifestoes as it affects Christian interest. The widely publicized exercise featured Chief M. K. O. Abiola (of the Social Democratic Party) a Muslim, responding to Idahosa's questions, pledging to protect Christian political interests if he won the elections. Based partly on the public support and endorsement of the PFN, the Christian populace in the country voted massively for Chief Abiola. He was believed to have won the elections but it was annulled by the military regime of Ibrahim Babangida.

The resultant crisis of the June 12 1993 election annulment further proved the PFN and CAN as potent political forces as well as beacon of hope and justice. Whereas some human rights and Muslim organizations compromised the fight for the de-annulment of the June 12 1993 election, PFN and CAN stood solidly for the actualization of Abiola's presidency. Rather unfortunately, Abiola died in prison custody in controversial circumstances. He died right in the presence of American delegation that came to negotiate his release. He was suspected to have been poisoned by the State in conspiracy with some international forces. The fact that the Christian populace supported and defended the interest of a Muslim-Muslim ticket (both the presidential and vice-presidential aspirants of the SDP were Muslims, contrary to erstwhile practice of religious balancing between Christians and Muslims), perhaps portrayed the confidence they had in the PFN. The June 12 1993 election annulment later threw the country into serious political impasse and further military rule many years after.

The peculiar advantage of the Pentecostal Fellowship of Nigeria is its wide/global appeal and composition which gives it relative advantage over the mission/evangelical churches which are strictly denominational. Pentecostal revival has drawn many members of these churches into the Pentecostal fold, in their search for better spiritual fulfillment. Any major Pentecostal assembly today will find in attendance, many Christians who do not belong to the Pentecostal churches. Some laterally convert, while some remain in their churches but attend special programs particularly camp meetings organized by Pentecostal churches. For example, the monthly 'Holy Ghost Service' of the Redeemed Christian Church of God draws attendance from virtually every church denomination in Nigeria and beyond. At the church's convention in 2000 tagged 'Open Heavens', it claimed to have gathered about six million people. The evolution of camp-evangelism has become the latest tool in enhancing the Christian network and globalization process. Through such assemblies, there is regular interaction between church as well as political leaders who attend the Church programs, as a forum for networking. This networking has facilitated the partial input/influence of the church in the Nigerian political process.

At local level, the PFN maintains a central headquarter with a Secretariat headed by the President, the current one being Mike Okonkwo, the founder and head of 'The Redeemed Evangelical Mission' (TREM). Each State has a branch Executive Committee, headed by a Chairman, who supervises the Local Government chapters which are directly in touch with the grass root churches. The PFN utilizes these layers to network the numerous Pentecostal Churches. Oftentimes, this network is enhanced by joint conferences, evangelistic crusades and workshops. The PFN is networked to the International Pentecostal Fellowship based in the United States of America. It also maintains relations with major Pentecostal organizations such as the 'Full Gospel Businessmen Fellowship International'.

A major global networking by the PFN was achieved by the invitation of the German preacher, Evangelist Reinhard Bonnke to General Olusegun Obasanjo's inauguration as President of the Federal Republic of Nigeria in May 1999. Following a prolonged military rule under successive Muslim Heads of State, the Churches rallied round under the collaborative arrangement of CAN and PFN in May 1999 to conduct a thanksgiving and dedication service to usher in the tenure of Obasanjo whom the Christians perceive as representative of Christian leadership. Apart from the active role of the (then) President of CAN (The Methodist Prelate Sunday Mbang) and the President of PFN (Mike Okonkwo), in the service, the prayerful role of Evangelist Bonnke, a non-Nigerian, can be viewed from the perspective of globalization. This is typical of the potential Nigeria-German collaboration. President Obasanjo reciprocated the German preacher's support by personally attending in Lagos, the open-air crusade conducted by the Evangelist. The presence of the Nigeria President at a public evangelistic rally in 2000 is indicative of the success of interaction between Pentecostal Christianity and politics in Nigeria.

However, subsequent events in the country's politics raised questions of the genuineness of Government-Church alliance. For instance, when more than one thousand Christians were massacred by Muslim *Sharia* fanatics in Kaduna in 2001, the President neither took immediate steps to rescue them, neither has anyone been prosecuted by the government for the heinous crime. Rather, the President is increasingly seen by many Christians as drifting favorably towards Muslim interests in a manner that raises questions about the influence of the Pentecostal preachers who surround and influence his policies. It is suspected that some Pentecostal churches have benefited from direct favors by the President in the approval granted them to run private Universities, which are run as commercial-profit oriented ventures, not as mission institutions. Their fees are far beyond the reach of middle class citizens, not even affordable by majority of the church members whose monies were used to set up such institutions.

Another local networking effort by the PFN was the consultative conference of selected Church leaders held at Abuja, the country's capital in 2000 to address in a practical manner, the emergent crisis arising from forceful imposition of Islamic *Sharia* legal system in the Northern parts of the country. At the meeting, initiated and sponsored by the PFN, were representatives of various Churches (Orthodox, Evangelical and Pentecostal), the 'Eclectic Movement' a Christian-political group in Nigeria, selected ethnic groupings and some respected elder statesmen. The communiqué of the conference presided over by the PFN President had far-reaching impact upon the attitude of the government towards Christian rights, particular as it affects the Christians areas in the Muslim-dominated Northern part of the country.

It is fast becoming a norm for many Pentecostal churches to demonstrate their globalization interest through the hoisting of flags of countries where their churches have networked or established branches. A typical church convention will feature several such flags on display to show their footholds in various parts of the world. To compliment this is another trend by many church leaders to invite foreign speakers (mostly from America and Europe) to their local programs. Perhaps this is deliberate to enhance their global outlook in the eyes of the public or to enable such leaders enjoy similar invitation to minister outside the country, of course with financial benefits. Although these new innovations may be interpreted as self-advertisement, it does show nonetheless that there is a growing consciousness by Nigerian Pentecostals to identify with religious globalization. Some Nigerian Pentecostal churches have vibrant branches in other nations. In the United Kingdom, Matthew Ashimolowo's 'Kingsway International Christian Church' is one of the largest and most prominent in London. The crusades of late Archbishop Benson Idahosa was global in dimension. The church planting initiatives of the 'Redeemed Christian Church of God' headed by Pastor E. A. Adeboye and the 'Deeper Christian Life Ministry' headed by Pastor W. F. Kumuyi have been of international repute. Bishop David Oyedepo's growing missionary endeavor is an outreach through the posting of preachers and missionaries to many nations of the world. All these efforts are sustained through effective networking. The internet has been an effective modern tool to enhance this move.

Heinz Hunke has recognized that many churches and faith organizations are on the Internet:

> In spite of the difficulties in getting an overall detailed and accurate global panorama, one can conclude that the church's presence on the electronic communication highways is considerable. But it comes across as a divided and segmented church. Next to the mainstream churches, there are hundreds of sites of small church communities. Next to ecumenical sites are those of strongly fundamental Christian groups.[29]

Many Nigerian Pentecostal and Mission churches are already on the Internet. This exposure is bringing them closer to global trends. Web sites have been created by major Nigerian Pentecostal churches such as Redeemed Christian Church of God, Deeper Life Bible Church, Christ Embassy, Winners Chapel, etc. Their services are also featured on satellite television, such as the Trinity Broadcasting Network (TBN) which is viewed globally. In the United Kingdom, not less than twenty Nigerian-led churches feature regularly on new television channels such as God Channel, Revelation, Daystar, etc. The concept of African reverse-mission to Europe appears to have been greatly enhanced through this electronic media networking.

PFN AND INTER-RELIGIOUS NETWORKING

> Pentecostalism provides new networks, both spiritual and material, which extend beyond local, ethnic, regional and even class considerations...At the local or national level, these networks provide a sense of belonging and common purpose...Networks extend beyond the national to the global...It carries with it the sense of belonging to a global movement or access...[30]

There are two levels of inter-religious interaction from the Christian perspective. First, is the Christian-Muslim relation and the second is the Christian-African Religion adherents relations. There have been concerted efforts by numerous Nigerian scholars of religion to advocate peaceful co-existence among adherents of the three major religious in Nigeria, viz. Christianity, Islam and African Religion (AFREL).[31] Opeloye focuses on how to enhance Christian-Muslim networking in Nigeria. He advocates common teaching of Islam and Christianity in schools and the provision for this in the curriculum of every educational institution. This is in order to inculcate the virtues of religious harmony. He also discourages what he terms aggressive proselytization by adherents of one religion over others. In this respect he refers to the characteristic proselytization zeal and methods of Christian Pentecostals in Nigeria. The members of PFN have been most vibrant in evangelism and have done this in spite of Muslim resistance. Even in the Muslim dominated Northern parts of the country the mutual suspicion over the issue of proselytization has been a common obstacle to Christian-Muslim networking in Nigeria. Our earlier study on 'Christian-African religious interactions in Nigeria'[32] established that although African Religion has a sizeable number of adherents, the most prominent and visible on the Nigerian socio-political scene are Christians and Muslims. It is between these two that religious misunderstanding and clashes have been common. AFREL by its very nature believes in religious networking because of its accommodating doctrine. The Yoruba adage *Oju orun to eye fo lai fi ara kan ra* (the sky is broad enough for birds of different species to fly without collision), is indicative of the 'live and let live' ideology of adherents of the traditional religion. AFREL itself is somewhat polytheistic (admitting and ready to still admit many more gods into its pantheon). Scholars like Bolaji Idowu and Ade Dopamu describe polytheism as an inappropriate description of the Yoruba pantheon, rather they argue that the term diffused monotheism is more appropriate to describe the religion. The various cults of divinities are expected to network to achieve a global harmony under the control of the Supreme God, *Olodumare* (of the Yorubas).

There are suspicions that some Pentecostal groups patronize AFREL centers for supernatural powers which are used to enhance their supernatural accomplishments which draw crowds into their assemblies. In this regard, it is feared among many, that the sources of supernatural powers displayed by some 'miracle preachers' are esoteric and unchristian. This possibility prompted the PFN to warn in its earlier referred communiqué, against questionable doctrinal practices by some of its members. Interaction at the social level, between Christianity and AFREL is inevitable for it is from the latter that traditional rulers and institutions draw their social relevance and strength. The traditional rulers (i.e. *Oba* in Yoruba or *Obi* in Igbo) are regarded as the custodians of the tradition and culture of their people, and father of their multi-religious subjects. They are the central connecting point in religious networking because in the traditional kingship institution, adherents of the various religions under their domain find confluence and interaction. Incidentally, there are several such rulers or Chiefs who are now Pentecostal Christians. Their presence is publicly recognized at huge Pentecostal gatherings. Here is an inherent institutional religious networking to achieve peaceful co-existence in the society. In times of religious crisis, the traditional rulers are the regular resource persons to effect amicable resolution of conflicts.

The Federal Government of Nigeria initiated a major inter-religious network in setting up the Advisory Council on Religious Affairs, to mediate between adherents of religions as well as advise government on sensitive religious matters. The body, comprising leaders of the Christian Association of Nigeria, leaders of Pentecostal Fellowship of Nigeria (on the Christian side) and leaders of the Nigeria Supreme Council for Islamic Affairs (a Muslim counter-part of CAN) was established at Kaduna in 1973. The Islamic team is led by the Sultan of Sokoto Emirate, who is traditionally seen as the Chief propagator of Islam in Nigeria. Despite the existence of this group, no major effective and positive networking has been achieved publicly because it became a toothless bulldog, unable to prevent recurrent violent Christian-Muslim clashes in parts of the North, the most recent of which was the *Sharia* riots in Kaduna in 2000. The Advisory Council on Religious Affairs was on ground when the then military government of Ibrahim Babangida finally registered Nigeria as full member of the Organization of Islamic Conference in 1986, yet it could do nothing to check this constitutional violation of Nigeria's Constitution regarding secularity. At a point the body itself was bedeviled by the problem it was meant to solve, members disagreed among themselves on which religion should provide its leadership. The PFN has not been able to comfortably network with Islam at this level. Whatever success is achieved on the terrain of inter-faith relationship in Nigeria is largely at personal/individual and family levels. For instance, it is common in Southern Nigeria to have a typical extended family composed of adherents of the different faiths.

Africans in the Diaspora have maintained Christian–AFREL networking to sustain their social relevance with their roots. As we noted elsewhere, Africans in Diaspora, out of patriotic zeal to identify themselves with their roots, found a way out by 'syncretizing' AFREL with Christianity. AFREL divinities were adopted and renamed after Roman Catholic saints...[33] The following adaptations were made by Brazilian and Cuban Africans:

Yoruba Deity	Roman Catholic Saints
Ogun (god of iron)	St. John the Baptist (in Cuba)
	St. Anthony (in Brazil)
Sango (god of thunder)	St. Jerome
Oshun (river goddess of Fertility)	Our Lady of Candlemas
Orisa Nla (Archdivinity)	Virgen de la Meroco (Virgin of Mercy)
Osoyin (god of healing)	St. Raphael
Ifa (divination divinity)	St. Francis of Assisi

We should remark that the characters of the above-adapted Saints are not necessarily compatible with the divinities in the

Yoruba traditional pantheon. It appears that the adaptation was effectively carried out by Africans in Diaspora to network their root and to use Roman Catholic Saints in expressing of their religion. Although Pentecostals do not believe in veneration of Saints, the above action is intended to show that there is a general desire by oppressed Africans (like other oppressed people elsewhere) to resist perceived elements of imperialism, albeit religious. This is part of the underlying motif in the current inculturation theology among African people.

Giddens aptly argues that globalization is the reason for the revival of local cultural identities in different parts of the world.[34] There is indeed a revival of cultural consciousness among various people or ethnic groups in Nigeria, even in religious circles. It appears that such conscious efforts to solidarize at group levels eventually evolve into identifying with the globalization process. The European Union, the unification of Germany and the formation of the African Union, even the 'Economic Community of West African States' (ECOWAS) are examples of group networks which ultimately evolve into globalization. A revolution was borne in Africa in the wake of this century when African Initiated Churches, prophetic in nature, emerged. Calvin Rieber regards indigenous Christianity as a form of an African Religion.[35] This is not exactly correct. Indigenous Christianity is essentially Christian and is distinct from African Religion. The process of contextualizing Christianity in African culture saw to the rapid use of African traditional songs, lyrics, music, dancing, clapping, charismatic attitude at worship and encouragement of manifestation of spiritual gifts such as prophecy, visions, faith healing, etc. in order to satisfy the psychological, inquisitive and highly emotional African mind. They want a Christianity that provides spiritual substitute to what they enjoyed in the ir indigenous religion. The Christ Apostolic Church (CAC), the Cherubim and Seraphim Church (C&S) and the Celestial Church of Christ (CCC) have been most prominent in meeting this need. Their large memberships have often been contacted to network with Pentecostal Fellowship of Nigeria for joint Christian programs.

The Nigerian academic sphere has also contributed to the networking of the adherents of the three religions in Nigeria. Apart from establishing inter-religious associations, virtually all Departments of Religious Studies in Nigerian Universities require students to offer courses in each of the three religions. The objective is to educate them about religions other than their own confession, hoping to achieve understanding and cooperation between adherents through dialogue. The ultimate viewpoint is to argue in the spirit of globalization, that there should be religious harmony in the world.

The Nigerian religious scene has been affected by the religious globalization process. Its direction at local levels has been influenced by international dynamics. The literature and tapes which influence Pentecostalism in Nigeria have been dominantly global. In any local church, Pentecostal leaders like Kenneth Hagin, and Reinhard Bonnke have some influence in the matter of faith, doctrine and Christian practice. Even some leading Pentecostal figures in Nigeria operate as 'surrogates' of their foreign 'godfathers' and mentors'. The face of Pentecostalism in contemporary Nigeria churches is somewhat westernized that a Nigerian Pentecostal will feel very well at home in an American Pentecostal gathering. There is what we can therefore call Pentecostal globalization, a move which also influences orthodox churches like the Anglican, Methodist, Baptist and even Roman Catholics (who now have vibrant charismatic/ Pentecostal sub-groups). However, in spite of dominant foreign presence on Nigeria's Pentecostal landscape, Pentecostalism in the Nigerian context today derives essentially from the initiatives and charisma of local founders and leaders. Today, Africa is in the process of re-evangelizing the Western world, which appears to have neglected a substantial part of their Christian heritage. In this respect, African Initiated Churches are active participants of the globalization process.

Giddens again submits that 'globalization is not incidental to our lives today. It is a shift in our very life circumstances. It is the way we now live'.[36] In the ongoing globalization process, the religious factor and dynamics may provide both explanation and direction for the future. In this context the thrust of Pentecostal perception of globalization is inevitably eschatological and apocalyptic; that the Messiah will in his millennial reign preside over a global government (Isa. 9:6-7, Ps. 2:8, 91:9; Rev. 11:17) and that even prior to this, there will be a global government to be controlled by an Antichrist. In other words, there appears to be a supernatural mastermind behind the globalization process on the comprehensive scale. Prigogine implies this when he states that '...the world is a system in construction to which we bring a modest contribution.'[37] The question is, who is constructing the globalization process? He contradicts himself later when he states that '...indeed, nobody has planned the networked society and the information explosion. It is a remarkable example of spontaneous emergence of new forms of society'.

This viewpoint has in fact made Pentecostals to be wary of the globalization process and ideology, and a resistance of this trend is one major impetus for increased Christian evangelism mostly by the Pentecostal churches before the consummation of the globalization project. O'Donovan puts it clearly in the following statement:

> What will be the final outcome of history? The Bible tells us where history is leading and how it will end. The Bible assures us that there will one day be a new heaven and a new earth...But what will happen before that golden age? The Bible predicts many things that will take place as the end of history approaches. These events are related to what God and Satan are doing in the present world.[38]

We submit that it is within this context that Pentecostal Churches in Nigeria interpret virtually every dimension of the globalization process thus far. Their disposition to it is neither of excitement nor zealous participation, but cautious observation and curious anticipation.

Bibliography

Akintola, I. L., *Shariah in Nigeria*, Ijebu Ode: Shebiotimo Press, 2001.

Asaju, D. F., 'Politicization of Religion in Nigeria', in Segun Johnson (ed.) *Studies in Selected Nigeria Problems*, Lagos: Okanlawon Press, 1990, pp. 105-130.

Ayegboyin, Deji, 'Religious Associations and the new Political Dispensation in Nigeria', in Aderibigbe G. and Ayegboyin D. (eds.) *Religion and Politics*, Lagos: NASRED, 1995, pp. 95-118.

Bryant M. Darol, 'Can there be a Muslim-Christian Dialogue Concerning Jesus/Isah?', in Bryant M.D. and Ali S. (eds.) *Muslim-Christian Dialogue*, Minnesota: Paragon House, 1998, pp. 168-180.

Constitution of the Christian Association of Nigeria

Constitution of the Christian Council of Nigeria

Constitution of the Federal Republic of Nigeria 1979, Lagos: Government Press, 1979.

Eldson, Ron, *Bent World: A Christian Response to the Environmental Crisis*, Illinois: Intervarsity Press, 1981.

European Commission, 1997.

Giddens Anthony, London, *Ruth/BBC Lecture Series*, 1999.

Hunke, Heinz, 'Churches and Faith Organizations on the Internet', *Echoes*, World Council of Churches, 12, 1997.

Liardon, Roberts, *God's Generals*, Kaduna: Evangel Publications, 1998.

Marshall-Fratani, Ruth, 'Mediating the Global and Local in Nigerian Pentecostalism', *Journal of Religion in Africa*, 28, 3, 1998, pp. 278-315.

Marshall, Ruth, 'Pentecostalism in Southern Nigeria: An Overview', in Paul Gifford (ed.) *New Dimensions in African Christianity*, Nairobi: All Africa Conference of Churches, 1992, pp. 7-32.

O'Donovan, Wilbur, *Biblical Christianity in African Perspective*, Carlisle: Paternosta Press, 1996.

Opeloye, M. O., 'Building Bridges of Understanding between Islam and Christianity in Nigeria', *Inaugural Lecture*, Lagos State University, 2001.

Opeloye, M.O. and Asaju, D. F., 'Christian-African Religion Interaction in Nigeria', *Studia Missionalia*, 43, 1994, pp. 295-312.

Oyalana, A. S., 'Ecumenical witnessing with special reference to Nigeria', in Asaju, D. F. (ed.) *Christianity and Selected Nigerian Issues*, Lagos: Lagos State University, 1994, pp. 75-90.

Prigogine, I., 'The Networked Society', *Journal of World Systems Research*, 6, 3, Fall/Winter, 2000.

Raiser, Konrad, 'Oikumene and Globalization', *Echoes*, World Council of Churches, 12, 1997, pp. 1-11.

Rieber, Calvin, 'Traditional Christianity as an African Religion', in Booth N. S., (ed.) *African Religions*, Lagos: N. O. K., 1979, pp. 255-274.

Robertson, Roland, 'Globalization, Politics and Religion', in J. A. Beckford and Thomas Luckmann (eds.) *Sage Studies in International Sociology*, 1989, pp. 11-23.

Stackhouse, Max. L., 'Politics and Religion', in Mircea Eliade (ed.) *The Encyclopaedia of Religion*, vol. II, New York: Macmillan, 1987, pp. 408-422.

Thomson Graham, 'Introduction: Situating Globalization', *International Social Science Journal*, 51, 1999, pp. 135-147.

Notes

1. Graham Thomson, 'Introduction: Situating Globalization', *International Social Science Journal*, 51, 1999, p.139.

2. Akin Jimoh, 'The Problem with Globalization', *The Guardian*, February 1, 2001, p.15.

3. Anthony Giddens, *Ruth/BBC Lecture*, London, 1999, p.1.

4. *European Commission*, 1997, p.45.

5. Konrad Raiser, 'Oikumene and Globalization', *Echoes*, WCC, 12, 1997, p.3.

6. Roland Robertson, 'Globalization, Politics and Religion', in J. A. Beckford and Thomas Luckmann (ed.) *Sage Studies in International Sociology*, 1989, p.12.

7. Robertson, p. 12.

8. Robertson, p. 12.

9. D. F. Asaju, 'Politicization of Religion in Nigeria', in Segun Johnson (ed.) *Studies in Selected Nigeria problems*, Lagos: Okanlawon Press, 1990, p. 112.

10. M. Darol Bryant 'Can there be a Muslim-Christian Dialogue concerning Jesus/Isah?', in M. D. Bryant and S. Ali (eds.) *Muslim-Christian Dialogue*, Minnesota: Paragon House, 1998.

11. The governments of Saudi Arabia, Iran and Libya were outspoken, through their respective Ambassadors in supporting the implementation of *Sharia* as State religion. Muammar Gaddafi of Libya advocated same during his visit to Nigeria in 1998.

12. *The Constitution of the Federal Republic of Nigeria*, 1979, Section 10.

13. I. L. Akintola, *Sharia in Nigeria*, Ijebu Ode: Shebiotimo Press, 2001, p. 200.

14. Max L. Stackhouse, 'Politics and Religion', in Mircea Eliade (ed.) *The Encyclopaedia of Religion*, Vol. II, New York: Macmillan, 1987, p. 410.

15. Stackhouse, p. 13.

16. Stackhouse, p. 13.

17. Robertson, p. 12.

18. Robertson, p. 16.

19. Ron Elsdon, *Bent World: A Christian Response to the Environmental Crisis*, Illinois: Intervarsity Press, 1981, p. 60.

20. Communique of the 6th Biennial Conference of the Pentecostal Fellowship of Nigeria (PFN), 6-8th February 2001. See *The Guardian*, February 22, 2001, p. 28.

21. Ruth Marshall, 'Pentecostalism in Southern Nigeria: An Overview', in Paul Gifford (ed.) *New Dimensions in African Christianity*, Nairobi: All Africa Conference of Churches, 1992, p. 7.

22. Roberts Liardon, *God's Generals*, Kaduna: Evangel Publications, 1998.

23. Liardon, pp. 254-255.

24. *Constitution of the Christian Council of Nigeria*, Section 2 (2).

25. *Constitution of the Christian Association of Nigeria* (CAN) Section 5: 6-8.

26. Deji Ayegboyin, 'Religious Associations and the new Political Dispensation in Nigeria', in Gbola Aderibigbe and Deji Ayegboyin (eds.), *Religion and Politics*, Lagos: Nigeria Association for the Study of Religious Education, 1995, p. 116.

27. A. S. Oyalana, 'Ecumenical Witnessing with Special reference to Nigeria', in D. F. Asaju (ed.), *Christianity and Selected Nigerian Issues*, Lagos: Lagos State University Christian Studies Unit, 1994, p. 75f.

28. Communique of the 6th Biennial Conference of the Pentecostal Fellowship of Nigeria (PFN), 6-8th February 2001. See *The Guardian*, February 22, 2001, p. 28.

29. 'Churches and Faith Organizations on the Internet', *Echoes* (WCC), Vol. 12, 1997, p. 29.

30. Ruth Marshall-Fratani, 'Mediating the Global and Local in Nigerian Pentecostalism', *Journal of Religion in Africa*, 28, 3, 1998, p.284.

31. M. O. Opeloye, 'Building Bridges of Understanding between Islam and Christianity in Nigeria', 12th Inaugural Lecture (20th March 2001), Lagos State University, pp. 66-67.

32. M. O. Opeloye and D. F. Asaju, 'Christian-African Religion Interaction in Nigeria', *Studia Missionalia*, 43, 1994, pp. 269-312.

33. *Ibid.*, 307-308

34. Giddens, p. 3.

35. Calvin Rieber, 'Traditional Christianity as an African Religion', in N. S. Booth (ed.) *African Religions*, Lagos: NOK, 1979, p. 269.

36. Giddens, p. 6.

37. I. Prigogogine, 'The Networked Society', *Journal of World Systems Research*, 6, 3, Fall/Winter 2000, p. 892.

38. Wilbur O'Donovan, *Biblical Christianity in African Perspective*, Carlisle: Paternosta Press, 1996, p. 342.

FEMALE RELIGIOUS LEADERSHIP IN NIGERIAN PENTECOSTALISM: EMBERS OR GALE?

Bolaji Bateye

INTRODUCTION

Pentecostalism has brought the advent of women in church leadership roles to become a major issue in Nigerian Christianity. Increasingly, churches are seen to be promoting women to leadership positions hitherto denied them. The question is whether this is just a temporary fad, a novelty, a display of tokenism that will soon pass away (likened to embers) or is part of an ongoing momentum that will become a permanent feature of Pentecostalism, if not the entire 'Christendom' in Nigeria (likened to a gale). This chapter attempts to come to grips with this issue by giving insight into the context of women in leadership roles among some Pentecostal Churches of South western Nigeria. Women taking up leadership roles for our purpose is meant that women act and function in the official church offices as General overseers, Bishops, Pastors and Teachers. They baptize, administer communion, perform marriages and funerals and generally do the work of ministers (McBeth, 1979:71). There are various terminologies used to depict a large number of African Initiated Churches, such as 'Independent Pentecostal Churches' (Hollenweger, 1972: 51), 'African Pentecostal Churches' (Anderson, 2002) and 'Pentecostal/ Charismatic' (Ojo, 1998: 4).

The Pentecostal churches that form the focus of our study lay emphasis on new birth experience, sanctification, holy living, evangelism, and monogamy as God's standard for marriage, restitution and the practice of spiritual gifts. In many ways they are in the process of metamorphosis from the old orthodox colonial church ways to those that are more liberal with respect to women and hence provide an opportunity for observing the dynamics of attitudinal changes toward women in leadership roles that are emerging from this context. The following questions are raised and addressed to direct this study viz: What was the image of women in the original colonial church setting? What are the motivations of the female leaders? What are the reactions towards the phenomenon of female leadership in the church? What are the prospects for female leadership?

COLONIALISM AND ITS IMPLICATIONS ON WOMEN IN THE CHURCH

It is deemed necessary to account for attitudes of Nigerian Christian converts before the appearance of the female religious leaders in question. The initial attitude of Christian converts was established with the introduction of Christianity in Nigeria. Colonialism brought in its wake missionaries and traders among others to the Nigerian coast ostensibly to proselytize and 'civilize' the African 'native'. The planting of Christianity was associated with European culture, for that was the culture of the missionaries. The missionaries regarded African culture as barbaric and prohibited African cultural practices from being expressed in the church. Hence, the culture of the early mission-oriented church was European. Understandably, European culture to the early African converts was synonymous with the practices of the church and hence had a 'divine mandate' as it was supposedly Bible based. This situation had definite implications on women. European culture does not permit polygamy and therefore the oppression suffered as a cause of polygamy was removed from the women. In this wise the church was considered as liberating in some aspects to the women. However, the European culture of that time was that of the Victorian era that upheld the attitude and accepted the idea that man was a superior being meant by God and nature to dominate the world, while women were meant to obey and serve (Lane, 1983: 67). Thus there was a kind of ambivalence on the part of the African woman convert towards European culture.

Nevertheless, overall, they had the attitude that European culture was more liberating, than oppressive for the African woman and that the demands of the European missionary church culture on them were much less rigorous than that of African culture. For them, women's experience in Africa was that of perpetuating servitude to the male. Accordingly, they were not discouraged from this stance by the seemingly justification of Scripture for the exclusion of women from leadership roles in the church. There has been a romanticized view of African culture as to whether being oppressive or otherwise to women, as depending on the person whose views were sought. The intriguing fact is those that would defend African culture in this light with respect to women are invariably the men. Exceptions, such as, the female scholar Zulu Sofola would like to defend African culture as favorable to women and regard the European culture as, 'alien and destructive to the African female psychic...unfortunately their alien culture descended upon us with their male-defined, male-centered and entirely male cosmology and dislodged the female component of African social order' (Sofola, 1994: 1). She and others like her would be put to the test to counter the observation of the feminist scholar Mercy Oduyoye that African culture is oppressive to women and that even to cite African heroines means to confirm the uniqueness of their contribution. Oduyoye went as far to state that, 'matriliny may give the impression of the structural dominance of women in certain parts of Africa, but (even where the marriage is not virilocal) no real power resides in the hands of the woman. As to political power, even the matrilineal, matrilocal Asante are not matriarchal' (Oduyoye, 1986: 123).

In summary, the advent of Christianity in Nigeria was a consequence of the proselytizing efforts of expatriate missionaries in the 1800's. The colonial churches were expatriate administered bodies that reflected the gender biases of the colonial masters that discriminated against women. The male dominated orientation of Islamic and western cultures dislodged the female component of the African social order (Bateye, 2002a: 86). After a period, schisms occurred in the colonial churches over the imposition that whites only be put in major leadership roles in the church. At that time, black African preachers were discriminated against even when they were men. The belief then was that black men and especially women were not qualified to lead a church. The whites saw themselves as 'saints' and the only qualified people who should lead the churches of God. This partly led some African converts to break away from the mother church and to found their own independent churches. One of the most significant developments of African Christianity in independent Africa is the emergence of the charismatic movements. Since the 1970's there had been a dramatic rise in the activities of Pentecostal and charismatic movements, most of which go by the name of ministries or fellowships or evangelistic associations (Ojo, 1998). Unlike the colonial churches, these Pentecostal churches were liberal in matters of women taking up leadership roles in the church, so much so that some churches are both founded and administered by women.

FEMALE RELIGIOUS LEADERSHIP MOTIVATION

A significant factor in the determination of whether the situation of female leadership is a case of embers or gale is to identify the particular motivations of female leadership in the church in question. The demise of female religious leadership would be inevitable if their motivation fails to cater for others. Accordingly, it is deemed necessary in this chapter to account for the motivation of female religious leaders in the promotion of female leadership in Pentecostal churches. To facilitate in clarifying this issue, two female religious leaders: Archbishop (Dr.) Dorcas Siyanbola Olaniyi and Dr. Stella Ajisebute both founders/leaders of churches in Ile-Ife are surveyed as examples of female religious leaders that display commitment to promoting female church leadership. Dorcas Olaniyi is selected on the basis of her success story, popularity and (contentment) intentions to encourage women by exposing church practices that discriminate against women as not being by divine mandate. The true Biblical representation of women is her clarion call and has inspired her major writings. Stella Ajisebute combines an academic career with ministry. Although her discipline is Microbiology and not in Theology or Religious Studies, her unique position as a University lecturer and a Pastor presents her in the unique position of interacting with both the ivory tower and public sphere. A lot stands to be gained, perhaps from questions probing her motivation for encouraging women to take up leadership roles in church ministry.

Archbishop Dorcas Olaniyi

Dorcas Olaniyi has achieved wide reputation as preacher and church founder. She is of Yoruba parentage and founder of the widely acclaimed Agbala Daniel Church in Nigeria. It has its headquarters at Ibadan with branches within Nigeria and abroad, the United States and Great Britain. Born in 1934 of Yoruba parentage, Dorcas Olaniyi spent her childhood under the care of white Baptist missionaries. She is from a polygamous family and the only child of her mother. As a child, she was prone to having visions. Her parents believed in the education of daughters as well as sons. She earned qualifications in Domestic Science and Midwifery and was for a time employed as a nurse and again as a teacher. These qualifications, as she later attested to, became useful in her church ministerial work. She believes that she was made a prophetess right from the time of her conception and therefore not surprisingly was prone to visions right from her earliest childhood, which she likened to receiving the staff of office from God. Among these prophetic gifts she received from her earliest memories was one that could be likened to an electric bulb, which gave her the abilities to predict the future. She claims to have predicted the flood that devastated Ibadan in 1980 twenty years before the occurrence. It is widely proclaimed by her congregations and others that the predictions of Mama Agbala (as she is fondly and popularly called) always come to pass.

Initially, Olaniyi was reluctant to obey the call of God on her life for ministry but embarked on a highly successful business career as a seamstress. After suffering some set backs which she interpreted as punishment for her disobedience, she decided to heed God's call. She attended Bible colleges to broaden her horizon and claimed to have launched out into full ministerial activities in 1977 after receiving a mandate from the Lord to go out and witness

to the whole world. The genesis of Agbala Daniel was as a consequence of a vision of Olaniyi at half past one in the afternoon of
the 7th day of November 1979 by God to establish a church to be
called Agbala Daniel Church (literally Daniels' courtyard). She has
since that time been 'shepherding' her flock and become famous for
a healing ministry. Olaniyi's mission pertaining to women from her
testimony is God given. She claimed:

> I was inspired by the spirit of God one morning and the
> hand of the Lord was upon me, the spirit kept telling me
> that he had a message for my female colleagues because
> a lot of them do not know God. The same voice told me
> that I should tell my female colleagues that the blood of
> Jesus as sacrifice for our sins has redeemed them (Olaniyi,
> 1988).

Olaniyi interprets her divine mandate to women as all-embracing
and promotes the self-actualization of women in the wider society
and to take up leadership roles in the church. Her crusade on
gender issues on behalf of women would correspond to what
Alison Weber defines as feminist consciousness:

> The awareness that women belong to a subordinate group
> that as members of such a group they have suffered.
> The recognition that their contribution of subordination
> is not natural but socially determined.
> The development of a sense of sisterhood.
> The articulation of specific goals and strategies for chang-
> ing their condition.
> (Weber, 1999)

Olaniyi's stand on the woman's role in the church is largely articulated in her publication, 'Woman I condemn you not, says Jesus. John
8: 11' (Olaniyi, 1980). In this work, Olaniyi looks for authorization
both in visions and biblical texts to lift up the self image of women
as being at par with men. She argues that women were not treated
as slaves in the Bible. Jesus proclamation on the cross 'It is finished'
(Jn. 19: 30) according to her was unambiguous and should settle
matters once and for all time concerning gender equality. The Bible
passage Mark 15: 37-38 'the veil of the temple' is interpreted by
Olaniyi as the door of mercy being opened to women to serve God
freely. She also uses these verses to come to grips with the issues

of the female monthly, menstrual cycle. She posits that it should be recalled that in the time of Moses women were not allowed to enter the temple because of their issue of blood (Lev. 15: 19-13) but Jesus who is most holy allowed the woman with the issue of blood to touch him and she became whole (Mt. 9: 18-22). Olaniyi argues retortingly, 'of what significance is the temple built with hands compared to Jesus?'. According to her, Jesus has set women free to use the temple as they please.

Olaniyi expressed her conviction that not only should women be allowed to preach but that they had no excuse for not doing so. She furthers her argument by locating women preachers within the biblical tradition. For example she places emphasis on her interpretation of Matthew 28:1-22, where Jesus told women to go and tell his brethren that he had risen. According to Olaniyi, this gives women the mandate to go and preach. Olaniyi also makes it known that her mission (as given her in a vision by Jesus) is to promote the attitude, especially among women that discrimination or subordination of women from leadership roles in the church is not by divine mandate. In answer to Paul's restriction on women (such as 1 Tim. 2: 11-12), Olaniyi insists that it was Paul's command to unruly women, but not to the 'godly' and virtuous, to keep silent in the house of the Lord. She pleads for women to take cognizance of where women did good in the Bible. For her as was the case with Teresa of Avila, the exclusion of women from an apostolic role contradicts the historical relationship between Jesus and his female followers (Weber, 1999).

Olaniyi developed strategies for changing the condition of women within the church. She established a school for ministers that teach gender equality right from the outset. She also makes effective use of the audio-visual media to promote the cause of women by encouraging them by example and precepts to meeting the challenges of today by removing the shackles of inhibitions on account of being a women from getting to the top in both the church and larger society. She encourages women to identify with other Pentecostal churches and preachers, for according to her Pentecostal churches are more filled with the Holy Spirit than others. Despite her determination to promote gender equality, Olaniyi is not a feminist by western standards. She believes a woman's first duty is to her family. Submission to husbands for her was mandatory. She however enjoins the husbands to be equally loyal and faithful to their wives.

STELLA AJISEBUTE

Stella Ajisebute, the founder and Minister-in-charge of Water from the Rock Church, Ile-Ife (a.k.a. Faith Covenant Church) also share the crusade for the upliftment of woman embarked upon by Dorcas Olaniyi. One distinguishing fact about her is that she is a career woman (female academic) as well as a minister of God. She once held the position of Acting Head of Department of Microbiology at the Obafemi Awolowo University, Ile-Ife. She holds a doctorate degree in Microbiology from the University of Bangor, North Wales. As was the case with Dorcas Olaniyi, Stella Ajisebute uses visions and spiritual experiences from the Lord to authenticate her ministry. Her first traumatic spiritual experience was as a child. The turning point in her life occurred in 1988 when she received a vision and a call to be an evangelist. She soon started exhibiting supernatural gifts, especially of healing. By 1999 she claimed to have been led by God to establish what later became known as the Water from the Rock Ministry at Ile-Ife. Her responses to penetrating questions on her motivations for ministry and encouragement to others are most intriguing as the following section shows.

ROLE MODEL AND GENDER ISSUES

Stella Ajisebutu believes in role models and advises women to follow and take to her example, a choice to be anchored on Scripture as well as on practical living experience. Her Biblical role model is Deborah, who is known as a Judge of Israel and for her commander-like leadership qualities. She also highly esteems Queen Esther for her high sense or resolve. Ajisebutu established an annual 'Esther Banquet' every last Wednesday of December on her church's ritual calendar. She also submitted to the mentoring of a male Pastor, Professor Imevburen of the Christ Apostolic Church Bethel, Ile-Ife. She however has no gender preference as to mentors. Ajisebute demands that equal opportunity be given to women and that no position should be exclusively reserved for men in both the sacred and secular setting. For her, women are entitled to aspire to all positions of human endeavors. She does not feel comfortable with 'idle women' but encourages them to labor with their 'hands.'

DILEMMA IN MINISTRY AND THEOLOGY

Ajisebute has personal views on the problem passages, namely some of the Pauline Epistles, about women in the Bible. Reacting to some of Paul's statements such as 'I do not permit a woman to teach nor to have authority over a man but to be in silence' (1 Tim. 2: 12) and 'Let your woman keep silent in the Church' (1 Cor. 14: 34), she is of the opinion that these are not binding on the Church today. In a critical tone, she maintains that they were made to keep order in that particular church at that time. Although from the foregoing, Stella Ajisebutu is emphatically emphasizing gender equality yet it must not be misconstrued that she is a feminist. In fact, she carefully evades comments as to being a womanist. She deplores feminist ethics that she feels promotes abortion and homosexual practices. An intriguing aspect of Ajisebutu's lifestyle is her resistance to 'sisterhood' networking, an endeavor she considers unnecessary.

REACTION TO FEMALE RELIGIOUS LEADERSHIP

Response to female leadership has tended to be highly favorable, so much so that it has made women's role in the church a major issue among Pentecostals. This has precipitated a new perspective among the pentecostal congregations on the issue of female leadership in the church. What follows is a further exploration of this new perspective, the reason for its emergence and the mode of its propagation.

THE NEW PERSPECTIVE

The impact of female religious leaders has been such as to instill attitudes into their members and other congregations challenging the mission churches' establishment on the treatment of women. They are persuaded that there is no divine order restricting women from taking preaching and teaching role in the church. They are of the view that objections to women carrying out such roles spring from social and culturally determined constructs. True Christianity has become for them one that is divorced of Jewish patriarchal influence and is based on equality and respect between the sexes. The number of those that would like to believe that such attitudes are a sign of apostasy is indeed shrinking, although such restrictive views are not unanimous among the Pentecostals. Doubts on the capacity of women to cope with the task of leadership appear to be universal. Writing on the American situation, Vashti Mckenzie (1996: 35) notes, 'there were doubts about whether women could administer and command the respect of a community. There were concerns about how a woman would handle natural physiological changes, such as pregnancies and menopause. There was still skepticism about whether a woman could preach a weekly schedule, manage a pastorate and a family without either one suffering'. Needless to say, in Nigeria as also in America, women have been found more than capable of meeting the task of combining successful careers in the ministry with carrying out domestic duties.

REASONS FOR EMERGENCE

The Baptist historian, Leon McBeth lists the following categorization as explanation for the emergence of Baptist women taking up leadership roles in the Church, namely: reinterpretation of scripture, abundance of prepared women, response to spiritual need, response to women's movements in society, expanding concept for ministry and response to denominations (McBeth 1979: 192). This categorization is also applicable in explaining this 'new perspective' of women's church leadership roles among Pentecostals within the Nigerian scene.

Reinterpretation of Scripture

A main reason for the change in attitude among Pentecostals towards women assuming authoritative roles in the church is the influence of the female use of biblical texts by religious leaders themselves. They use biblical texts to authenticate their preaching and teaching roles in the church. Although they accept the authority of the Bible in its entirety as the word of God, they nevertheless attempt to persuade members of their congregations to 'realize that it is not enough merely to accept the Bible, one must interpret honestly and accurately' (McBeth, 1979: 21). They attempt to persuade their listeners to accept the Bible in a new light favorable to women.

They especially interpret scriptures that restrict or exclude women in the light of 'slavish' cultural influence or the social context of the time and not as being the will of God. Scriptures, such as, 1 Tim. 2: 11-12 forbidding women to teach men, and 1 Cor. 14: 33-35 that command women to keep silent in the church fall under this category. They also interpret texts that are not so obvious in ways to validate their assumption of pastoral and teaching roles. Dorcas Olaniyi uses the text, 'Women I condemn you Not' (John 8:11) in ways that persuade women that they are redeemed by the blood of Jesus and are therefore free from all gender inhibitions and restrictions. Emphasis is laid especially on what Myrtle Langley defines as, Paul's freedom manifesto- Galatians 3: 26-28. This according to her addresses the issues of fundamental human rights (Langley, 1989: 27). It states:

> For you are all children of God through faith, in Christ Jesus. For as many of you as were baptized into Christ have put on Christ. There is neither Jew nor Greek; there is neither slave not free; there is no male and female. For you are all one in Christ.

It becomes obvious that the female religious leaders have to pick and choose stance towards Paul. They are prone to promote what they consider as favorable and ignore or wisely keep silent on what is generally accepted as the 'devastating anti-feminine polemic posterity attributed to Paul in 1 Tim. 2: 11-14 (Manus, 2002: 72). Dennis Carmody goes as far as to attest that, pseudo-Paul has on his head guilt for a significant amount of the violence and humiliation women have suffered throughout the Christian era (Carmody, 1998: 147).

Abundance of Prepared Women

The co-educational system that calls for daughters also to be educated, and again the large increase in the intake to higher institutions has produced an expanding Nigerian elite class of followers. Many of them, like their American counterparts, are as highly motivated to Christian service as men are (McBeth, 1979: 21). The Nigerian Christian elites are also eager to explore new doctrines and find a fascination with teachings of female religious leaders. The access and appropriation of new media technologies such as the Internet, foreign religious literature and female televangelists from abroad have had a great impact on many women. An on-going research by this author points to the fact that the new generation Christian especially the youths are greatly influenced by foreign tele-evangelists like Joyce Meyer, Paula White, Juanita Vynum, Diane Bish, Darlene Zschech and a host of others.[1]

Response to Spiritual Needs

There are those that identify with the words of Jesus that 'the harvest is ripe but the laborers are few' (Luke 10: 2). They are therefore supportive of the individual that is willing to join the labor force for God, regardless of which half of humanity that the 'servant' represents. Evidence abounds from personal interviews with some religious leaders that they eventually yielded to the call of God upon their lives mainly to bring a harvest of souls to Christ. The spiritual yearnings are also seen in the light of the women's social locations. In this wise, women's experience of poverty, rape, marginalization and battering among other ills, are grounded in an emerging theology of vitality. This is largely embedded in a context ravaged by wars, growing insecurity and the HIV/AIDS pandemic.[2]

Response to Women's Movement in Society

The effects of globalization have virtually turned the world into a global village. There is a great awareness and sensitization of both the Nigerian elite and even semi-illiterates to the liberation of women mainly from entrenched patriarchal hegemonies. There is also a great drive for the mobilization of women in the Gospel Ministry. These bring the concept that models for church ministry have greatly expanded. This is because many of these female gospel singers see and address themselves as preachers, evangelists and teachers of the gospel, especially through the medium of songs. Some of them established music schools that are meant to prepare 'men and women of God' in the line of ministering through songs. They go as far as assuming such titles as Reverend (Dr.), Lady-Evangelist, etc. Good examples of such are Lady Evangelists Dr. Bola Are, Dupe Olulana (formerly Solana); Funmi Aragbaiye and Toun Soetan who have made waves in south western Nigeria. Among the budding stars are Lady Evangelist Ayodele Makun, Bose Beulah, Tope Alabi and Felicia Ogunsola.

Response to other Denominations

There is a great awareness in both women's secular and religious movements. Various societies demand women's better treatment, justice and equity. It is inferred that in the ecclesial circles a form of resentment could build up in the female members of denominations who felt that in other denominations, possibly the less gifted were enjoying the privilege of pasturing while they were denied. The temptation to move to other pastures would eventually begin to mount up unless the issue was properly addressed.

MODE OF EXPRESSION

A major practical consequence of the new perspective acquired by the 'new generation churches' in support of women in leadership roles was that they no longer took the Bible at face value. Both men and women began to refer directly to the Bible on matters of female leadership as to whether indeed there were examples that Jesus was different from others in His treatment of women, and there were examples of women that took leadership roles in the Bible. They ceased taking things for granted. They now take time to sort things out for themselves namely by the depth interpretation – 'for the letter killeth but the spirit giveth life' (II Cor. 3: 6). A recent survey shows that there are now more women taking up leadership roles especially in Pentecostal circles. Men are now generally less skeptical and are ready to support female leadership.

Among today's youth, the presence of female religious leaders stirs up topical debates and discussion. Nevertheless, these women are more often than not regarded as role models. Conformity to group presence, tends to be internalized and brought to the fore when the youth is alone. The print and audio-visual also helps in shaping attitudes and values. Female religious leaders have greatly utilized this medium where they exert great influence. Some, like film stars, have good and respectable reviews of their personality and missions. Pastor Bimbo Odukoya's TV program, *Singles and Married* is a delight to many although some still criticize what they termed her 'westernized model of freedom' which could give room to spiritual laxity, while others are criticized by gossip columns. For example, the estrangement and divorce of Bola Odeleke, founder of *Agbara Olorun Kii Ba ti* (The Power of God never fails) was headline news for several weeks in leading newspaper and magazines in Nigeria.

The youth and women among others are also adapting to the fashions of women in religious leadership roles. For example, the once touchy issue of 'head covering' is becoming less controversial as men and women especially the youth are imitating female religious leaders that preach and teach without head covering, a practice which is alien to African culture. But some now read the Bible to find in it their 'true' identity. They interpret it to distinguish what is sinful from what is cultural and what God ordained. It is generally believed that in America, opposition to women in the pulpit does not come from the men but from the women themselves. 'One of the reasons given for this attitude is that men are better at directing women's growth and development' (McKenzie, 1996: 36). However, Pentecostal women in Nigeria behave differently. Women feel represented at the pulpit because of the 'female' who is at the pulpit. They believe that she would have an understanding of their shared problems as African women, which stem from their cultural environment.

WOMEN'S RITUAL POTENCY

This highlights what ritual women are expected to undergo as depending on what they are passing through. 'Old habits are said to die hard'. This statement is definitely applicable to the lingering attitudes on culturally imposed taboos in respect of women. In spite of their belief in the efficacy of 'the blood of Jesus', there are those that lack 'faith' for its potency to nullify cultural inhibition. For example the issue of menstruation appears to be a 'stumbling block' for many post New Testament faiths. The act of menstruation is stigmatized as unclean and as such would pollute the sanctuary of the holy assembly. This attitude had Biblical sanction as in (Lev. 15:19-24) specifically referring to menstruating women as untouchable, 'If a woman has an issue in her flesh the blood shall be put apart seven days; and whosoever toucheth her shall be unclean until the evening'. Such statements are indeed seen to be harsh on women, and these Old Testament texts were used to subjugate women rather than resort to texts that ensure their 'liberty in Christ'.

The issue of menstruation and other cultural practices such as female circumcision and the rights of widows are receiving attention by the majority due, in no small measure, to the activities of the new generation churches, female religious leaders who as women have greater empathy with these issues than men. Female religious leaders are propagating the attitude that menstruation is neither a sickness, nor a disease and should therefore not be treated as such. They assert that women should be allowed to officiate in whatever capacity regardless of whether or not they are undergoing a menstrual circle. Female religious leaders are even propagating the attitude among their congregations that it is a paradox that while menstruation is pictured as repulsive and repugnant (to some), it nevertheless is a good sign that women are able to bear children which the cultural context in which they live exalts and extols.

MIXED CLIENTELE

In most traditional African societies, it is believed that if a man dies well it means both he and his spouse did well. This credo is applicable to the new attitude female religious leaders are instilling into both men and women in their congregations. Field work evidence carried out by this author shows that men are generally responding favorably to women in leadership roles and indeed in many instances have come out openly to support it. From the testimony of their converts and our survey, there is indeed an upsurge in the number of men accepting female religious leadership. No longer is it thought to be 'unmanly' for a man to be pastured by a woman or taught the Scripture by a woman (cf. Bateye 2001, 2002b).

PROSPECTS FOR FEMALE LEADERSHIP

The activities of female religious leaders are viewed by an increasing number of men as creative and redeeming contributions from the women themselves on the issue of women's subordination in the church. The female leaders on the current scene are removing the barriers of inhibitions, sexism and patriarchy to women taking up church leadership roles. This on-going momentum has passed the epileptic phase of 'stops and starts'. The emergence of an outstanding female religious leader from a Pentecostal/Charismatic setting or even from among the Aladura churches is heard almost on a monthly basis. The appearance of the female leader in church, on radio, television or even in the print media has ceased to be a novelty in Nigeria. Female religious leaders are currently enjoying a visible and supportive public image, whether as guest preachers at camp meetings, churches, revival grounds or on civic occasions. Opposition to female religious leadership that are of substantial significance is on moral and ethical rather than doctrinal or theological grounds. There is a marked proliferation of Bible Colleges and mass enrolment of women seeking careers in ministry. In other words, there is renewed enthusiasm for women taking up careers in Ministry.

CONCLUSION

There is little doubt that female religious leaders have faced a lot of challenges. They are pioneers in an on-going 'battle' of highlighting the question of gender inequality to the Nigerian public. Their refusal to be complacent but to cry out has catapulted the issue of gender inequality to be sustained as a crucial topical issue not only in the church but also the larger Nigerian society. The motivation of female religious leaders for taking up governing roles can be discerned as generally based on supernatural experiences (visions) and their claim of biblical justification in support of such. It can be deduced that they have begun to create their own biblical hermeneutics to support their notion of gender parity. Whether this stance as a correct interpretation of Scripture will win acceptance by not only the male but also the female followers themselves (not of the particular denominations of the female religious leaders) is largely a matter of conjecture. This is because prominent female figures placed in leadership positions in the Bible could be argued were regarded in their own times and according to biblical context as a rarity. Nevertheless, they have had a measure of success in winning their cause for the equality of women as the ranks of their followership continues to swell.

The implication of this study is that there is an on-going awareness among Pentecostal women of the need not only to challenge old notions on the subordination of women but also to actively install them into positions of religious authority at par with men. Female religious leaders have largely been the instigators of this perception and the popular acceptance in Pentecostal churches and other denominations. Attitudes among Pentecostals have changed so radically that rather than making a case for women to take up active leadership, it is the denial of such rights that seeks justification. There is no sign that the impetus to install women into leadership positions in the church will be short lived. Nevertheless, this issue of women taking up pastoral or ordained roles in Nigerian pentecostal churches has reached a point of no return. It is not the case of dying embers of coal but that of a gale that is sweeping away every obstacle in its path towards change, which nevertheless is at the ebb, but still causing a change.

Bibliography

Ajisebutu, S., *At Eventide*, Ibadan: Yadah, 2000.

Anderson, A., 'The Globalization of Pentecostalism', Paper presented at the Commission Meeting of the Churches Commission on Mission, Bangor/Wales, Sept. 14-16, 2002.

Bateye, B. O., 'Female Leaders of New Generation Churches as Change – Agent in Yoruba land', Unpublished PhD Dissertation, Department of Religious Studies, Obafemi Awolowo University, Ile – Ife. 2001.

Bateye, B.O., 'Reclaiming a Lost Tradition, Nigerian Women in Power and Resistance', in Akintunde, D. and Labeodan, H. (eds.) *Women and the Culture of Violence in Traditional Africa*, Ibadan: Sefer.2002 (a), pp. 79-91.

Bateye, B.O., 'The Impact of Female Leaders of New Generation Churches on their followers among the Yoruba of South – Western Nigeria', in G. A. Ojo (ed.) *Women and Gender Equality for a Better Society in Nigeria*, Lagos: Leaven Club. 2002(b), pp. 219 – 234.

Bateye, B.O., 'African Women's Christian Practices and Theologies', (forthcoming).

Bateye, B.O., 'Jesus Online and Women Identity: The Impact of the Internet and Cable Networks on Yoruba Women's Spirituality', (forthcoming).

Beyer, E., *New Christian Movements in West Africa: A Course in Church History*, Ibadan: Sefer, 1998.

Hollenweger, W., *The Pentecostals*, London: SCM, 1972.

Lane, P., 'Women Radicals – Early "Women's Lib", in *Radicals and Reformers*, London: B.T. Batsford, 1973.

Manus, C.U., 'Gender Bias against Women in some Sacred Narratives: Re-reading the texts in our times', in Ojo, G.A. (ed.) *Women and Gender*

Equality for a Better Society in Nigeria, Lagos: Leaven Club. 2002(b), pp. 63-82.

McBeth, L., *Women in Baptist Life*, Nashville: Broadman, 1979.

McKenzie, V.M., *Not Without a Struggle: Leadership Development for the African American Women in Ministry*, Cleveland: United Church, 1996.

Oduyoye, M., *Hearing and Knowing: Theological Reflections on Christianity in Africa*, Maryknoll: Orbis, 1986.

Ojo, M., 'The Church in the African State: The Charismatic/Pentecostal Experience in Nigeria', *Journal of African Christian Thought*, 1, 2, 1998, pp. 25-32.

Olaniyi, D. S.,'Woman, I Condemn You Not, Says Jesus, John 8: 11', Ibadan: Agbala Daniel Church Ministry, 1988.

Sofola, Z., 'Feminism and the Psyche of African Womanhood', a paper presented at the First Conference on Women in Africa and the African Diaspora, University of Nigeria, Nsukka, 1992, pp. 1-40.

Webber, A.,'The Fortunes of Ecstasy: Teresa of Avila and The Discaked Carmelite Reform', 28, 4, 1999.

Notes

1. See Bateye, B.O., 'Jesus Online and African Women Identity' (forthcoming).

2. See Bateye, B.O.,'African Women's Christian Practices and Theologies' (forthcoming).

ONLINE FOR GOD:
MEDIA NEGOTIATION AND
AFRICAN NEW RELIGIOUS
MOVEMENTS

Afe Adogame

INTRODUCTION

The media play a crucial role in establishing, maintaining and changing collective representations (cf. Pickering 1984; Rothenbuhler 1998). Global 'mediazation' facilitates the worldwide marketing of goods, symbolic forms, and 'life styles'. This chapter seeks to examine the inter-connectedness between religion and media in the practices of everyday life. The contemporary world has witnessed a rapid development, expansion and convergence of communication technologies in religious, economic, political and socio-cultural spheres. One of the most prevalent forms of new technology is the use and appropriation of the computer-mediated communication technology, the Internet. This chapter shows how African New Religious Movements (ANRMs) have engaged the media, especially the Net, as conduits for the communication of their religious messages, as well as a means of developing new and sustaining old relationships and community. Since media texts now serve as significant maps through which the ANRMs see themselves on local and global religious landscapes; the methods, levels of appropriation and the impact of the communication media will be investigated.

AFRICAN NEW RELIGIOUS MOVEMENTS

Our definition of new religious movements from the African context marks a departure from the 'popular' definitions already adduced to delineate the phenomenon.[1] Our definitional category of ANRMs may not necessarily eliminate all the criterion and characteristics employed by anti-, pro- and counter-cultists or new religious movements. However, most (if not all) of the NRMs in our category do not come under the umbrella of cults and sects, and shall therefore not be described as such in this chapter. From a historical-descriptive point of view, African new religious movements refer to the various religious initiatives that emerged in different parts of Africa especially from the wake of the twentieth century onwards. It cuts across Christian, Islamic and African traditional religion. It also includes spiritual science movements that are now making their impact felt on the African religious landscape. The religious movements which fall under this wide categorization may not be entirely new in terms of their doctrines and ideology, but they are considered new in the sense that these indigenous religious initiatives and creativities are historically unprecedented in the African religious context.[2] For instance, within Christianity, new religious movements refer to the newer forms of Christianity which succeeded mission or mainline Christianity, and which has reshaped, contextualized and revitalized Christianity in contemporary time. This includes the so-called African Indigenous Churches (AICs), the African Pentecostal and Charismatic movements. Many other new movements have emerged from Islam, the traditional religion, but for the purpose of this chapter, examples will be drawn mainly from the Christian new religious movements.

ANRMS AND THE NEW MEDIA: THE INTERNET

Our conceptualization of the mass media has been rendered more complex with the growth in 'new' technologies. Thus, the media landscape has been somewhat altered and widened from

the print, film, radio, music, and television we are used to, with
the development of computer networks, digital technologies, and
the interactive cable television. We may think of the relationship
between media and religious movements as a transaction between
two complex systems, each trying to accomplish a particular goal.
Movements ask and employ the media to communicate their
message to the public, while the media look to movements as one
potential source of 'news'. On the former, religious movements
usually need the mass media (Internet) not only to widely publi-
cize their activities, but also as a recruitment strategy and medium
towards the enlargement of their clientele. Such appropriation of
and coverage by the media may in some respect help to mobilize
support, achieve validation and acquire some kind of legitimization
and credibility within and around the socio-cultural environment
they find themselves.

One significant asset of the so-called 'new media' in contradis-
tinction with the previous generation of mass media lies in their
capability and use for interactive communication. Instantaneous
communication and interaction can be carried out over far dis-
tances (space-time compression). New media technologies provide
the populace and potential clients with the technical apparatus to
do more than just receive information. They can respond to messages they receive, ask further questions or seek for clarifications,
select which images they want to receive, or even send out their own
messages. The Internet, the World Wide Web (WWW) provides
computer links between people for either electronic conversation
or the transfer of data and images. The computer Internet is the
site of many 'home pages' for religious movements as well as a home
to many discussion groups and home pages that focus on religious
and spiritual issues. But how and to what extent has the ANRMs
exploited this to their own corporate advantage?

The use of media is not at all a novel feature among the ANRMs.
Several movements have vigorously used and still continue to use
the print, electronic and 'personal' mediums, at different stages of
their developmental histories. What is however a recent phenomenon is their deliberate effort towards making their presence known
and felt on the WWW. Thus, particularly in the last decade, several
ANRMs are increasingly employing the use of the Internet for religious communication. As we have argued elsewhere, the recourse

to new, alternative evangelistic strategies is intricately tied to new, global socio-cultural realities. The somewhat individualistic nature of the Western societies for instance has largely rendered some of the known conventional modes inept and far-less productive.[3] Thus, the 'personal' modes of communication (i.e. door to door, street to street, marketplace and bus evangelism) is giving way systematically to more 'impersonal', 'neutral' modes (i.e. computer web sites, electronic mail, fax). The relevance and urgency which these alternative modes of communication demand in the western context, lends credence to why virtually all the web sites of these churches have been established, developed and maintained in Europe, USA or elsewhere outside Africa. Closely related to this is the fact that a large percentage of their members in Africa do not have access to the World Wide Web, or are totally unaware of the existence of these church web pages. ANRMs' engagement of the Internet can be more closely examined through the structure and scope of their web pages, and more importantly the strategies and initiatives adopted to reach out to the virtual-minded public, and to maintain their own religious communities as well. We shall conclude this section by highlighting the methodological enigma this phenomenon is posing to scholars of religion and media. Which opportunities and what research materials do the WWW offer us? What problems are likely to emerge from this new focus and what appropriate tools can be used to address this?

VISUAL AND STRUCTURAL FEATURES OF WEB PAGES

A careful surfing of the web for ANRMs sites reveals a variety, from professionally built, relatively flashy and well developed sites, providing a lot of information; to poorly designed, emerging web sites. The earlier employs colorful graphics, texts which consist largely of programmatic statements of their mission, *raison d être*, belief and ritual systems, foundational histories, prerequisites for membership, information on the various program of events, and links to branches and several other related groups or networking bodies. Other characteristics include on-line shopping (audio, video, books), free brochures, directories, site host, search engines, guest book, chat room, testimony/petition corner, prayer site and avenues for prayer rituals, reading lists, announcement page, photo gallery, email addresses and lists, music and sound bites in real audio and video from choir group or other gospel singers, sermon texts, messages from founders and leaders, multi-language texts, information on US Green Card Lottery and Immigration procedures etc. Most of these sites offer ways of establishing further contact to obtain more materials (i.e. pamphlets, books, tapes, videos, holy water, and anointing oil) and to access courses, lectures, and other religious programs, either by electronic mail, fax, telephone or mailing addresses. Examples of professionally-built websites of Pentecostal churches are those of the Redeemed Christian Church of God, Winners Chapel and the Kingsway International Christian Center.[4]

Most of the web sites are officially owned by the various movements, although some of them have been created and generated privately by members, but later taken over by the religious authorities (leadership) as the official web sites of the respective groups.[5] Some of the sites have been professionally designed by computer specialists who are at the same time members of the group. Other groups have commissioned individuals, mainly members, with expertise in computer designs to build their sites. In some cases, the movement is directly involved in the process, such as the RCCG Internet Outreach Project. Most of these sites simply replicate, in appearance and content, the kind of material available in other publications by these groups, and the web materials are often meant to be downloaded as a ready substitute for more conventional publications.[6]

SELF-PACKAGING AND THE STRATEGY TOWARDS RELIGIOUS TRANSMISSION

Dawson and Hennebry (1999:26) have shown that the primary use of the web is clearly a way to advertise the groups and to deliver information about them cheaply. Although the web sites act as a new and relatively effective means of outreach to the larger community, most of these groups who appropriate it do so in order to also draw potential clientele or membership. Such intentions are clearly portrayed in their introductory statements.

The CCC[7] seeks to create a global network through the use of Internet websites and electronic mail.[8] In a 'web release' on 15 December 1997, announcing its (Riverdale, USA site) presence on the Internet, it stated inter alia,

> Halleluyah!!! ... Celestial Church of Christ now has a
> dominant presence on the World Wide Web. The main
> focus of this page is to present a unified and cohesive
> communication vehicle for Celestial Church as a whole,
> world-wide ... As the web site evolves, we hope to use it as
> a vehicle to communicate news about Celestial Church of
> Christ on a global basis, both information geared toward
> Celestians and non-Celestians alike.

The UK site complements this objective through her mission
statement which partly states:

> To introduce CCC to the whole world ... to bring all the
> parishes together by obtaining free e-mail addresses for
> interested parishes and contribute to the free flow of
> information in the church ... to use the medium of the
> Internet as a vehicle to recruit new members ....

The official web site[9] of CLA was established in 1999. One
introductory statement of this site is that 'the Church of the Lord
(Aladura) is conscious of her mission to spread the good news of
our Lord Jesus Christ to every nook and corners of the world'. It
describes the four tenets of the church as 'Pentecostal in Power,
Biblical in Pattern, Evangelical in Ministry, and Ecumenical in
Outlook'. The Internet could serve as a kind of status booster for
the CLA as it contains a long list of local and international religious
and ecumenical organizations to which it belongs or is affiliated
to. This in our view gives some kind of religious credibility to the
group, especially in a society where such a group could be easily
'demonized' and waved off as a cult or sect.

In the RCCG[10] Internet Outreach, the introductory statement
on the Parish directory states inter alia:

> Over the years The Redeemed Christian Church of God
> has experienced an explosive growth with branches being
> planted all over the world. It has become pertinent to create
> a directory and online data base for all The Redeemed
> Christian Church of God parishes worldwide... This will
> enable us do a complete, relational online database that
> will be useful for the Body of Christ. Furthermore online
> database will help us in our evangelism, fellowship and
> interaction among member parishes. It will also serve to

assist travellers in their efforts to find a place of worship wherever they find themselves.

The vision and goals of the members as expressed in the RCCG 'Mission Statement' published on their site includes:

> It is our goal to make heaven. It is our goal to take as many people as possible with us. In order to accomplish our goals, holiness will be our lifestyle. In order to take as many people with us as possible, we will plant churches within five minutes walking distance in every city and town of developing countries; and within five minutes driving distance in every city and town of developed countries. We will pursue these objectives until every nation in the world is reached for JESUS CHRIST OUR LORD.

Although, these goals may appear too ambitious, idealistic and utopian to attain, yet one point of significance here is the fact that the church has demonstrated optimism and enthusiasm towards the realization of its global vision. The church is not only concerned with the local setting but what transpires beyond it, within so-called 'developing' and 'developed' countries.

Another common feature of the ANRMs web sites is the presence of Discussion Forum, Question and Answer Sheet, Testimony Forum, Visitors' Form, Feedback Form etc. Closely related to this is the recent creation of free-web based emails for branches (parishes), interested members and visitors to the site. What does this portend for the group? One of the main reasons for providing and offering free email services to interested persons is in order to establish contact and maintain link through the web. By supplying personal data and contact information, the group is able to keep close, intimate contact with the visitor with the end purpose of a probable recruitment.

INTERNET RECRUITMENT AND A METHODOLOGICAL ENIGMA?

It would appear that Internet users (web browsers) are drawn largely from the young adult population or the upwardly mobile youths, educated elites, students etc. As Dawson & Hennebry (1999:30) aptly remark, 'Access to computing technology and to the Internet, as well as sufficient time and knowledge to use these resources properly is still largely a luxury afforded the better-off segments of our society'. The situation becomes much more complex in the case of Africa where even many of the so-called 'better-offs' have virtually little or no access to the Internet. With the Internet fast emerging as a new public space, it may be hasty to conclude that many people are recruited to the ANRMs through the Internet. While this may have been one of the reasons for setting up official web pages, there is however a paucity of evidence which suggests so. Moreover, it is this attempt at garnering empirical evidence to test this assertion that raises an enigmatic methodological issue in academic research.

Since the Internet represents a new public space that is open to a wide, borderless community, how can we effectively measure the extent of recruitment via the net? It may not be difficult to identify persons within an existing group who joined as a consequence of surfing the web, but how do we reconcile the several other web browsers who have gained access to sites for various reasons without necessarily enlisting their membership? This further raises the question whether the simple display of information on a site and the access to it by browsers can lead in any specific, endearing commitment of the viewer. A possible answer to this may be that such available information on the site may be attractive to a potential member depending on how well it is packaged, convincing and exhibited. On the other hand, the information may be grossly inadequate and unconvincing to draw the interest of a potential convert. Where this is the case, such provision of information must necessarily be followed up by much more personal forms of interaction, telephone, electronic mail. This largely explains why most of these sites as we have pointed out above provide feedback (follow-up) pages and electronic mail services in order to establish and maintain contact with potential viewers. As the use of the Internet develops and becomes more and more popular, the tendency of assuming a vital channel of recruitment may become clear.

GOD DIGITAL (THE GOD CHANNEL) AS A GLOBAL RELIGIOUS NETWORK

Another way through which the ANRMs have used the new technologies is through their space appropriation in global religious TV-networks. A glaring example here is the Kingsway International Church Center (KICC) with headquarters in London. The KICC founded and led by the Nigerian-born Pastor Matthew Ashimolowo, is often described as one of the largest Pentecostal Church in the UK. They are known for their prodigious appropriation of the new media technology. As the church asserts '...We recognise the effectiveness of using the media to communicate and draw the attention of the world to the good news. We do this by Winning Ways Program.'[11] The Winning Ways Television program is claimed to be transmitted across 21 European nations and has a potential viewing audience of several millions in Europe as well as Africa. The programs can be viewed or heard on the following channels: Europe (Christian Channel Europe (now God Digital), Premier Radio London, BBC Radio Leicester), Nigeria (NTA 2 Channel 5, NTA Channel 10, OGTV Channel 22 and PRTV Channel), and Ghana (Ghana TV).

God Digital (formerly known as 'the Christian Channel Europe'), the Christian Television and Radio Service of the Dream Family Network Ltd., was founded in 1995 by a South African couple, Rory and Wendy Alec in the United Kingdom. The God Digital, on cable and satellite, operates 24-hour Television Channels such as The God Channel, Revival Channel (which incorporates Revival Europe and the Worship Channel), and the proposed Channel 'God 24 SEVEN'. The vision for a Christian TV in Europe started as, 'a two hour program broadcast from their kitchen table and grew to be a multi-channel network of Christian TV and Radio programs broadcasting to a potential 80 million people in 58 nations across the UK, Europe, Scandinavia, Western Russia, North Africa and the Middle East', from its purpose built studios in (Sunderland) the North East of England. The primary mission claim of God Digital was 'to take the message of salvation – the message of the Gospel of the Lord Jesus Christ to a lost and dying Europe'.[12] To realize this objective, the electronic medium is being used as the basic vehicle of religious communication and transmission. In recognition of this, they claim that 'In our modern, fast paced, instant access, technology driven world, the media has become the single most powerful tool of influence in the battle for the hearts of 21st century mankind'.[13] An interesting feature of the God Digital is their prodigious use of catching phrases, martial, bellicose metaphors like 'God Digital: Safe viewing in a secular world', 'Hook on to God's Spiritual Air Force', 'Battle for Britain', and 'God's Army (Air Force) in the spiritual battle in Europe', 'The enemy and God's Spiritual Air Force' etc., in their daily religious communication.

Matthew Ashimolowo is on the Board of Reference of the God Digital (Christian Channel Europe), and the KICC religious programs are screened from time to time on 'the God Channel' TV network. In this way, KICC targets and communicates its religious message to a wider, multi-ethnic public that is far beyond the constituency of Africans back in the continent as well as the African diaspora communities. The church is involved in intra-religious networks, and organizes conferences and crusades which draw local and international audiences. The annual conference tagged 'Gathering of Champions', a forum that attracts an international audience of leaders and Christians from the global Pentecostal landscape suggests a remarkable tendency towards religious internationalism and transnationalism.

Religious Video Technology

Haynes (2000) aptly remarks that Nigeria video[14] films, a phenomenon less than a decade old, are now being produced at a rate of nearly one a day. As he argues, 'Only the daily press and weekly news magazines rival the videos as media for telling the story of Nigeria in the 1990s' (p. xv). He noted further,

> The videos offer the strongest, most accessible expression of contemporary Nigerian popular culture, which is to say the imagination of Africa's largest nation. They are a prime instance of the interpenetration of the global and the local through the international commerce in cultural forms...And they are a prime instance of African modernity... (p. 4).

Partly corroborating the above assertion, Ogundele (2000: 97) submits that 'The ubiquitous presence of the video play in Nigeria, plus its popularity, point to its importance as a new medium for the production, dissemination, and consumption of one specific form of popular culture, with its ideology and aesthetic'.

A complex variety of video films now abound within the new, emerging 'video culture' that may render a simple categorization as somewhat preposterous. While they may bear some similarities in terms of using same local stars (actors), similar scenes or story-lines, the themes and paradigms which characterize them are as variegated as the titles themselves. Some of their very visible particularities are along the ethnic, religious, socio-political dichotomies. A remarkable chunk of this output 'video boom' is what Oha (2000: 192-199) describes as 'Nigerian Christian Videos'. It is with one of this burgeoning strand of 'religious home videos' that this chapter is concerned with here.

However, it is significant here to begin with a distinction with respect to our categorization of religious videos. There are several genres that may be loosely classified under this rubric. The first refer to movies or religious drama that are written, produced and projected to the general public by religious organizations, ministries. The second video genres are movies that are secular in nature and outlook but which are overtly suffused with religious symbolism and connotations. Another interesting category are the religious musical videos, which can be further classified into: independent local gospel artistes, gospel singers and or choir groups within existing religious groups, musical videos of foreign gospel singers, and lastly what I term 'cross-over (secular) gospellers'.[15] The growing video documentation and commodification of religious festivals, revivals, services, ritual ceremonies and other events for both public and private consumption represent yet another genre of video films. However, depending on the genre, such films are ostensibly produced and marketed either for evangelistic (religious), entertainment, recreation (social) and commercial (economic) ends or in most cases for a combination of all these factors.

Oha has shown that most of the Christian narratives that make up these video plays are situated within the locus of spiritual warfare, a conflict between benevolence (God's forces) and malevolence (Satan and its cohorts) in the affairs of human beings.[16] He continued,

> Such spiritual warfare is made the explanation for human problems such as poverty, disease, childlessness, impotence, barrenness and divorce. The Christian videos that promote this view are becoming important instruments of evangelisation in Nigeria and are shaping attitudes in a social context of fear, uncertainty, helplessness, and hopelessness (p. 193).

We add here that the significance which these 'religious movies' have come to assume is not limited to Nigerians and within Nigeria alone, but is increasingly becoming a household feature among the African diaspora (especially Nigerians and Ghanaians but also other Africans) communities in Europe, America and elsewhere. The home video industry has expanded within the diaspora communities due to their increasing commodification especially through African shops, entertainment centers, cybercafés, phony centers, and also through centers of ethnic and religious socialization within the host societies. Religious video products are not only largely consumed by Africans in diaspora, but they are also partly sponsored, produced and commodified by them as well.

We contend that one way through which the ANRMs have used the new technologies is through the production and distribution of what has been called the Christian home videos. We shall demonstrate with the case of the Mount Zion Faith Ministries International (MZFMI) headquartered in Ile-Ife (Nigeria), showing how religious video dramas or video movies produced by them are consumed locally and internationally by Christians and non-Christians alike.

The MZFMI describes itself as 'a full-time evangelical drama and film ministries' whose mission is 'to evangelize the word through drama'.[17] In 1996, MZFMI was duly registered as a religious organization with Nigeria's Corporate Affairs Commission. It comprised five major organs namely: the Drama Outreach, Institute of Christian Drama, Film productions, Publications and Production Studios. The first Christian motion picture made was by the MZFMI in 1994. The relative success of its pioneer film *Agbala Nla* generated enough impetus for further works, like the English version 'Ultimate Power' and 'The Blood Covenant'.[18] These and many other films have become very popular in sub-Saharan Africa (particularly Nigeria and Ghana) through domestic and public screening, as well as among African Diaspora communities. The religious and social impact of these video genres on the viewers cannot be underestimated.[19] A sub-section within the MZFMI web site is devoted to 'testimonies' and 'comments' of wide ranging viewers. The fact that such testimony genres emanate from Africa, Europe, America and other parts of the world explains the local-global nexus these 'home videos' have come to assume.

CONCLUSION

ANRMs' web sites act as a new and relatively effective means of outreach to a larger, global community. It provides a convenient point of access to a seemingly elite segment of our society and enhances tremendously the public profile of each of these movements. While some of the available online-literature is offered free-of-charge, in other cases it adds to the revenue obtained through the sale of books, tapes and other paraphernalia. Although the 'mission statements' of several ANRMs elucidates their intents, cogency and determination towards appropriating the Internet for membership recruitment, there seems yet no substantial empirical evidence to suggest that ANRMs have succeeded in using it as a viable medium of recruiting members. Our tentative conclusion deriving from our investigation is that recruitment to ANRMs seems to happen primarily through pre-existing social networks, interpersonal bonds as well as through other conventional evangelistic strategies such as revival sessions, musical concerts and jamborees, prayer and healing sessions etc. (Cf. Dawson 1996, 2000, 2001). Thus, the Internet could serve more as a complementary vehicle not as a replacement for other mediums.

Bibliography

Adogame, Afe, 'Betwixt Identity and Security: African New Religious Movements and the Politics of Religious Networking in Europe', in *Nova Religio. The Journal of Alternative and Emergent Religions*, 7, 2, 2003, pp. 24-41.

Adogame, Afe, 'Traversing Local-Global Religious Terrain: African New Religious Movements in Europe', in *Zeitschrift für Religionswissenschaft*, 10, 2002, pp. 33-49.

Adogame, Afe, *Celestial Church of Christ: The Politics of Cultural Identity in a West African Prophetic-Charismatic Movement*, Frankfurt a/M: Peter Lang, 1999.

Dawson, Lorne L. and Hennebry, Jenna, 'New Religions and the Internet: Recruiting in a New Public Space', in *Journal of Contemporary Religion* 14, 1, 1999, pp. 17-39.

Dawson, Lorne L., 'Doing Religion in Cyberspace: The Promise and the Perils', *The Council of Societies for the Study of Religion Bulletin*, 30, 1, 2001, pp. 3-9.

Dawson, Lorne L., 'Researching Religion in Cyberspace: Issues and Strategies', in J.K. Hadden and D. Cowan (eds.) *Religion and the Internet: research Prospects and Promises* (Religion and the Social order, vol. 8), Greenwich, Conn.: Elsevier, 2000, pp. 25-53.

Dawson, Lorne L.,'Who joins New Religious Movements and Why. Twenty Years of Research and What Have We Learned?', in *Studies in Religion* 25, 1996, pp. 193-213.

Haynes, Jonathan (ed.), *Nigerian Video Films*, Athens: Ohio University Center for International Studies, 2000.

Larkin, Brian,'Hausa Dramas and the Rise of Video Culture in Nigeria', in Haynes, J., *Nigerian Video Films*, pp. 209-242.

Oha, Obododimma,'The Rhetoric of Nigerian Christian Videos: The War Paradigm of *The Great Mistake*', in Haynes, J. (ed.) *Nigerian Video Films*, pp. 192-199.

Ogundele, Wole, 'From Folk Opera to Soap Opera: Improvisations and Transformations in Yoruba Popular Culture', in *Nigerian Video Films*, pp. 89-130.

Pickering, William S., *Durkheim's Sociology of Religion: Themes and Theories*, London: Routledge and Kegan Paul, 1984.

Rothenbuhler, Eric W., *Ritual communication: From everyday conversation to mediated ceremony*, Thousand Oaks: Sage, 1998.

Ukah, Asonzeh, *Religion and Mass Media: A Sociological Perspective*, M.A Thesis, Department of Religious Studies, University of Ibadan, 1997.

Notes

1. For a concise treatment of the varied delineation of NRMs, see Afe Adogame, 'Traversing Local-Global Religious Terrain: African New Religious Movements in Europe', in *Zeitschrift für Religionswissenschaft*, 10, 2002, pp. 33-49.

2. Afe Adogame, 'Traversing Local-Global Religious Terrain', p. 34. See also Afe Adogame, Betwixt Identity and Security: African New Religious Movements and the Politics of Religious Networking in Europe', in *Nova Religio. The Journal of Alternative and Emergent Religions*, 7, 2, 2003, pp. 25.

3. Afe Adogame,'Traversing Local-Global Religious Terrain, p. 44.

4. See their official websites at http://www.rccg.org , http://www.winnerscanaanland.org and http://www.kicc.org.uk respectively.

5. Cf. the Celestial Church of Christ (CCC) website at: http://www.celestialchurch.mcmail.com

6. The CCC Constitution can now be downloaded directly from their official website at: http://www.celestialchurch.com.

7. For details on the use of media by the CCC, see A. Adogame, *Celestial Church of Christ: The Politics of Cultural Identity in a West African Prophetic-Charismatic Movement*, Frankfurt a/M: Peter Lang, 1999, pp. 82-89.

8. See for instance the website addresses: http://www.celestialchurch.com (operated by a parish in Riverdale, USA); http://www.celestialchurch.mcmail.com (administered from the United Kingdom), and http://mageos.ifrance.com or http://www.ChristianismCelest.com (administered from France). Their electronic mail addresses are webmaster@celestialchurch.com, celestialchurchofchrist@mcmail, and jl_degnide@hotmail.com respectively.

9. See the official Church of the Lord (Aladura) web page at the address: http://www.aladura.de. It was created and managed by Dr. Rufus Ositelu, who was the founder and leader of the Langen-Frankfurt (Germany) branch and also the General Overseer of the European branches of the church. He is currently the Primate of the CLA Worldwide. The web administrator still remains the incumbent Primate as his email address show: aladura-rufus.ositelu@t-online.de, rufus-ositelu@beta.linkserve.com, and primate-cla@beta.linkserve.com.

10. See the official website of the RCCG in http://www.rccg.org created and maintained by the RCCG Internet Project, Houston Texas, USA. See also UK parish web sites http://www.jesus-house.org.uk/ and http://www.rccgarea4.org.uk/.

11. The Winning Ways Program on Radio/Television is a program aired on TV both within and outside the UK. This is produced from the various teachings of Pastor Matthew Ashimolowo. The Winning Ways Program is categorized into TV/Radio, T.O.P 1000 Club, Video Technical, Audio Technical and Tape Production. See details at http://www.kicc.org.uk

12. See 'The Call' and 'Mission field' at God Digital website www.god-digital.com/rory&wendy3.htm

13. See details of 'What is God Digital?' at www.god-digital.com/getgod1.htm. The God Digital is seen as the first daily Christian broadcaster in Europe. It is regarded in some circles as a 'fundamentalist Christian Channel' Sky/Cable (Information gleaned from the Netscape web search-engine).

14. Haynes (2000) describes video films as – dramatic features shot on video and marketed on cassettes, and sometimes also exhibited publicly with video projectors or television monitors (p. xv), and as 'something between television and cinema' and which 'do not fit comfortably within

the North American structures of either' (p. 1). Larkin (2000: 210) describes video dramas (cassette or video culture) as a new genre of fictional drama made specifically for video consumption.

15. Cross-over gospellers best describes secular-musicians turned gospel-musicians such as Sonny Okosun of the Ozzidi fame, Ebenezer Obey of Juju fame etc. in Nigerian musical scene.

16. Oha (2000: 192-199) used the example of the video film titled 'The Great Mistake' (produced by the Mount Zion Faith Ministries International) in his exposition of 'The Rhetoric of Nigerian Christian Videos' to demonstrate inter alia the use of spiritual paraphernalia in an ensuing spiritual warfare projected in the narrative.

17. The MZFMI started in Nigeria but now has branches in Europe and America. As at today, it has produced at least 20 films including *Agbara Nla*, *Perilous Time*, *Ide Esu* etc.

18. See Ukah, A., *Religion and Mass Media. A Sociological Perspective*, M.A Thesis, Department of Religious Studies, University of Ibadan, 1997, p. 144.

19. See details of testimonies and views expressed on the Testimony Section of the MZFMI website at http://www.mzfm.org/.

Fused Sound–
Globalization and Gospel
Music in Zimbabwe

Ezra Chitando

Introduction

One of the areas where the effects of globalization are clearly discernible is music. The cliché that music is universal has a ring truth and is illustrated by how music easily transcends ethnic boundaries. Music generated in Africa has been consumed in North America, while reggae music has been popularly accepted worldwide. However, music also provides an opportunity to highlight the complex interaction between the global and the local. The incorporation of religious themes in gospel music makes it a particularly relevant area of research. This study examines the influence of globalization on gospel music in Zimbabwe. Music with Christian themes has become increasing popular in some African countries. Gospel music has a wide following in Nigeria and Ghana (Hackett, 1998: 263), Malawi (van Dijk, 1992: 69), Zimbabwe (Chitando, 2000: 301), South Africa and other countries. Gospel music highlights the impact of globalization on Christianity in Africa. The rapid movement of music styles, religious ideas, chants, dance routines and other features can be discerned in gospel music. However, local religious ideas, languages and concerns force themselves into African gospel music. This study seeks to demonstrate the fascinating interplay between the global and the local by utilizing the specific case of gospel music in Zimbabwe.

AN OVERVIEW OF INTERNATIONAL INFLUENCES ON ZIMBABWEAN MUSIC

It requires a longer narrative to trace the historical development of music in Zimbabwe (Turino, 2000). However, it is possible to highlight the international influences in Zimbabwean music. Since gospel music has been directly affected by developments in Zimbabwean music, there is need to rethink the sacred-profane dichotomy. In addition, international influences on Zimbabwean music show the limitations of regarding globalization as a recent phenomenon. Whilst the concept of globalization became popular in the 1990s, the process it seeks to name had been under way for much longer. Although it is difficult to define globalization with precision, this study adopts the understanding of globalization as connoting the deepening capitalist integration (Hoogvelt, 1997: 115). The technological revolution has resulted in the increased mobility of persons, ideas, goods and services. The growing power and influence of corporate business has meant the commercialization of virtually all aspects of life. However, as this study will illustrate, globalization has not achieved uniformity in culture. Cultural diversity continues to thrive (Berger and Huntington, 2002) and local values remain important. The interplay between global influences and indigenous trends is well illustrated in Zimbabwean gospel music. Various traditional instruments have been used in Zimbabwean music (Jones, 1992) and there were internal changes due to borrowing across various types, and compositions that brought together different instruments (Berliner, 1981: 25).

It should be acknowledged that colonialism brought dramatic changes to Zimbabwean music. As a number of leading ethnomusicologists have noted, urban popular musical styles in Africa developed out of three types of colonial institutions, namely, mission schools, churches and military bands (Waterman, 1990). Fred Zindi (1997: 1) notes that in Zimbabwe, Western instruments such as the guitar, the banjo, the harmonica and accordion began to replace indigenous instruments in the late 1930s. Churches became instrumental in suppressing indigenous music and dances, as well as mediating Western musical practices. Although individual missionaries and denominations differed in their approaches to indigenous music, it is fair to suggest that the dominant thread was one of condemnation. African music was considered inferior and pagan, while Western music was adopted as Christian (Axelsson, 1974: 91). African dance routines were censured as being too sexually suggestive, while indigenous instruments were discouraged. In the area of popular urban music, the forces of commercialization were asserting themselves on African music during colonialism. The emergence of African programs and field staff of the Rhodesian Broadcasting Corporation (RBC) by the end of the 1950s led to more airplay of indigenous Shona music (Turino, 2000: 77). Municipalities and private companies aided the commercialization of African music by paying performers (Dube, 1996: 106).

It was also during the colonial period that more foreign influences appeared in Zimbabwean music. American films were influential in popularizing foreign styles (Turino, 2000: 132). Other influences came from migrant workers from Zambia and Malawi, as well as touring Zairian rhumba bands. As a result, Western pop and rock, reggae, rhumba, South African *mbanganga* and other foreign musical styles become an integral part of Zimbabwean music (Zindi, 1997: 4). The different foreign musical styles that were already prevalent in Zimbabwean music were carried over to gospel music.

GLOBALIZATION AND GOSPEL MUSIC IN ZIMBABWE

Gospel music may be loosely defined as music that utilizes Christian themes and is connected to hymns, choruses and popular tunes (Chitando, 2000a: 149). It is directly connected to developments in Zimbabwean music as outlined above. Although a detailed history of the development of gospel music lies outside the scope of this study (Chitando, 2002b), it is important to note that the church has provided space for the development of African artistic talent. The role of the mission school in education also ensured that many people were familiar with Christian music.

Starting in the late 1970s, music with Christian themes became available on radio. African-American and South African gospel artists were also played on Zimbabwean radio stations.

Since globalization thrives on the mass media, it is important to consider the impact of radio on music and the recording industry in Zimbabwe (Scannell, 2001). When gospel music became the most popular music type in the country in the 1990s, foreign gospel musicians like Sipho Makhabane, Rebecca Malope, Itani Madima and others were receiving extensive airplay. The television has also played an important part by mediating foreign influences on Zimbabwean gospel music. As Knut Lundby (1998: 88-90) has shown, Zimbabwean television has a distinctly Christian outlook. Programs such as *The Psalmody* and the *Prime Gospel Show* were dedicated to gospel music and played video tapes showing British, African-American, South African and other foreign gospel artists. Furthermore, television was also an avenue for accessing the global music industry in general. Zimbabwean gospel artists were, therefore, open to these influences. Cultural closure was not a viable option as the forces of globalization were self-asserting.

Globalization has left an indelible mark on Zimbabwean gospel music. Machanic Manyeruke, one of the leading performers, has taken gospel to international audiences and has held shows in North America and Western Europe (Chitando, 2002b: 51). Shuvai Wutawunashe, a pioneering female gospel musician, has also enjoyed considerable external exposure. Her husband, Jonathan Wutawunashe, is a career diplomat and gospel artist. He has held diplomatic posts in a number of countries, allowing their group, *The Family Singers*, to attain an international profile. The versatility of the group may be attributed to their mobility and transnational connections. Globalization has ensured that Zimbabwean gospel musicians have attained some commercial success outside the country's borders. Worldbeat or world music seeks to inspire 'increasing adoption of cosmopolitan aesthetics and style in order to succeed on the international markets' (Turino, 2000: 334). Groups like *The Family Singers* perform some of their music in English and have gained considerable following within the region and abroad. Furthermore, 'universal' Christian themes make it possible for adherents of the religion in different parts of the world to identify with Zimbabwean gospel music.

A number of groups have also appropriated reggae in performing gospel music. Bob Marley popularized reggae in the country when he was the prime entertainer at the independence celebrations in 1980. Subsequently, prominent reggae artists and groups like Don Carlos, Misty in Roots, UB40 and others have toured the country. *The Black Saints* played reggae gospel in the mid-1980s and early 1990s. Their name signifies black consciousness, while their dreadlocks were consistent with their reggae beat. Playing popular hymns and choruses, the group illustrates the extent to which religious music is open to transformation.

Following the saturation of local television by American hip hop, rap soul, rhythm and blues and other styles in the late 1990s, a number of youthful groups fused these into gospel music. They retained the rhythm, but brought in specifically Christian lyrics. It was also clear at gospel music concerts that African American performing artists heavily influence local youths. They appropriated their chants and dance styles although they blended them with local variations. Other mature artists like Olivia Charamba incorporated jazz into their gospel music, highlighting the variety emerging from global influences.

THE PENTECOSTAL APPROPRIATION OF MEDIA TECHNOLOGIES IN ZIMBABWE

Pentecostal groups dominate Zimbabwean gospel music. As Rosalind Hackett observes with reference to Pentecostals in Nigeria and Ghana, creative utilization of the mass media largely accounts for the rapid expansion of Pentecostalism (Hackett, 1998). Gospel musicians emerging from Pentecostal churches have been aggressive in marketing their products because of their ability to appropriate media technologies in the era of globalization. Elias Musakwa, a gospel musician, producer and businessman, is indicative of this trend. His recording company, *Ngaavongwe Records*, is well connected in the Southern African region. He distributes gospel music video and audiocassettes across the region.

Although gospel groups affiliated to Protestant and African Independent Churches also make use of the media, they are not as adept as the Pentecostals. It is the Pentecostals who have been instrumental in advertising gospel music concerts on radio and television, as well as putting up glossy posters. In line with the connection between Pentecostalism and globalization (Droogers, 2001), artists from other countries perform at Zimbabwean gospel music concerts. In November 2002, South African and Ghanaian gospel musicians were star attractions at well marketed, sold out shows. Transnational Pentecostal networks are visible in such religious and commercial activities.

Gospel music is understood as an integral part of the Pentecostal sense of mission. At gospel music concerts, trade in Christian literature is actively encouraged. In most instances, Christian books, magazines and pamphlets from North America and Nigeria are on sale. Public address systems, video recorders, amplifiers and the latest gadgets are employed at such gatherings. Pentecostals do not regard technological advancement as an evil to be resisted. Rather they harness technology in their endeavor to ensure that the gospel message reaches as many people as possible. A number of gospel musicians affiliated to Zimbabwean Pentecostal churches have also visited branches of their churches that are based overseas. As Gerrie ter Haar (1998) has shown, African Christian churches in the Diaspora are growing. Preparations for shows in Europe and North America are made by utilizing modern communication strategies availed by globalization, such as the Internet. Artists and groups like Charles Charamba, Gospel Trumpet, Appointed and others thrive on such transnational links. In an economy characterized by severe shortages of foreign currency, external branches support the home church by buying gospel music tapes and hosting musicians for specific periods.

The dominant 'message' of globalization is one of wealth and accumulation. Pentecostalism has been instrumental in portraying genuine Christians as those who enjoy prosperous lives. This ideology has been described as the gospel of prosperity. As Pentecostalism has spread rapidly over the last two decades, this message has also attracted many converts (Coleman, 2000). In Zimbabwean gospel music, videos show artists driving the latest car models, staying in up market houses and wearing designer clothes. These are shown as symbols of divine approval, characterizing the new life in Christ. Globalization has also allowed Zimbabwean gospel to address international concerns in their compositions. Through the radio, television, newspapers and magazines, artists have become aware of developments in other parts of the world. Images of war, famine, racism and others are beamed into their homes by global media networks. In their music, Zimbabwean artists plead with God to end suffering in various parts of the world. Cultural workers like Charamba, are therefore, able to name Africa's afflictions due to their exposure to global images.

Successful utilization of media technologies ensured the ascendancy of gospel music in Zimbabwe in the mid-1990s. Pentecostal groups disseminated their cultural products through television, cassettes and other forms to an appreciative audience. This challenged main-line church groups who began to join the trend. In the late 1990s the Catholics released church music in the form of tapes. Prior to this, Catholic church' music was for performance and consumption in well defined religious spaces (Mushayapoku-vaka, 1997). The Pentecostal challenge forced Catholics to redefine gospel music.

CONTESTING HOMOGENEITY: THE INFLUENCE OF THE LOCAL CONTEXT

The project of globalization has not resulted in the obliteration of local identities. Instead of worldwide imitation, global visions have often instigated creative appropriations in local contexts. Thus, 'Global trends can be restated in terms of contributing to cultural diversity; they can be strategically harnessed for the new opportunities they offer' (Lundby and Dayan, 1999: 399). Gospel music in Zimbabwe has not entirely succumbed to globalization influences. Local contexts have asserted themselves and Zimbabwean gospel music reflects these influences. In this way, there is a creative interplay between the global and the local. Thus:

> The dichotomy of global versus local is a major key to the understanding of these issues. In other words, the whole world is tied up in the proceedings and happenings of the global arena, while at the same time – and with sometimes very different results and outcomes – the music makes a statement on the local ground (Kirkegaard, 2002: 11).

Alongside foreign musical styles, indigenous styles are prevalent in Zimbabwean gospel music. Following the Africanization of church music, traditional instruments like drums, horns, rattles and others found their way back into the church. These instruments are heavily used in gospel music from the United Methodist Church. Although there is a lot of improvization, the buying public identifies such music as having a local origin. While the *mbira* has been strongly identified with the ancestor cult, it has been transformed into a Christian musical instrument. Christianity's radical descralization, also seen in taking over traditional sacred sites, is underlined in the use of *mbira* in Christian workshop. As a globalizing religion and assertive cultural force, Christianity has appropriated the instrument and given it a new interpretation. Although some denominations remain wary of *mbira*, Catholics have accepted the instrument. A number of gospel groups also play the instrument, insisting that all instruments proceed from God and should be used in praise (Psalm 150: 3-6).

The choice of rhythm for mournful tunes in Zimbabwean gospel music is also indicative of sensitivity to the local context. A form-critical analysis shows that many of the songs are adapted funeral hymns and choruses. In the 1990s, the HIV/AIDS pandemic resulted in numerous deaths. This resulted in the high circulation of songs addressing the theme of death (Chitando, 1999: 337). Independent gospel artists like Cephas Mashakada recorded such songs and were careful to preserve the mournful tone. One would have expected globalization to wipe out such local concerns. Gospel music in Zimbabwe thus illustrates the impact of the local context. Artists address indigenous Zimbabwean spiritual issues like witchcraft, avenging spirits and other oppressive forces. They call upon the Holy Spirit to come down and neutralize negative spirits so as to ensure prosperity. Gospel song tracks show how adherents of the traditional religion struggle to appease the ancestors and invite them to join Christianity. Pentecostal gospel musicians emphasise the need for Africans to make a radical break with indigenous spirituality (Meyer, 1998).

A number of artists call upon Africans to unite in the face of marginalization in the global economy. Globalization does not represent God's last word on Africa, they claim. Olivia Charamba calls upon Africa to restore her identity, arguing that Africa is not the devil's workshop. For her, Africa has the capacity to shake off her negative image. An African Independent Church group, Apostolic Melodies, recorded the song, *Messiah Sunungura Africa* (Messiah Save Africa) in which they note that disease, hunger and death stalk Africa. However, they urge Africans to fight the negative effects of globalization and enjoy abundant life.

Female gospel musicians also address the local context in their compositions. While women have not enjoyed a high profile as musicians in Zimbabwe, gospel music has facilitated the rise of many female artists. Artists like Charamba, Wutawunashe, Fungisai Zvakavapano and others have emerged as competent female cultural workers (Mapuranga, 2000). Although they address general themes, they devote considerable attention to Zimbabwean women's issues. In a video shot by a young artist, Dzidzai, sexual abuse against the girl child is clearly portrayed. This is a burning local issue as some men believe that having sex with a virgin will cure them of HIV/AIDS. Female gospel musicians also seek to counsel women who have been abused. These local concerns assert themselves in music that has a cosmopolitan outlook.

Perhaps the most significant dimension of the importance of the local context is the adoption of African languages. Zimbabwean gospel musicians largely use their own languages, including minority languages (Chitando, 2002b: 80-82). Although groups like *The Family Singers, Gospel Trumpet, Shingisai Suluma* and others have used English, indigenous languages dominate gospel music in Zimbabwe. Using the vernacular allows artists to express themselves clearly and profoundly. Some artists employ story telling, riddles, proverbs and other techniques available from indigenous oral literature. They utilize such art forms to communicate the Christian message, demonstrating their sensitivity towards the local context.

GOSPEL MUSIC, GLOBALIZATION AND AFRICAN IDENTITY

This study has highlighted the impact of globalization on gospel music in Zimbabwe and the influence of the local context on cultural production that employs Christian themes. At a conceptual level, one could assume that there is tension between globalization and localization in gospel music. The formulation of a 'global' Christian identity appears to be based on the rejection of local identities. However, gospel music in Zimbabwe illustrates the extent to which communities of faith succeeded in holding the two in creative tension. The co-existence of international and local influences in gospel music show how individuals and communities 'play with identities in contemporary music in Africa' (Palmberg and Kirkegaard, 2002).

The fusion characterizing gospel music in Zimbabwe is also a challenge to both cultural nationalists and uncritical champions of globalization. Cultural nationalists nostalgically yearn for 'uncontaminated' African culture, while uncritical champions of globalization prophetically envisage a single global culture. Gospel music in Zimbabwe has been heavily influenced by globalization in terms of new musical styles, marketing, foreign languages and other factors discussed in preceding sections. However, it has also embraced indigenous music styles, local themes and is expressed in African languages. A Zimbabwean gospel music cassette is, therefore, an epitome of hybridity. It eloquently testifies to the complex negotiation that goes on in shaping postcolonial African identities. Thus:

> The notion of hybridity challenges the ideas of the existence of separate bounded cultures, and the idea of the possibility to retrieve the "real" and "unspoiled" African culture. The notion of hybridity also challenges the prediction of the doomsday prophets regarding the fate of African culture production in the age of globalization (Baaz 2001:14).

The fused sound that has been consumed widely in Zimbabwean gospel music also shows the impact of Christianity on popular culture. As the discussion on the development of music during colonialism shows, the mission school played a key role in disseminating Christian beliefs and practices. As a result, the buying public in Zimbabwe can readily identify with music that is inspired by Christian themes, although many may no longer actively participate in church life. In addition, others enjoy gospel music for the memories that it brings since HIV/AIDS has resulted in many deaths. Hymns, choruses and chants that are common at funerals are electronically recorded and released as gospel music. Christianity's dominance on the market of religions has ensured the ascendancy of gospel music in Zimbabwe and in other African countries.

The influence of Christianity on popular culture in Zimbabwe is also discernible in sculpture, literature, dance and other spheres of life. Christianity has therefore become a component of African identity. However, it is important to acknowledge that its influence has not been complete and decisive. David Maxwell's (2002: 22) claim that 'by the turn of the twenty-first century it had become the corner stone of African culture and society' overlooks the persistence of indigenous traditions. In gospel music, traditional instruments, dance routines, as well as the call and response formula have all found their place. Furthermore at the same family event where the cosmopolitan gospel music is being consumed, ancestors may also receive their libation.

The popularity of gospel music with its multiple influences has also not resulted in abandoning local styles and themes. In appropriating jazz, reggae, country and other foreign musical styles, gospel artists are demonstrating their versatility. However, an examination of their texts shows a preoccupation with pressing local issues like HIV/AIDS, unemployment, inflation and other themes. This is a result of the fact that gospel musicians have received more formal education than other popular musicians in Zimbabwe. Their political and economic literacy levels are, therefore, higher than those of the other musicians. Consequently, compositions that wrestle with issues like globalization, African identity and others are more pronounced in gospel music than in other genres. The other popular music style, sungura, is mainly cherished for its fast, punchy electric guitar (Eyre, 2001: 95).

The presence of young, educated professionals in Zimbabwean gospel music has major implications for discourses on African identity. It is these cosmopolitan youths who sing about the value of Christianity while utilizing indigenous instruments. Comfortable in performing for both the congregation in London and in the dusty growth point in Zimbabwe, these musicians are sophisticated cultural workers. They challenge the popular portrayal of the 'real' African as the 'raw native' who can be captured in the rural areas.

CONCLUSION

Although globalization accelerated the effects of international influences on Zimbabwean music in the 1990s, a historical survey shows that local music has always been open to innovation and adoption of external styles. This study shows how the colonial period witnessed the entry of musical styles from North America, Europe and other African countries. When gospel music asserted itself in the 1990s, it utilized these foreign styles, as well as appropriating the latest media technologies. Zimbabwean gospel music has become commercially successful due to its efforts to address the local context. This study shows how indigenous instruments, styles and local themes have left an imprint on gospel music. Alongside the forces of globalization, forces of localization have expressed themselves on the gospel music scene. Zimbabwean gospel music is, therefore, fused sound that borrows eclectically from multiple global and local sources.

Bibliography

Axelsson, Olof E., 'Historical Notes on Neo-African Church Music', *Zambezia* 3, 2, 1974, pp. 89-102.

Baaz, Maria Eriksson, 'Introduction: African Identity and the Postcolonial', in Maria Eriksson Baaz and Mai Palmberg (eds.), *Same and Other: Negotiating African Identity in Cultural Production*, Uppsala: Nordiska Afrikainstitutet, 2001, pp. 5-21.

Berliner, Paul F, *The Soul of Mbira: Music and Traditions of the Shona People of Zimbabwe*, Chicago: University of Chicago Press, 1981 (1978).

Berger, Peter L., and Huntington, Samuel P., *Many Globalizations: Cultural Diversity in the Contemporary World*, Oxford: Oxford University Press, 2002.

Chitando, Ezra, 'Complementary Approaches to the study of Religion: An application to a study of Gospel Music in Zimbabwe', *Scriptura* 71, 4, 1999, pp. 331-341.

Chitando, Ezra, 'Songs of Praise: Gospel Music in an African Context', *Exchange* 29, 4, 2000, pp. 296-310.

Chitando, Ezra, '"Jesus Saves!" Gospel Music as a Mode of Identity Formation in Zimbabwe', *Swedish Missiological Themes* 90, 2, 2002a, pp. 149-162.

Chitando, Ezra, *Singing Culture: A Study of Gospel Music in Zimbabwe*, Uppsala: Nordiska Afrikainstitutet, 2002b.

Coleman, Simon, *The Globalization of Charismatic Christianity: Spreading the Gospel of Prosperity*, Cambridge: Cambridge University Press, 2000.

Droogers, André, 'Globalization and Pentecostal Success', in André Corten and Ruth Marshall-Fratani (eds.), *Between Babel and Pentecost: Transnational Pentecostalism in Africa and Latin America*, Bloomington: Bloomington University Press, 2001, pp. 41-61.

Dube, Caleb, 'The Changing Context of African Music Performance in Zimbabwe', *Zambezia* 23, 2, 1996, pp. 99-120.

Eyre, Banning, *Playing with Fire: Fear and Self Censorship in Zimbabwean Music*, Copenhagen: Freemuse, 2001.

Hackett, Rosalind I.J., 'Charismatic/Pentecostal Appropriation of Media Technologies in Nigeria and Ghana', *Journal of Religion in Africa* 28, 3, 1998, pp. 258-277.

Hoogvelt, A., *Globalization and Postcolonial World: The New Political Economy of Development*, London: Macmillan, 1997.

Jones, Claire, *Making Music: Musical Instruments in Zimbabwe, Past and Present*, Harare: Academic Books, 1992.

Kirkegaard, Annemette, 'Introduction', in Mai Palmberg and Annemette Kirkegaard (eds.) *Playing with Identities in Contemporary Music in Africa*, Uppsala: Nordiska Afrikainstitutet, 2002, pp. 7-18.

Lundby, Knut *Longing and Belonging: Media and the Identity of Anglicans in a Zimbabwean Growth Point*, Oslo: Development of Media and Communication, 1998.

Lundby, Knut and Daniel, Dayan, 'Mediascape Missionaries? Notes on Religion as Identity in a Local African Setting', *International Journal of Cultural Studies* 2, 3, 1999, pp. 398-417.

Mapuranga, Tapiwa P., 'The Rise of Gospel Music in Zimbabwe with Special Reference to the Role of Women', Unpublished BA Honours Dissertation, University of Zimbabwe, 2000.

Maxwell, David, 'Introduction: Christianity and the African Imagination', in David Maxwell and Ingrid Lawrie (eds.), *Christianity and the African Imagination: Essays in Honour of Adrian Hastings*, Leiden: Brill, 2002, pp. 1-24.

Meyer, Birgit, '"Make a Complete Break with Past": Memory and postcolonial Modernity in Ghanaian Pentecostalist Discourse', *Journal of Religion in Africa* 28, 3, 1998, pp. 316-349.

Mushayapokuvaka, Cecilia, 'Development of Shona Liturgical Music in the Catholic Church in Zimbabwe, 1890-1997', Unpublished BA Honours Dissertation, University of Zimbabwe, 1997.

Palmberg, Mai and Annemette Kirkegaard (eds.), *Playing with Identities in Contemporary Music in Africa*, Uppsala: Nordiska Afrikainstitutet, 2002.

Scannell, Paddy, 'Music, Radio and the Record Business in Zimbabwe Today', *Popular Music* 20, 1, 2001, pp. 13-27.

Ter Haar, Gerrie, *Halfway to Paradise: African Christians in Europe*, Cardiff: Cardiff Academic Press, 1998.

Turino, Thomas, *Nationalists, Cosmopolitans and Popular Music in Zimbabwe*, Chicago: University of Chicago Press, 2000.

Van Dijk, Richard, 'Young Born Again Preachers in Post–Independence Malawi: The Significance of an Extraneous Identity', in Paul Gifford (ed.), *New Dimensions in African Christianity*, Nairobi: All Africa Conference of Churches, 1992, pp. 55-79.

Waterman, Christopher, *Juju: A Social History and Ethnography of an African Popular Music*, Chicago: University of Chicago Press, 1990.

Zindi, Fredi, *Music Ye Zimbabwe: Zimbabwe versus the World*, Harare: Fred Zindi and Morgan Chirumiko, 1997.

LIST OF CONTRIBUTORS

Afe Adogame holds a PhD in History of Religions from the University of Bayreuth, Germany. Prior to his appointment in 2005 to the lectureship in World Christianity, he was Teaching/Senior Research Fellow at the Department for the Study of Religion and Institute of African Studies, Bayreuth University from 1995–1998 and from 2000–2005. His current research interests include religion in the new African diaspora, religious transnationalism, religion and youth, and religion in prison. One of his most recent publications is (co-edited) *Religion Crossing Boundaries: Transnational Religious and Social Dynamics in Africa and the New African Diaspora* (Brill 2010).

Allan Anderson is Head of the School of Philosophy, Theology and Religion and Professor of Global Pentecostal Studies at the University of Birmingham, England, where he has been since coming from Southern Africa in 1995. He is author and co-editor of several books on Pentecostalism and African independent churches, the latest being An Introduction to Pentecostalism (Cambridge, 2004), Spreading Fires (SCM & Orbis, 2007) and Studying Global Pentecostalism (University of California Press, 2010).

Dapo Asaju is Professor of New Testament and Church History at the Department of Religions, Lagos State University, Ojo-Lagos, Nigeria. His research focus and specialization includes: New Testament Studies, Church History, African Christian Theology and Missiology. He is an ordained priest of the Church of Nigeria, Anglican Communion. His publications include *Olabayo: Life and Ministry of an African Prophet* (1996); *F. Akinbola: Life and Ministry of an Anglican Bishop* (1996); and *Re-Enthroning Theology as Queen of Sciences: Global Missiological Challenges of African Biblical Hermeneutics* (2005)

Deji Ayegboyin is Professor of Church History and African Christianity, Department of Religious Studies, University of Ibadan, Former editor of ORITA, Ibadan Journal of Religious Studies. He is currently President, Nigerian Baptist Theological Seminary, Ogbomoso. His publications include as co-editor of *African Indigenous Churches: An Historical Perspective (1997)*; *Rediscovering and Fostering Unity in the Body of Christ: The Nigerian Experience* (2000)

Bolaji Bateye teaches Religious Studies & Gender Studies at the Department of Religious Studies, Obafemi Awolowo University, Ile-Ife, Nigeria. She is also a Resource Person at the OAU Center for Gender and Social Policy Studies. She is widely published in books and journals and some of the most recent include: 'Forging Identities: Women as Participants and Leaders in the Church among the Yoruba', Studies in World Christianity (2007); 'Paradigmatic Shift: Reconstruction of Female Leadership Roles in New Generation Churches in South-western Nigeria" in Afe Adogame, et al. (eds.) The Appropriation of a Shattered Heritage: Christianity in Africa and the African Diaspora. (2008).

Ulrich Berner is professor of Religious Studies (Religionswissenschaft) at the Faculty of Cultural Sciences, University of Bayreuth, Germany. His main interests are European Religious History, African Christianity, and method and theory in the study of religion. He is also a principal investigator in the Bayreuth International, Graduate School of African Studies (BIGSAS).

Ezra Chitando is Associate Professor and teaches History and Phenomenology of Religion in the Department of Religious Studies, Classics and Philosophy at the University of Zimbabwe.

He is Consultant for the World Council of Churches' Ecumenical HIV and AIDS Initiative in Africa (EHAIA). He is author of *Singing culture: a study of Gospel music in Zimbabwe* (2002). He has also published widely on the Church's response to HIV and AIDS in Africa and on gender. Living with Hope: African Churches and HIV/AIDS, Acting in Hope: African Churches and HIV/AIDS (2007).

Umar Danfulani is Professor (History of Religions) in the Department of Religious Studies, University of Jos, Nigeria. He teaches African Traditional Religion, Phenomenology of Religion, Interaction of Religions and World Religions at the University of Jos since 1984. He earned his PhD from Uppsala University, Sweden (1994). He is the author of *Pebbles and Deities: Pa Divination Among the Ngas, Mupun, and Mwaghavul in Nigeria* (1995) and *The Sharia Issue and Christian-Muslim Relations in Contemporary Nigeria* (2005)

Rosalind Hackett is Professor at the Department of Religious Studies of the University of Tennessee, Knoxville, USA. She has published widely on new religious movements in Africa (*New Religious Movements in Nigeria*, ed. 1987), religious pluralism (*Religion in Calabar*, 1989), art (*Art and Religion in Africa*, 1996), gender, the media, and religion in relation to human rights (*Religious Persecution as a U.S. Policy Issue*, co-ed., 1999). She has also edited, *Proselytization Revisited: Rights Talk, Free Markets, and Culture Wars* (London: Equinox, 2008)

Ogbu Kalu was Henry Winters Luce Professor of World Christianity and Mission, McCormick Theological Seminary, Chicago, USA. He authored and edited 16 books, including: *African Pentecostalism: An Introduction; Power, Poverty and Prayer: The Challenges of Poverty and Pluralism in African Christianity, 1960-1996; History of the Church in the Third World: Vol. III*, and *African Christianity: An African Story*. He also edited and published more than 150 articles in journals and books.

Jacob Olupona is Professor of African Religious Traditions, with a joint appointment as Professor of African and African American

Studies in the Faculty of Arts and Sciences, Harvard University, USA. His current research focuses on the religious practices of the estimated one million Africans who have emigrated to the United States over the last 40 years. He has authored or edited eight other books, including, most recently, *Òrìsà Devotion as World Religion: The Globalization of Yorùbá Religious Culture*, co-edited with Terry Rey.

Asonzeh Ukah holds a Ph.D. and lectures at the University of Bayreuth, Germany. His research interest includes African Pentecostalism, religious media and visual culture. He is currently involved in a research project on "Sacred Economy of Space" in South Africa. He is the author of *A New Paradigm of Pentecostal Power: A Study of the Redeemed Christian Church of God in Nigeria* (2008).

INDEX